▌▌spring into ▌▌▌

PHP 5

D1517143

■■❙spring into❙❙❙ series

Spring Into... a series of short, concise, fast-paced tutorials for professionals transitioning to new technologies.

Find us online at **www.awprofessional.com/springinto/**

Spring Into Windows XP Service Pack 2
Brian Culp
ISBN 0-13-167983-X

Spring Into PHP 5
Steven Holzner
ISBN 0-13-149862-2

Spring Into HTML and CSS
Molly E. Holzschlag
ISBN 0-13-185586-7

Spring Into Technical Writing for Engineers and Scientists
Barry J. Rosenberg
ISBN 0-13-149863-0

Spring Into Linux®
Janet Valade
ISBN 0-13-185354-6

YOUR OPINION IS IMPORTANT TO US!

We would like to hear from you regarding the Spring Into... Series. Please visit **www.awprofessional.com/springintosurvey/** to complete our survey. Survey participants will receive a special offer for sharing their opinions.

From the Series Editor
Barry J. Rosenberg

A few years ago, I found myself in a new job in which I had to master many new skills in a very short time. I didn't have to become an instant expert, but I did have to become instantly competent.

I went to the bookstore but was shocked by how much the publishing world had changed. At a place where wit and intelligence had once been celebrated, dummies were now venerated. What happened?

Photograph courtesy of Ed Raduns

Well, I made a few phone calls, got Aunt Barbara to sew up a few costumes, and convinced Uncle Ed to let us use the barn as a stage. Oh wait… that was a different problem. Actually, I made a few phone calls and got some really talented friends to write books that clever people wouldn't be ashamed to read. We called the series "Spring Into…" because all the good names were already taken.

With Spring Into…, we feel that we've created the perfect series for busy professionals. However, there's the rub—we can't be sure unless you tell us. Maybe we're hitting the ball out of the park and straight through the uprights, bending it like Beckham, and finding nothing but net. On the other hand, maybe we've simply spun a twisted ball of clichés. Only you can tell us. Therefore, if anything—positive or negative—is on your mind about these books, please email me at

barry.rosenberg@awl.com

I promise not to add you to any email lists, spam you, or perform immoral acts with your address.

Sincerely,
Barry

▌▌spring into ▐▐▐

PHP 5

Steven Holzner

✦Addison-Wesley

Upper Saddle River, NJ • Boston• Indianapolis • San Francisco
New York • Toronto • Montreal • London • Munich • Paris • Madrid
Capetown • Sydney • Tokyo • Singapore • Mexico City

The publisher offers excellent discounts on this book when ordered in quantity for bulk purchases or special sales, which may include electronic versions and/or custom covers and content particular to your business, training goals, marketing focus, and branding interests. For more information, please contact:

U. S. Corporate and Government Sales
(800) 382-3419
corpsales@pearsontechgroup.com

For sales outside the U. S., please contact:

International Sales
international@pearsoned.com

Visit us on the Web: www.awprofessional.com

Library of Congress Catalog Control Number: 2004118156

Copyright © 2005 Pearson Education, Inc.

ISBN 0-13-149862-2
Text printed in the United States on recycled paper at R.R. Donnelley in Crawfordsville, Indiana.
First printing, April 2005

To Nancy, now and always!

Contents

CHAPTER 7 **Object-Oriented Programming and File Handling 199**

CHAPTER 8 **Working With Databases 235**

Preface

Welcome to PHP! This book has been written to be as comprehensive—and as accessible—as a book on PHP can be. It puts the power of PHP to work for you, pushing the envelope as far as it can go. The best way to learn any topic like PHP is by example, and this is an example-oriented book. You'll find dozens of tested examples here, ready to go to work.

PHP is quickly gaining popularity these days. Web page authors are requiring more and more power, and PHP is the answer. Not content to simply handle web pages in browsers any more, people are turning to the server side to do things you just can't do in a browser. Using PHP, you have total control over your web applications—and the good part is that they're not any harder to write than a typical web page.

PHP is an amazing package, and you're getting into it at the right time, when the excitement level is soaring. You'll see more PHP here than in any similar book, doing things you won't see other places, such as drawing images on-the-fly on the server and then sending them back to the browser.

Who Should Read This Book?

This book is for you if you truly want to develop all the power of web applications. If you want to start using cookies instead of just having your browser accept them, if you want to handle buttons, text fields, check boxes and more in your web pages, if you want to track users with sessions, or if you want to connect to a database on the server, then look no further. This book lets you take control of the server side of things.

In addition, this book is specially written so that you don't need a lot of experience to use it. The only real requirement for this book is familiarity with HTML. You don't need to be an HTML expert, but you'll need to know some.

How Is This Book Organized?

This book contains nine chapters:

- Chapter 1 provides a foundation, getting you started with PHP.

- Chapter 2 is all about using operators and flow control in PHP to begin handling your data.

- Chapter 3 handles text strings and organizes data into arrays.

- Chapter 4 introduces functions, which let you wrap up PHP into manageable sections that can be called by name.

- Chapter 5 starts using PHP to work with HTML controls such as text fields and buttons in web pages.

- Chapter 6 shows how to create web applications in more detail by checking what type of browser the user has, how to check the user's data, and more.

- Chapter 7 introduces object-oriented programming in PHP and shows how to handle files on the web server.

- Chapter 8 discusses something that PHP does well: working with databases on the server. In this chapter, we'll work with MySQL.

- Chapter 9 covers a number of important web techniques: using cookies, sessions, FTP, email, and more.

- We have included a bonus chapter on the Web site that shows how to draw graphics interactively on the web server and send them back to the browser. To download this chapter, go to www.awprofessional.com/title/0131498622.

All you need to read this book is some knowledge of HTML. You don't need to know anything about server-side programming. You get all the material you need right here.

As far as software goes, we'll be using PHP 5.0, and I'll show you where to download it for free. All you need to do is to download and install the required software (the installations are easy, unlike some larger software packages).

You don't need Internet access to learn PHP from this book. If you want, you can develop and test your PHP pages all on the same computer. However, if you want to put your PHP code on the Internet, you'll need to use an ISP that supports PHP. Check with your ISP to find if they support PHP—more and more ISPs are doing so every day.

What's Unusual About This Book?

This book—like other books in the Spring Into… Series—includes the following elements:

- Each topic is explained in a discrete one- or two-page unit called a "chunk."

- Each chunk builds on the previous chunks in that chapter.

- Most chunks contain one or more examples. I believe that good examples provide the foundation for almost all useful technical documents.

- Many chunks contain sidebars that provide helpful, ancillary material.

In addition, this book is filled with examples—dozens of them—because seeing a working example is the best way to learn this material. Here are just a few included topics:

- Reading data from a web page's text fields, radio buttons, check boxes, and list boxes on the server

- Creating and handling image maps

- Tracking users with sessions and cookies

- Writing data to files on the server (such as guest books)

- Recovering from errors without crashing

- Connecting to databases on the server

- Using SQL to work with databases

- Drawing images on-the-fly and sending them back to the browser

- Handling strings and arrays

- Working with the PHP operators

- Creating functions

- Creating classes and objects

- Using FTP from PHP

- Sending email from PHP

- Using sessions to preserve data between page accesses

- The complete PHP syntax

There's a lot to PHP, and there's a lot to this book. Our plan is to cram as much PHP into the book as we can.

Where Can You Download Examples Used in This Book?

The code in this book is available for download at http://www.awprofessional.com/springinto. All the code examples have been tested by the author and tech editor on different machines.

This book is designed to be at the top of the PHP field. If you have comments and suggestions for improvements, please write to me, care of Prentice Hall. This book is designed to be the new standard in PHP programming books, more complete and more accessible than ever before. Please keep in touch with ways to improve it and keep it on the cutting edge. Thanks.

Who Helped Me Write This Book?

A book like this is the work of many people. Besides your local author, Mark L. Taub and Barry Rosenberg helped create and design the book. Matt Wade and Eugenia Harris did excellent reviews of the manuscript.

That's it. We're ready to dig into PHP on Chapter 1.

About the Author

Steven Holzner has been writing about online programming since before the Internet became the Internet. He's worked extensively with PHP and many other online languages and is the author of 88 programming books. His books have included many bestsellers, have sold over two million copies worldwide, and have been translated into 18 languages. He's also been a contributing editor for *PC Magazine*. Online programming topics, such as PHP, Perl, JavaServer Pages, servlets, and others, are his specialty.

About the Series Editor

Barry Rosenberg wrote *KornShell Programming Tutorial* (Addison-Wesley, 1991), which pioneered many of the chunk-oriented techniques found in the Spring Into... Series. He is the author of more than sixty corporate technical manuals, primarily on programming. An experienced instructor, Barry has taught everything from high-school physics to weeklong corporate seminars on data structures.

Most recently, he spent four semesters at MIT where he taught advanced technical writing. Barry is also a professional juggler who has performed more than 1,200 shows, including a three-week run in Japan. Juggling serves as the backdrop for his novel, *Cascade* (not yet published). Barry currently works as the documentation manager at 170 Systems.

CHAPTER 1

Essential PHP

Welcome to PHP! "PHP" officially stands for "PHP: Hypertext Preprocessor," but millions of people still know it by its original name, *Personal Home Page*, and that's what it's all about—creating your own interactive web pages in the easiest possible way. No longer will web pages have to be static, unchanging things. Now you can send the user new web pages tailored to what he or she wants to see in real time. You can handle button clicks, checkbox selections, and radio buttons and can even draw graphics interactively and store data in a database. It's all up to you—the lid is off the box.

This is where you make your web pages come alive.

We'll be using PHP version 5, whose web site is www.php.net, in this book. PHP is specially designed to make creating your own web pages a snap. In this book, we're going to work from the server side by installing PHP scripts on your web server. Users will be able to open those scripts in a web browser, seeing everything they'd expect from a fully fledged page: text fields, tables full of data created on-the-fly from databases, and fluid graphics—everything you might see on the most professional interactive web page is now within your grasp.

With static web pages written in simple HTML, a web server will just pass the HTML in a web page back to the browser, and the user can see pictures and text, but that's about it. When you write sever-side scripts in PHP, on the other hand, you actually tell the server what you want to do—read what the user entered in a text field, see which checkboxes were clicked, and so on. Then you can decide what to do next, and you can create the web page to send back on-the-fly. That's the name of the game here—being able to respond dynamically.

PHP has become a huge success—more than 15 million web pages use it now. In the following pages, we'll see how to make the web server do what we want with PHP.

Getting PHP

The first step to creating your own interactive web pages is to get access to a web server that runs PHP. In fact, your Internet Service Provider (ISP) probably supports PHP already. You can find out by asking your ISP's support staff, or you can test for PHP yourself in one of two ways.

First, if you can open a command prompt by connecting to your web server using a Telnet, SSH, or SSH2 application (don't worry if you don't know what these applications are—you won't need them in this book), you can try typing php -v at the command line (we'll use a % sign for a generic command prompt in this book). If you have PHP installed, you'll see something like this:

```
%php -v
PHP 5.0.0 (cli) (built: Jul 13 2004 21:39:58)
Copyright (c) 1997-2004 The PHP Group
Zend Engine v2.0.0, Copyright (c) 1998-2004 Zend Technologies
```

The other way to determine whether you have PHP installed is by trying out an actual PHP script. To do that, take a look at the section "Creating Your First PHP Script" in this chapter. If that script works, you've got PHP installed, and you're all set.

NOTE

If you want a list of ISPs that already run PHP, take a look at www.php.net/links.php#hosts.

Installing PHP Locally

It's a good idea to install PHP on your own computer so that you can test your PHP scripts as you develop them. This way, you won't have to take the time to upload your PHP scripts to your ISP, check them by downloading them in your browser, make changes, and then start the whole cycle again. If you develop your PHP scripts locally, you can get things running a lot faster, but you'll need to install PHP on your own machine.

Some operating systems, such as Linux and many versions of Unix, now come with PHP installed by default. In others, such as Windows and Mac OSX, you'll have to download and install PHP yourself. The first step is to check if you already have PHP available locally—try the php -v command at the command prompt (for example, in Windows, open a DOS window and type php -v). If it works, you're all set.

If you don't have PHP already installed, you can install it yourself. Prebuilt "binary" versions are available for download and immediate installation for a number of operating systems: Windows, Mac OSX, Novell NetWare, OS/2, RISC OS, SGI IRIX 6.5.x, and AS/400. You can find the binary installation package for Windows at `http://www.php.net/downloads.php`, along with links to the binaries for the other operating systems mentioned.

NOTE

Binaries are no longer distributed for Linux and Unix because PHP is usually pre-installed. If you want, you can build your own PHP installation from source code. Go to `http://www.php.net/downloads.php` to get the source code for PHP.

You can find the installation instructions for PHP in the PHP documentation, which is online at `http://www.php.net/docs.php` (you can download the complete PHP documentation from `http://www.php.net/download-docs.php`). You can also find installation instructions in an installation file (named, for example, install.txt) when you uncompress the PHP download. Because the instructions change every time PHP changes, and because there are so many possible variations of operating systems and web servers, you should read the current installation instructions and use them. Listing all the instructions here would take 20 pages, and they'd be obsolete by the time you read them.

Briefly, here's how things might work in Windows XP (all this can be found in full detail in the downloadable installation instructions). You first need a web server, such as the Apache web server or Microsoft's Internet Information Server (IIS). You can get a Windows installer file for Apache (apache_2.0.52-win32-x86-no_ssl.msi) at `http://httpd.apache.org/download.cgi`; when you download and double-click this file, it installs Apache. Or you can install IIS in Windows XP by using the Add/Remove Programs icon in the Control Panel, clicking the Add/Remove Windows Components button, and then selecting IIS.

PHP can be installed in two different ways for Windows, and you can download what you need for both methods from `http://www.php.net/downloads.php`. There's a Windows installer executable file, php-5.0.x-installer.exe, with basic PHP support (which includes standard PHP but no external extensions). This installer will automatically configure servers such as IIS, PWS, and Xitami, and it has instructions for manual configuration of other servers such as Apache.

The other installation technique uses a .zip file, php-5.0.x-Win32.zip, which contains the full PHP installation and allows for external extensions (this option is better if you want to do everything covered in this book). Download and unzip this file; you'll find all the installation instructions included. Depending on your operating system, you typically copy php.exe to the directory from which you intend to run it, for example.

The next step is to connect your PHP installation to your web server. If you've unzipped the PHP .zip file in Windows XP and you're using Apache, you should edit the Apache http.conf file, following the directions in the installation instructions. If you're using IIS, you configure IIS with its management console (select Start > Settings > Control Panel > Administrative Tools > Internet Services Manager in Windows XP), also following the directions in the installation instructions. For the full details, see the instructions, which take you through everything step by step.

Setting Up Your Development Environment

To create PHP pages, you'll need a text editor of some kind to create PHP files, which are a mix of HTML and PHP. All kinds of text editors are available on numerous operating systems that can serve the purpose, such as vi, emacs, pico, Macintosh's BBEdit or SimpleText, and Windows Notepad or WordPad. By default, PHP files are given the extension .php (as in myBigTimeWebPage.php).

The text you enter into our pages is just plain text, a mix of HTML and PHP. You can see an example in Figure 1-1; to create this PHP-enabled page, you just enter the text as it appears in the figure and save it as a file with the extension .php. As you can see, this example is mostly HTML; the PHP part is the script that appears between the <?php and the ?>. When you navigate to this document in your browser, the PHP-enabled server will read the document, find the PHP part between the <?php and the ?>, and execute it automatically. In this case, our PHP is just the single line phpinfo();, which will display an HTML table full of information about the PHP installation on the server, as we're about to see in "Creating Your First PHP Script."

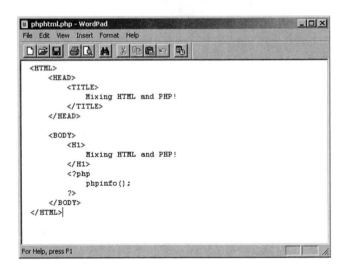

FIGURE 1-1 Creating a PHP page with HTML in it.

In fact, you can even use a word processor such as Microsoft Word to create PHP documents if you save your documents in *plain text format*, not in some other format such as .doc (for example, in Microsoft Word, you'd select the Text Only option from the Save as type drop-down list box in the Save As dialog). It's much better to stick with a plain text editor than a word processor, however, because unless you're careful, word processors will add all kinds of features and decorations that will get in the way.

You can also use a PHP integrated development environment (IDE) to create your PHP pages. IDEs give you all kinds of tools that simple text editors don't, such as checking what you've written automatically to make sure it's valid PHP, automatic syntax highlighting (where items such as PHP keywords appear in various colors, making it easy to pick out what's going on at a glance), and automatic deployment, where the IDE can upload your PHP pages to your ISP when you click a button or select a menu item.

Here's a starter list of IDEs available online that can handle PHP. Note, however, that most of them cost money, and although they have some nice features, we won't rely on those features in this book:

- Komodo (www.activestate.com/Products/Komodo) runs on Linux and Windows.

- Maguma (www.maguma.com) runs on Windows only.

- PHPEdit (www.phpedit.com/products/PHPEdit) is free, but runs on Windows only.

- Zend Studio (www.zend.com/store/products/zend-studio.php) runs on Windows and Linux. This one is created by the same people who created the Zend software "engine" that actually runs at the core of PHP itself.

If you're working with an ISP, you'll also need some way of transporting your PHP pages to the ISP, as you would with standard web pages. You can use a File Transfer Protocol (FTP) program or a web interface if one is provided by your ISP. If you haven't uploaded web pages before, ask your ISP support team what they recommend because they will often point you to an FTP program that they support or a web interface they've set up to allow people to upload web pages. You upload and run PHP pages just as you would standard HTML pages, as long as your server supports PHP.

Creating Your First PHP Script

Here's where all the action starts—creating your first PHP scripts. With PHP, which will be run on the web server, you can make all kinds of things happen that couldn't happen before. You can have your PHP retrieve data from databases, check someone's password, print out customized greeting text, use cookies, write a guest book, create interactive games, calculate sales tax, or even build your own shopping cart or chat room web applications. And all these things can run by themselves, 24 hours a day, even while you're peacefully sleeping in bed.

Our first PHP page is going to be a simple one, enclosing a simple PHP script. You can mix PHP and HTML in the same web page, but you've got to have some way to keep them apart. To do that, you enclose your PHP inside special *tags* <?php and ?>:

```
<?php
        .
        . Your PHP goes here....
        .
?>
```

NOTE

Actually, you can shorten this even more if you turn on *short tags* in php.ini, the PHP configuration file, in which case you can enclose your PHP between <? and ?>. I don't recommend doing that, however, because that usage often means scripts can be used on other web servers beside one you've specially configured, and you may run into conflicts with other scripting languages.

Inside these tags, PHP scripts are made up of PHP *statements*, which end with a semicolon. The semicolon is important because it tells PHP when the current line is ended, and PHP will complain if you don't use it. You may have seen other scripting languages, such as JavaScript, where the semicolons were optional at the ends of lines, but in PHP, they're required.

Our first PHP script is the standard one—we'll use a single statement here, just phpinfo(). As we're going to see, PHP statements can do all kinds of things. This one uses the phpinfo *function* to display information about the version of PHP you're using. A function is a set of statements—sometimes hundreds of them—that are given a convenient name, such as phpinfo, by which you can invoke them. When you call such a function by name, all the statements in the function are run. The phpinfo function is one of the many functions built into PHP, ready for us to use. Because hundreds of lines are wrapped up into a single function, all we have to do is call that function by name.

In this case, the `phpinfo` function will create an HTML table holding information about your PHP installation. Here's how we call this function in our script's single statement:

```php
<?php
    phpinfo();
?>
```

Enter this PHP script in your text editor now, as shown in WordPad in Figure 1-2, and save this file as phpinfo.php. Don't forget to make sure you're saving this file as plain text—if it's not plain text, PHP will have a problem with it (one way to check is by typing out the file to take a look at what's in it, such as by using the type command in a DOS window in Windows).

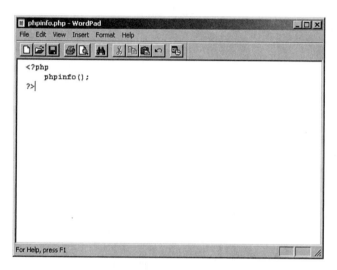

FIGURE 1-2   Creating a PHP script.

Congratulations, you've created your first PHP script! Not bad. Now that you've created phpinfo.php, the next step is to store it in the web server where that server can read it. If you're working with an ISP, upload phpinfo.php to where you store your standard web pages on your ISP as you'd normally upload a web page, using an FTP application or web page interface.

If you're working locally and have PHP and a web server already installed on your own machine, store phpinfo.php where the server can find it. In Apache, it's htdocs in the directory where Apache has been installed. For IIS, it's inetpub/wwwroot. In Linux, it may be /var/www/html. After making sure your web server has been configured to work with PHP, as detailed in the PHP installation directions from www.php.net, start your web server.

Running Your First PHP Script

To run phpinfo.php, just open it in your browser as you would a standard web page that you've uploaded—that is, navigate in a browser to the URL for phpinfo.php, such as `http://www.yourisp.com/username/phpinfo.php`. If you're using PHP locally, navigate to `http://localhost/phpinfo.php` after starting your local web server.

NOTE

Do *not* open phpinfo.php directly in your browser using a menu item such as File > Open because that would open the file without running it through the web server, so the PHP script wouldn't run. Make sure you enter the appropriate URL in the browser's navigation bar instead.

If all is well, you should see a table packed full of information about PHP, as it appears in Figure 1-3 in the browser. Congratulations, you're a PHP developer! There are a number of tables here; it's worthwhile scrolling down to take a look at the information on your PHP configuration. If you're ever in doubt about what your PHP version has installed, this is a good place to check.

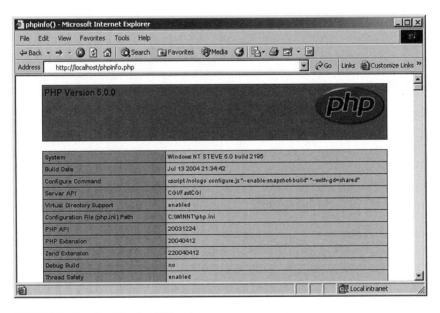

FIGURE 1-3   Results of the first PHP script.

What If It Doesn't Work?

Unfortunately, plenty of things can go wrong when you first try to get PHP running. If things aren't working right, don't panic; it'll just take a little extra time. You may get a blank page, a file-not-found error, or another kind of error, but the problem can be tracked down.

The first thing to check is whether PHP is running, which, if you're using PHP locally, is easy to check. At the command prompt, change directories to the PHP install directory and run php -v. If the PHP is version displayed, PHP is running. If you can open a command prompt on your ISP using a Telnet or SSH2 application, you can run the same test.

The next item, and the most common issue, is that PHP may not have been installed correctly as far as your server is concerned. This is the problem if you get a blank page, and when you do a "view source" in the web browser, you can see the source code of your PHP script. This means that the web server did not pass the script to PHP to be run. This can be a little finicky, which is why the instructions from www.php.net are so extensive. The best idea is to go through those directions again, line by line, to make sure you did everything just as it's listed.

Then make sure that phpinfo.php is where your web server expects to find it. As mentioned earlier, in Apache, this location is htdocs in the directory where Apache has been installed. For IIS, it's inetpub/wwwroot. In Linux, it may be /var/www/html. The actual directory may be different on various servers; on one PHP server I use, the correct directory is /httpdocs/ROOT, so ask your ISP's tech support. If you've uploaded phpinfo.php to the usual directory on your ISP for your HTML pages and it's not working, ask your ISP's tech support; sometimes they have to enable support on a directory-by-directory basis. For that matter, some ISPs require that you use a different extension for PHP 5 scripts, such as .php5.

NOTE

Do you need any special Unix file protection level for PHP scripts? Must they be set as executables? No, simple 644 protection (not 755) will do.

If you're using IIS, also check php.ini for the line cgi.force_redirect = 0, which must be set as indicated in the installation directions. If you don't see it there, add it.

Finally, take a look at the "Problems?" section in the installation instructions for a troubleshooting guide. The PHP Frequently Asked Questions (FAQ) is at www.php.net/ FAQ.php, and it handles many such problems, as does the PHP installation Frequently Asked Questions (FAQ) at www.php.net/manual/faq.installation. You might also check the PHP install archives at http://marc.theaimsgroup.com/?1=php-install&r=1&w=2, or the news groups alt.php or comp.lang.php.

Mixing In Some HTML

PHP files are most often mixtures of HTML and PHP scripts. Putting HTML and PHP scripts into the same document is no problem because you put your PHP statements inside a script bounded by <?php and ?>, which means the server can pick them out easily.

You already know how the HTML in web pages work; when you insert some HTML that displays text, for example, that text is displayed when the web server reaches the line with the text in the web page as it's sending the web page back to the browser. In the same way, if a PHP script creates some text to be inserted in the web page sent back to the browser, that text is inserted into the web page at the location of that script.

For instance, take a look at Example 1-1, phphtml.php. This file contains a mix of HTML and PHP. As you can see, the HTML sets the title of the document (which will appear in the browser's title bar) and uses an <H1> HTML header to display the text Mixing HTML and PHP! in large bold font.

EXAMPLE 1-1   Mixing HTML and PHP

```
<HTML>
    <HEAD>
        <TITLE>
            Mixing HTML and PHP!
        </TITLE>
    </HEAD>

    <BODY>
        <H1>
            Mixing HTML and PHP!
        </H1>
        <?php
            phpinfo();
        ?>
    </BODY>
</HTML>
```

After the <H1> header HTML element, the server will encounter our PHP script, which means that the output of the phpinfo function will be inserted into the web page we're sending back to the browser exactly at that point. As you know, the phpinfo function creates the HTML for a table holding information about the PHP installation, so the result is what you see in Figure 1-4—the HTML header appears first, followed by the PHP information table.

Want to make your PHP page look more official? You can find some "Powered by PHP" logos at http://www.php.net/download-logos.php. Just download them and add them to your web page using an <IMG> element like this:

```
<HTML>
    <HEAD>
        <TITLE>
            Mixing HTML and PHP!
        </TITLE>
    </HEAD>

    <BODY>
        <H1>
            Mixing HTML and PHP!
        </H1>
        <?php
            phpinfo();
        ?>
        <IMG SRC="php-power-white.gif">
    </BODY>
</HTML>
```

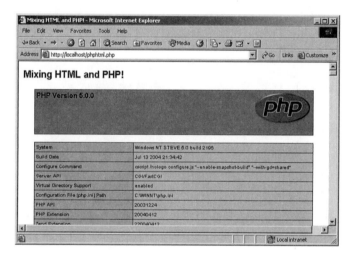

FIGURE 1-4   Mixing PHP and HTML.

You can see an example in Figure 1-5, where we've downloaded php-power-white.gif and are displaying it in a PHP-enabled web page.

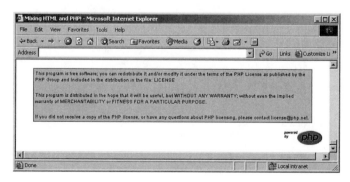

FIGURE 1-5   Adding a PHP logo.

How About Printing Out Some Text?

The echo statement, which inserts text into a web page, is just about the most versatile and common statement in PHP. We're going to be using this statement a lot to display the results of doing something with PHP, so let's get started now.

You use the echo statement simply with the keyword echo and by giving it some quoted text to display. You can see how the echo statement might display the text "Hello from PHP." in this script:

```
<HTML>
    <HEAD>
        <TITLE>
            Using the echo statement
        </TITLE>
    </HEAD>

    <BODY>
        <H1>
            Echoing some text:
        </H1>
        <?php
            echo "Hello from PHP.";
        ?>
        .
        .
        .
```

Because you can intersperse PHP scripts throughout an HTML page, you can echo text at multiple locations in a web page using PHP, as you see in Example 1-2, echo.php.

EXAMPLE 1-2   Using the echo statement

```
<HTML>
    <HEAD>
        <TITLE>
            Using the echo statement
        </TITLE>
    </HEAD>

    <BODY>
        <H1>
            Echoing some text:
        </H1>
        <?php
            echo "Hello from PHP.";
        ?>
        <H1>
            Echoing some more text:
```

```
        </H1>
        <?php
            echo "Hello from PHP again!";
        ?>
        <IMG SRC="php-power-white.gif">
    </BODY>
</HTML>
```

The results appear in Figure 1-6.

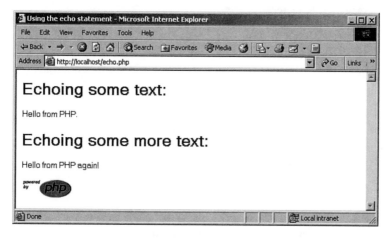

FIGURE 1-6   Using echo.

You can enclose the text you want to echo in single quotes or double quotes, and you can also echo numbers without having to quote them at all, like this:

```
echo 111555;
```

Because what you're echoing goes to a web page (unless you're executing PHP on the command line), it's also useful to echo HTML tags back to the browser. For example, if you want each word to appear on a different line, you can use HTML <BR> elements like this:

```
echo "Hello<BR>from<BR>PHP.";
```

More Printing Power

There's a difference between displaying text at the command line and displaying text in a browser. In a browser, you use HTML elements such as <BR> and <P> to format your text. When you print out text at the command line, you can use special characters for formatting if you enclose that text in double quotes. Here are those special characters:

\n	Newline character
\r	Carriage return
\t	Tab
\\	Displays a \
\$	Displays a $
\"	Displays a "
\0 to \777	Displays a character corresponding to a hexadecimal (base 8) code
\x0 to \xFF	Displays a character corresponding to a hexadecimal (base 16) code

For example, echo "Line 1\nLine 2" will display "Line 1" on one line and "Line 2" on the next—if you're running PHP at the command line. In a browser, the \n newline character means nothing. For the same result, you should use echo "Line 1
Line 2".

NOTE

This is an important item to remember—if you're displaying text in a browser, you must format that text using HTML tags. Just sending line breaks in your text won't do anything because the browser will take those line breaks out automatically, just as it would in any web page. To format your text as you want it, you must use your PHP scripts to send proper HTML to the browser.

If you want, you can break up a long quoted string across various lines in your script, and the line breaks will be preserved—if you're printing at the command line. If you print to a web page, the line breaks will be ignored:

```php
<?php
echo "This text
spans
multiple
lines.";
?>
```

You can also separate the items you want printed with commas, like this:

```php
echo "Hello", "this", "is", "PHP.";
```

All the items you want printed this way are printed, one right after another:

```
HellothisisPHP.
```

If you want to include spaces between the words, do something like this:

```
echo "Hello ", "this ", "is ", "PHP.";
```

This would give you:

```
Hello this is PHP.
```

If you want to print a sensitive character such as a " without telling PHP that you're ending your text (which a " mark would otherwise do), you can use \" instead this way:

```
echo "He said, \"I like ice cream.\"";
```

This is called *escaping* the quotation mark so that PHP will display it instead of treating it as marking the end of a text string.

In PHP, you can also assemble text strings together into one string using a dot (.). Here's an example:

```
echo "Hello " . "this " . "is " . "PHP.";
```

In this case, PHP takes your expression "Hello " . "this " . "is " . "PHP." and assembles it together (this is called concatenation) into one single string, "Hello this is PHP.", and then passes that string on to the echo statement.

Here are a few echo examples:

```
echo 11115555;                    Displays: 11115555
echo "Hello from PHP.";           Displays: Hello from PHP.
echo 'Hello from PHP.';           Displays: Hello from PHP.
echo "Hello", "from", "PHP.";     Displays: HellofromPHP.
echo "Hello " . "from " . "PHP."; Displays: Hello from PHP.
```

Besides echo, you can also use the PHP print statement using the same syntax, like this: print "Hello from PHP.";. What's the difference between print and echo? Not much, really; print is more like a PHP function (see Chapter 4, "Breaking It Up: Functions"), so it *returns* a value, which is always set to 1. As with other functions, you can read this value, but in this case you can't do much with it. For most practical purposes, echo and print work the same way in PHP, so which one you use is up to you.

Printing "Here" Documents

Here's another printing option: you can also create "here" documents, which cause echo or print to display everything it reads until it encounters an end token you specify (usually END), which must be placed at the very beginning of a line. You can see what this looks like in Example 1-3, phphere.php.

EXAMPLE 1-3   Printing a here document

```
<HTML>
    <HEAD>
        <TITLE>
            Displaying here Documents
        </TITLE>
    </HEAD>

    <BODY>
        <H1>
            Displaying here Documents
        </H1>
<?php
echo <<<END
This example uses
"here document" syntax to display all
the text until the ending token is reached.
END;
?>
        <BR>
        <BR>
        <IMG SRC="php-power-white.gif">
    </BODY>
</HTML>
```

The result of this here document appears in Figure 1-7.

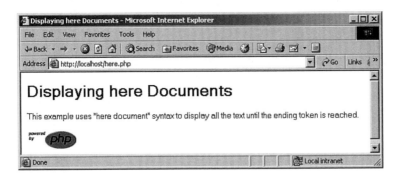

FIGURE 1-7   Displaying a here document.

Running PHP on the Command Line

Besides connecting PHP to a web server so that the web server can read your scripts and run them, you can also run PHP on the command line. This can be great for testing things out before you go through the whole rigamarole of uploading files to an ISP.

PHP is an interpreted language, which means that when you run it, the PHP interpreter reads your script and interprets each statement, converting it into code your computer can run. In PHP 5.0, the program that actually does the interpretation on the command line is called the Command Line Interpreter (CLI) and is named php. The program that runs with a web server is called php-cgi.

You can run PHP on the command line with the command php. You've got to make sure that the computer can find php, which means either making sure that php (in the PHP bin directory) is in your computer's path or giving the full path to php when you run it. For example, say you had this script, echo.php:

```
<?php
    echo "Hello from PHP.";
?>
```

If php is in your path, you can run this from the command line like so (where % is a generic, cross-platform command-line prompt, and this example assumes you're in the same directory as echo.php):

```
%php echo.php
```

If this works, you'll see:

```
Hello from PHP.
```

If it doesn't work, you can specify the exact location of php, which might look like this in Unix or Linux:

```
$/usr/local/bin/php echo.php
```

And something like this in Windows:

```
C:\>C:\php\php echo.php
```

The CLI has many *command-line options*, which you can use to customize its operation. In fact, php can tell you all about its options if you enter php -h to get the full list:

```
%php -h
Usage:  php [options] [-f] <file> [--] [args...]
        php [options] -r <code> [--] [args...]
        php [options] [-B <begin_code>] -R <code> [-E <end_code>] [--] [args...]
        php [options] [-B <begin_code>] -F <file> [-E <end_code>] [--] [args...]
        php [options] -- [args...]

  -a                   Run interactively
  -c <path>|<file>     Look for php.ini file in this directory
  -n                   No php.ini file will be used
  -d foo[=bar]         Define INI entry foo with value 'bar'
  -e                   Generate extended information for debugger/profiler
  -f <file>            Parse <file>.
  -h                   This help
  -i                   PHP information
  -l                   Syntax check only (lint)
  -m                   Show compiled in modules
  -r <code>            Run PHP <code> without using script tags <?..?>
  -B <begin_code>      Run PHP <begin_code> before processing input lines
  -R <code>            Run PHP <code> for every input line
  -F <file>            Parse and execute <file> for every input line
  -E <end_code>        Run PHP <end_code> after processing all input lines
  -H                   Hide any passed arguments from external tools.
  -s                   Display colour syntax highlighted source.
  -v                   Version number
  -w                   Display source with stripped comments and whitespace.
  -z <file>            Load Zend extension <file>.
```

For example, if you want to get a simple text version of the information the phpinfo function prints out, use the -i option this way: %php -i. And you already know you can get the version of PHP with the -v option (note the (cli) in the output, indicating that we're using the CLI):

```
%php -v
PHP 5.0.0 (cli) (built: Jul 13 2004 21:39:58)
Copyright (c) 1997-2004 The PHP Group
Zend Engine v2.0.0, Copyright (c) 1998-2004 Zend Technologies
```

In Linux and Unix, you can run PHP scripts simply by typing the name of the script on the command line if you indicate where to find PHP with a line that begins with #! (and give the script execution permission):

```
#! /usr/bin/php
<?php
    echo "Hello from PHP.";
?>
```

Commenting Your Scripts

The lines in a PHP web page so far have been either HTML or PHP scripts, which are meant to be read by computers. But there's also a component that's meant to be read only by people—comments.

Comments are annotations you add to your PHP pages to tell the story of what's going on to a human. This is important because when you come back to a long and complex script years from now, you probably won't remember what was happening in it. Or you might pass your script around for others to use. That's where comments come in. With comments, you can describe exactly how a script behaves so that you can pick it up instantly later on.

There are three types of comments in PHP. The first kind lets you write multi-line comments, beginning with /* and ending with */ like this:

```php
<?php
/* Start by displaying a
   message to the user */

    echo "Hello from PHP.";
?>
```

You can surround each line with /* and */ to make the comment look like a block, which will attract more attention:

```php
<?php
/* Start by displaying a  */
/* message to the user  */

    echo "Hello from PHP.";
?>
```

But one thing that will make PHP choke is *nesting* comments inside each other, so don't do this:

```php
<?php
/* Start by
   /* displaying a */
message to the user  */

    echo "Hello from PHP.";
?>
```

This won't work because PHP looks for */ to end a comment, and when it sees that, it assumes the comment is ended—which is a problem because the comment isn't actually ended, but PHP will suddenly see what it thinks is plain text where there should be PHP statements.

The other types of comments are one-line comments, designed to hold text that will fit on a single line. You can use either // to start these comments, or a #:

```php
<?php
// Start by displaying a
# message to the user

    echo "Hello from PHP.";
?>
```

These kinds of comments are also useful because they can be placed on lines that also contain code. In that case, PHP will ignore anything after the # or //, like this:

```php
<?php
    echo "Hello from PHP.";          //Display a message
    echo "Hello from PHP again!";    #Display another message
?>
```

You can also use these comments to make blocks:

```php
<?php
// Start by displaying a
// message to the user

    echo "Hello from PHP.";
?>
```

Or, to make something that will really stand out, try this:

```php
<?php
########################
# Start by displaying a #
#/ message to the user #
########################

    echo "Hello from PHP.";
?>
```

These days, single-line comments, which are easier to write because you don't have to keep track of where they end, are prevailing. The multi-line comments still have their uses, though, and are often used at the beginning of programs to form a comment block that explains what the program is all about. They're also sometimes used when you define your own functions so that a comment-style block can indicate what the function does and how you use it.

It's a good idea to use as many comments as needed to clarify what a script is doing. Using too many comments can cloud the issue, but not using enough is worse.

Getting a Handle on Data: Variables

So far, the messages we've displayed have been fixed and unvarying, like this:

```php
<?php
    echo "Hello from PHP.";
?>
```

This just displays some string text and not much more—and if that's as far as you could go with PHP, you might as well stick with HTML. But PHP is actually about handling your data in a dynamic way, and we're going to start taking a look at how that works now, using *variables*.

Variables are containers for your data. For example, say you are selling party hats on the web, and you want to check your current total inventory in all three of your warehouses—Chicago, Tokyo, and Paris. To do that, you'll need to be able to add together those three separate values. PHP comes with all kinds of support built in for performing math operations on your data, including adding. So, to add values, you can use the + operator—for example, the following script will print out "I have 6 tomatoes":

```php
<?php
    echo "I have " , 1 + 2 + 3 , " tomatoes";
?>
```

Note that we're using numbers here, which is different from straight text–because the numbers aren't text, they're not quoted. This result is fine, but again, it's static because we've simply put 1 + 2 + 3 in our PHP script. How about being able to add the number of party hats in your warehouses in Chicago, Tokyo, and Paris when the script runs?

That's where variables come in. Variables can hold current data and make that data accessible to you at run time. In PHP, variables start with a dollar sign, $. Variables can store data, so if you're storing the number of party hats in variables named $chicago, $tokyo, and $paris, here's how you could add together those values at run time:

```php
<?php
    echo "I have " , $chicago + $tokyo + $paris , " party hats!";
?>
```

In PHP, a valid variable name starts with a letter or underscore, followed by any number of letters, numbers, or underscores, and the name can be of any length. Here are some valid variable names: $pizza_temperature, $_number_of_tigers, $planet_number_9.

As you can see, variables act as repositories for data. But how do you store that data in variables in the first place?

Assigning Values to Variables

In PHP, when you want to create a variable, you *assign* data to it using an *assignment operator*. We'll see all the PHP assignment operators in Chapter 2, "Gaining Control With Operators and Flow Control," but for now, the most common one is the equals sign, =. Here's an example that uses the equals operator to assign values to new variables (after this runs, $temperature will hold 69, $pi will hold 3.1415926535, and so on):

```
$temperature = 69;
$number_of_earths = 1;
$pi = 3.1415926535;
$reassurance = "No worries.";
```

Note that we're assigning numbers to some variables and text to other variables here. In some languages, you need to specify the variable type, such as string or integer, but not in PHP, which makes it much easier.

NOTE

Internally, however, the computer does use various data types for storage, so in some cases you should know what issues can arise because of data typing. For more on data types, see "Handling Data Types" in this chapter.

Take a look at an example, phpvariables.php, which appears in Example 1-4. In this case, we're assigning a value of 1 to a variable named $apples and displaying the value stored in that variable:

```
echo "Setting number of apples to 1.<BR>";
$apples = 1;
echo "Number of apples: ", $apples, "<BR>";
          .
          .
          .
```

Next, say we want to increase the number of apples we have by three. You can do that by assigning $apples the current value in $apples plus 3 and displaying the new result:

```
echo "Setting number of apples to 1.<BR>";
$apples = 1;
echo "Number of apples: ", $apples, "<BR>";
echo "Adding 3 more apples.<BR>";
$apples = $apples + 3;
echo "Number of apples now: ", $apples, "<BR>";
```

EXAMPLE 1-4   Assigning values to variables

```
<HTML>
    <HEAD>
        <TITLE>
            Assigning values to variables
        </TITLE>
    </HEAD>
    <BODY>
        <H1>
            Assigning values to variables
        </H1>
        <?php
            echo "Setting number of apples to 1.<BR>";

            $apples = 1;

            echo "Number of apples: ", $apples, "<BR>";

            echo "Adding 3 more apples.<BR>";

            $apples = $apples + 3;

            echo "Number of apples now: ", $apples, "<BR>";
        ?>
    </BODY>
</HTML>
```

You can see the results in Figure 1-8. Now you can do math at run time, storing data in variables and manipulating that data as needed.

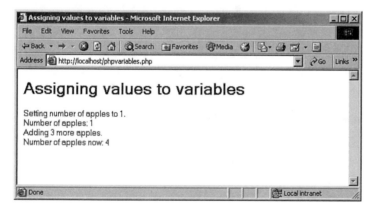

FIGURE 1-8   Assigning values to variables.

Interpolating Variables in Strings

You can display the values of variables like this:

```
$apples = 1;
echo "Number of apples: ", $apples, ".";
```

However, there's a shortcut that you can use to make this easier. The values in variables can be *interpolated* if you put them into double-quoted (not single-quoted) strings, which means that their values are inserted directly into the string. This technique enables you to convert the example from the previous chunk:

```
$apples = 1;
echo "Number of apples: $apples.";
```

This example prints out Number of apples: 1. You can see the complete previous example, which displays variable values after assignment, converted to use variable interpolation in Example 1-5, phpinterpolation.php.

EXAMPLE 1-5   Expanding variables in strings

```
<HTML>
    <HEAD>
        <TITLE>
            Interpolating variables
        </TITLE>
    </HEAD>
    <BODY>
        <H1>
            Interpolating variables
        </H1>
        <?php
            echo "Setting number of apples to 1.<BR>";

            $apples = 1;
            echo "Number of apples: $apples <BR>";
            echo "Adding 3 more apples.<BR>";
            $apples = $apples + 3;
            echo "Number of apples now: $apples <BR>";
        ?>
    </BODY>
</HTML>
```

The results of this example appear in Figure 1-9.

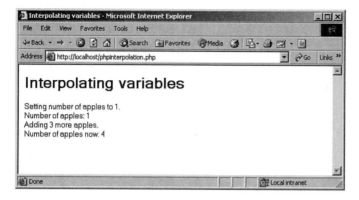

FIGURE 1-9   Interpolating variable values.

Interpolation gives you a quick way of displaying the contents of a variable, but there's an issue to watch here. For example, what if the variable $text held the text "news", and you wanted to put the word "newspaper" into the output? You might try this:

```php
<?php
    $text = "news";

    echo "Where's the $textpaper <BR>";
?>
```

But PHP isn't going to understand that because it looks like you're using a variable named $textpaper. Here's the error you get:

```
PHP Notice:  Undefined variable:  textpaper in C:\php\t.php on line 4
```

The correct way to handle this situation is to enclose the variable you're interpolating, $text, in curly braces, { and }, as in Example 1-6.

EXAMPLE 1-6   Expanding variables in strings

```
<HTML>
    <HEAD>
        <TITLE>
            Interpolating variables
        </TITLE>
    </HEAD>
    <BODY>
        <H1>
            Interpolating variables
        </H1>
        <?php
            $text = "news";

            echo "Where's the {$text}paper.";
        ?>
    </BODY>
</HTML>
```

Creating Variable Variables

That's not a typo—PHP lets you create *variable variables*. A variable variable is one that holds the *name* of a variable. Here's how it works: you create a variable named, say, $apples:

```php
<?php
    $apples = 4;
        .
        .
        .
?>
```

Then you can create a new variable, which we'll name $fruitname, that holds the *name* of the $apples variable:

```php
<?php
    $apples = 4;
    $fruitname = "apples";
        .
        .
        .
?>
```

Now you can refer to the value in $apples as $$fruitname:

```php
<?php
    $apples = 4;
    $fruitname = "apples";
    echo "Number of apples: ", $$fruitname;
?>
```

This script displays:

```
Number of apples: 4
```

You have to be more careful when using double-quotation interpolation, however, because PHP will have trouble with an expression such as $$fruitname in double quotes. To fix that, you use curly braces like this: ${$fruitname}.

Example 1-7, phpvariablevariables.php, shows how this works.

EXAMPLE 1-7   Using variable variables

```
<HTML>
    <HEAD>
        <TITLE>
            Using variable variables
        </TITLE>
    </HEAD>
```

```
<BODY>
    <H1>
        Using variable variables
    </H1>
    <?php
        $apples = 4;
        $oranges = 3;
        $fruitname = "oranges";

        echo "Number of oranges: ${$fruitname} <BR>";

        $fruitname = "apples";

        echo "Number of apples: ${$fruitname} <BR>";
    ?>
</BODY>
</HTML>
```

The results of this example appear in Figure 1-10.

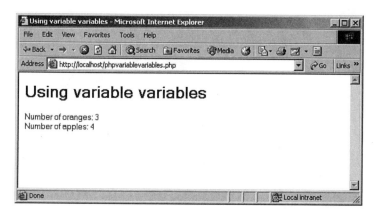

FIGURE 1-10 Interpolating variable variables.

If you hadn't used the curly braces in Example 1-7, you would have gotten this result:

```
Number of oranges: $oranges <BR>
Number of apples: $apples <BR>
```

Variable variables are important to understand, although they might not look like much more than a curiosity right now. In particular, they're very useful when you work with loops and arrays, as we'll be seeing in Chapter 3, "Handling Strings and Arrays."

Creating Constants

Sometimes you don't want variables to be variable—you want their value to be fixed. For example, say you have a variable named $pi that holds the value of pi. It's possible that such a value may be inadvertently modified, which is not good. The solution is to create a *constant*, whose value can't be altered.

You create constants with the define function, giving it the name of the constant and the value you want to assign to it like this: define ("pi", 3.1415926535);. The name of the constant is always quoted, but the value you assign to the constant is only quoted if it's a string. Take a look at phpconstants.php in Example 1-8, which creates the constant named pi and displays it—note that when you use the constant, you *don't* prefix it with a $. The results of this example appear in Figure 1-11.

EXAMPLE 1-8 *Creating constants*

```
<HTML>
    <HEAD>
        <TITLE>
            Using PHP constants
        </TITLE>
    </HEAD>

    <BODY>
        <H1>
            Using PHP constants
        </H1>
        <?php
            define ("pi", 3.1415926535);

            echo "The constant pi holds " , pi,  "<BR>";

        ?>
    </BODY>
</HTML>
```

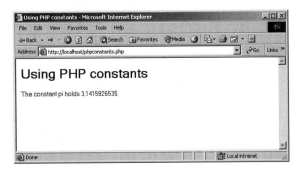

FIGURE 1-11 *Using constants.*

If you try to alter the value of this constant (like this: pi = 3.14), PHP won't accept it and won't even start the script.

Because you don't prefix constants with a $, PHP can become confused if you use a constant with the same name as one of the reserved keywords in PHP. These keywords appear in the following list:

PHP Keywords

__CLASS__	__FILE__	__FUNCTION__	__LINE__	__METHOD__
and	default	endif	global	print
array	die	endswitch	if	require
as	do	endwhile	include	require_once
break	echo	eval	include_once	return
case	else	exception	isset	static
cfunction	elseif	exit	list	switch
class	empty	extends	new	unset
const	enddeclare	for	old_function	use
continue	endfor	foreach	or	while
declare	endforeach	function	php_user_filter	xor

Also, a number of predefined constants are available to your scripts. We'll use these constants as we need them. Here's a sample:

__LINE__	The current line number of the file.
__FILE__	The full path and filename of the file.
__FUNCTION__	The function name. (This was added in PHP 4.3.0.)
__CLASS__	The class name. (This was added in PHP 4.3.0.)
__METHOD__	The class method name. (This was added in PHP 5.0.0.)
PHP_VERSION	The PHP version.
PHP_OS	The operating system.
DEFAULT_INCLUDE_PATH	Where PHP will search for what it needs.

For example, using echo __LINE__ at a particular position in a script will display the current line that's executing.

Handling Data Types

You don't decide the way your data is stored internally—PHP does. Behind the scenes, it supports eight internal data types (we'll see all these types in this book):

- boolean. Holds true/false values

- integer. Holds numbers such as -1, 0, 5 and so on

- float. Holds floating-point numbers ("doubles") such as 3.14159 or 2.7128

- string. Holds text such as "Hello from PHP."

- array. Holds arrays of data items

- object. Holds programming objects

- resource. Holds a data resource

- NULL. Holds a value of NULL

You usually don't have to worry about these data types because PHP determines a variable's type based on the kind of data you assign to it. For example, this makes $variable a string:

```
$variable = "No worries.";
```

This makes it a float value:

```
$variable = 1.2345;
```

This makes it a boolean value:

```
$variable = TRUE;
```

Because PHP selects the data type based on the data you assign to a variable, there's no problem here. The trouble starts when you mix data types by, for example, adding new values to the value in $variable using the + (addition) operator, which we'll see in Chapter 3. Here are some examples:

```
<?php
$variable = "0";              // $variable is a string set to "0"
$variable = $variable + 2;    // $variable is now an integer set to 2
$variable = $variable + 1.1;  // $variable is now a float set to 3.1
$variable = 2 + "8 apples";   // $variable is now an integer set to 10
?>
```

If you want to avoid potential data type troubles, don't mix data types. Even if you do, PHP does the right thing almost every time (such as converting the result of adding an integer and a float into a float value, which is the right thing to do), but if you need to explicitly specify the type of a variable to PHP, you can always use a *type cast*. Casts appear inside parentheses and come right before the name of the variable whose type you want to specify. Here are a few examples:

```
$int_variable = (integer) $variable;
$float_variable = (float) $variable;
$string_variable = (string) $variable;
```

Some hints about mixing data types: when you're converting to the boolean type, these values are considered FALSE (more on these items, like arrays, is coming up in the book):

- The boolean FALSE
- The integer 0
- The float 0.0
- The empty string, and the string "0"
- An array with zero elements
- An object with no member variables
- The special type NULL (including unset variables)

Every other value is considered TRUE (including any resource). When you're converting to the integer type:

- Boolean FALSE will yield 0 (zero), and boolean TRUE will yield 1 (one).
- Float values will be rounded toward zero.

When you're converting to the float type, the conversion is the same as if the value was converted to an integer and then to a float. You can also convert from string to the numeric types, but that's somewhat involved—see Chapter 3 for all the details.

In the next chapter, we're going to start getting control over the data in our PHP scripts by using operators and the PHP statements that control program flow and looping—all vital items for any PHP programmer.

Summary

PHP makes your web pages come alive in ways no static page can match. Here are some of the significant points about getting started:

- The PHP installation instructions vary by operating system and version and can be very involved. To install PHP, use the instructions that come with the PHP download.

- To test your installation of PHP, try typing php -v on the command line; if you see PHP version information, you've been able to access PHP.

- To work with PHP, you have to set up your development environment, which includes a text editor or PHP IDE. Your development environment should also include some way of installing PHP pages where the server can reach them.

- PHP scripts enclose executable PHP between the markup <? and ?>. You can add HTML to the same page, as long as it's outside the <? and ?>.

- The echo statement echoes text to the browser.

- Here documents let you echo every word in them until the end token is encountered.

- There are three types of comments in PHP: /* */, //, and #.

- You prefix variable names with a $, and a valid variable name starts with a letter or underscore, followed by any number of letters, numbers, or underscores.

██ CHAPTER 2 ███

Gaining Control with Operators and Flow Control

C hapter 1, "Essential PHP," brought you the basics of PHP, and in this chapter, we're going to really get to work with PHP. The previous chapter was about getting started; this chapter is about making things happen. Everything we'll see in this chapter is an essential skill we'll use throughout the book.

We're going to start by working with the PHP *operators* that let you manipulate data in this chapter. For example, when you work with numerical data, you have a whole set of operators to work with—the + operator adds numbers ($variable + 5 adds 5 to the value in $variable), the * operator multiplies numbers ($variable * 2 multiplies the value in $variable by 2), and so on. All the operators appear in Table 2-1, and knowing how to use these operators is essential knowledge in PHP.

Besides putting the PHP operators to work, we're also going to start taking command of *flow control* in this chapter. Flow control lets you make decisions based on your data's values, which can include data that the user enters. For example, if the value in $temperature is greater than 80, you can echo "Too hot!" like this:

```
if ($temperature > 80){
    echo "Too hot!";
}
```

Flow control statements such as the if statement in this case give the PHP author a great deal of power because you can use them to make decisions at run time, based on the current value of the data you want to work with. They are also one of the primary ways in which PHP-enabled pages differ from static HTML pages.

Another set of flow-control statements that we'll see is *loops*. Computers excel at working with large amounts of data, and a loop will let you handle all the data in a huge set by working on each data item in turn. How this works will become more apparent when we work with arrays in Chapter 3, "Handling Strings and Arrays," which are designed to hold data in a way that makes it easy for loops to handle that data. Using a loop, you can handle each data item in a large set, such as the contents of a database.

The Math Operators

We'll start with the math operators, which are the most basic of all operators:

- `+` Adds two numbers

- `-` Subtracts one number from another

- `*` Multiplies two numbers together

- `/` Divides one number by another

- `%` Returns the remainder when one number is divided by another (modulus).

You can see them all at work in phpmath.php; here's the PHP:

EXAMPLE 2-1   Using the *Math* operators, phpmath.php

```
<HTML>
    <BODY>
        <H1>The math operators</H1>
        <?php
            echo "5 + 2 = ", 5 + 2, "<BR>";
            echo "5 - 2 = ", 5 - 2, "<BR>";
            echo "5 * 2 = ", 5 * 2, "<BR>";
            echo "5 / 2 = ", 5 / 2, "<BR>";
            echo "5 % 2 = ", 5 % 2, "<BR>";
        ?>
    </BODY>
</HTML>
```

The results, all as expected, appear in Figure 2-1.

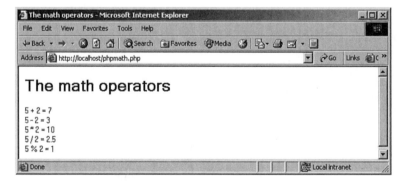

FIGURE 2-1   The math operators.

The Math Functions

Besides the math operators, PHP comes with all kinds of math functions built in—here's the list of what's available to you in your scripts:

- abs. Absolute value
- acos. Arc cosine
- acosh. Inverse hyperbolic cosine
- asin. Arc sine
- asinh. Inverse hyperbolic sine
- atan2. Arc tangent of two variables
- atan. Arc tangent
- atanh. Inverse hyperbolic tangent
- base_convert. Converts a number between bases
- bindec. Converts binary to decimal
- ceil. Rounds fractions up
- cos. Cosine
- cosh. Hyperbolic cosine
- decbin. Converts decimal to binary
- dechex. Converts decimal to hexadecimal
- decoct. Converts decimal to octal
- deg2rad. Converts the number in degrees to the radian equivalent
- exp. Calculates the exponent of e
- expm1. Returns exp(number) - 1
- floor. Rounds fractions down
- fmod. Returns the floating point remainder of the division of the arguments
- getrandmax. Shows the largest possible random value
- hexdec. Converts hexadecimal to decimal
- hypot. Returns sqrt(num1*num1 + num2*num2)
- is_finite. Determines whether a value is a legal finite number

- is_infinite. Determines whether a value is infinite

- is_nan. Determines whether a value is not a number

- lcg_value. Combined linear congruential generator

- log10. Base 10 logarithm

- log1p. Returns log(1 + number)

- log. Returns the natural logarithm

- max. Finds the highest value

- min. Finds the lowest value

- mt_getrandmax. Shows the largest possible random value

- mt_rand. Generates a better random value

- mt_srand. Seeds the better random number generator

- octdec. Converts octal to decimal

- pi. Gets the value of pi

- pow. Exponential expression

- rad2deg. Converts the radian number to the equivalent number in degrees

- rand. Generates a random integer

- round. Rounds a float

- sin. Sine

- sinh. Hyperbolic sine

- sqrt. Square root

- srand. Seed the random number generator

- tan. Tangent

- tanh. Hyperbolic tangent

Here's an example, using sqrt to get a square root:

```php
<?php
    echo "sqrt(49) = ", sqrt(49);
?>
```

Here's what you get when you run this script:

```
sqrt(49) = 7
```

If you ever need some advanced math, PHP has the situation covered.

The Assignment Operators

The main assignment operator is =, which assigns a value to a variable:

```
$oranges = 12;
```

That's one we've already seen. You can do some tricky stuff with the = operator, such as the following, where we're setting three variables to the same value, 1:

```php
<?php
    $a = $b = $c = 1;
    echo $a, ", ", $b, ", ", $c;
?>
```

Here's what you see when you run this script:

```
1, 1, 1
```

Besides the basic assignment operator, there are "combined operators" for all the binary arithmetic and string operators that allow you to use a value in an expression and then set its value to the result of that expression. Here are the combined operators (we'll see the various operators that are combined with the = sign here in this chapter):

```
+= -= *= /= .= %= &= |= ^= <<= >>=
```

These operators can save you a step; for example, say you wanted to add 10 to the value in the variable $my_CD_collection. You could do that like this:

```
$my_CD_collection =  $my_CD_collection + 10;
```

Using the combination operator += gives you a shortcut, letting you combine the addition and the assignment into one operation:

```
$my_CD_collection +=  10;
```

Not bad. Here's another example, using the string concatenation operator, ., and the division operator, /:

```php
<?php
    $text = "No ";
    $total = 150;
    echo $text .= "worries.<BR>";
    echo "Average = ", $total /= 3, "<BR>";
?>
```

Here's what you get from this script:

```
No worries.<BR>Average = 50<BR>
```

Incrementing and Decrementing

A common thing to do in PHP scripts, especially in the loops we'll see later in this chapter, is to increment the value in a variable by adding one or to decrement the value in a variable by subtracting one. In PHP, the incrementing operator is ++, and the decrementing operator is --.

For example, if $bananas holds 0, then using the ++ operator like this: $bananas++ leaves a result of 1 in $bananas. If $apples holds 11, then $apples-- leaves 10 in $apples.

You can use ++ and -- *before* or *after* a variable name, such as ++$bananas (this is using it as a *prefix operator*) or $bananas++ (this is using it as a *postfix operator*). If you use ++$bananas, the value in $bananas is incremented, and that incremented value is then used in the rest of the statement. If you use $bananas++, then the original value in $bananas is used in the rest of the statement, and *then* the value in $bananas is incremented. Here's an overview of the difference:

++$value	Pre-increment	Increments $value by one, then returns $value.
$value++	Post-increment	Returns $value, then increments $value by one.
--$value	Pre-decrement	Decrements $value by one, then returns $value.
$value--	Post-decrement	Returns $value, then decrements $value by one.

In other words, if you use ++$bananas, the value in $bananas is incremented *before* that value is passed on for use in the rest of the current statement. If you use $bananas++, the current value in $bananas is passed on for use in the rest of the statement, and only *then* is the value incremented.

You can see this difference in Example 2-2, phpincrementing.php, which works through the various possibilities, using ++ and -- as both a prefix and postfix operator.

EXAMPLE 2-2   Incrementing and Decrementing, phpincrementing.php

```
<HTML>
    <HEAD>
        <TITLE>
            Incrementing and Decrementing
        </TITLE>
    </HEAD>

    <BODY>
        <H1>
```

```
                Incrementing and Decrementing
        </H1>
<?php
    $a = $b = $c = $d = 1;

    echo "\$a++ gives ", $a++, "<BR>";

    echo "++\$b gives ", ++$b, "<BR>";

    echo "\$c- - gives ", $c--, "<BR>";

    echo "- -\$d gives ", --$d, "<BR>";
?>
    </BODY>
</HTML>
```

The results appear in Figure 2-2. As you can see, it makes a difference whether you use ++ and -- as prefix operators or postfix operators.

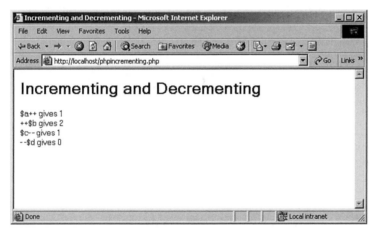

FIGURE 2-2   Using the increment and decrement operators.

If you just want to make sure you increment or decrement the value in a variable without worrying about whether the value will be incremented or decremented before being used in the rest of the statement, use ++ and -- as prefix operators.

Operator Precedence

Now that we've got all these new operators floating around—+, -, ++, %, and so on—a new question arises: if you use a bunch of these operators at the same time, which comes first? For example, what's the result of the following script?

```php
<?php
    echo 4 + 2 * 9;
?>
```

Will the + part be evaluated first, giving 4 + 2 * 9 = 6 * 9 = 54, or will the * part be evaluated first, giving 4 + 2 * 9 = 4 + 18 = 22?

The answer is 22 because the * operator has *precedence* over the + operator when you mix them up like this. You can see the complete list of PHP operator precedence in Table 2-1. The operators with the highest precedence are at the top, and the lowest are at the bottom. As you can see in the table, the * operator is above the + operator.

TABLE 2-1 Operator Precedence

Operators
new
[
! ~ ++ -- (int) (float) (string) (array) (object)
@
* / %
+ - .
<< >>
< <= > >=
== != === !==
&
^
|
&&
||
? :
= += -= *= /= .= %= &= |= ^= <<= >>=
print
and
xor
or
,

If operator precedence is interfering with your goal, you can always clarify how you want items to be evaluated by using parentheses. For example, you'll get 22 when you run this script:

```
<?php
    echo 4 + 2 * 9;
?>
```

But you can use parentheses to tell PHP what to do. If you change this expression to (4 + 2) * 9, then you'll get 6 * 9 = 54. Take a look at phpprecedence.php in Example 2-3 to see this at work.

EXAMPLE 2-3   Incrementing and Decrementing, phpprecedence.php

```
<HTML>
    <HEAD><TITLE>Setting operator precedence</TITLE></HEAD>
    <BODY>
        <H1>Setting operator precedence</H1>
<?php
    echo "4 + 2 * 9 = ", 4 + 2 * 9, "<BR>";
    echo "(4 + 2) * 9", (4 + 2) * 9, "<BR>";
    echo "4 + (2 * 9)", 4 + (2 * 9), "<BR>";
?>
    </BODY>
</HTML>
```

The results, where we've set our own execution precedence, appear in Figure 2-3.

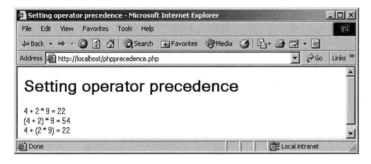

FIGURE 2-3   Setting execution precedence.

The Execution Operator

Here's a cool one—the *execution operator* lets you run operating system commands and programs. All you've got to do is to enclose the command you want to run in backticks (`—not the same as a single quote!). Here's an example that runs the date system command, captures the output, and displays it:

```
<?php
$output = `date`;
echo $output;
?>
```

Here's the kind of result you might see under Unix, using the bash shell:

```
-bash-2.05b$ php t.php
Thu Aug 12 10:53:28 PDT 2004
```

Because date is also a command in DOS, here's what you might see in a DOS window:

```
C:\php>php t.php
The current date is: Thu 08/12/2004
Enter the new date: (mm-dd-yy)
```

What if you want to pass an argument to the system command? Include the argument in the backticks too, as in the following, where we're executing the command dir c:\temp in Windows:

```
<?php
    $output = `dir c:\\temp`;
    echo $output;
?>
```

The result appears in Figure 2-4.

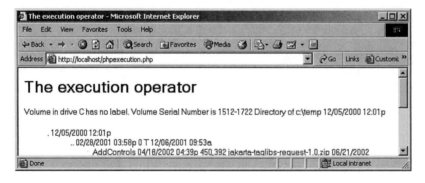

FIGURE 2-4 Executing system commands.

String Operators

PHP has two string operators. The first is the concatenation operator (.), which we've seen before, which joins its right and left operands into one string. The second is the concatenating assignment operator (.=), which appends the operand on the right side to the operand on the left side.

You can see an example of each in pphpstringop.php, Example 2-4.

EXAMPLE 2-4   Using the string operators, pphpstringop.php

```
<HTML>
    <HEAD><TITLE>The string operators</TITLE></HEAD>
    <BODY>
        <H1>The string operators</H1>
<?php
$a = "No ";
echo "\$a = ", $a, "<BR>";
echo "\$b = \$a . \"problem \"<BR>";
$b = $a . "problem ";
echo "Now \$b = ", $b, "<BR>";
echo "\$b .= \"at all.\"<BR>";
$b .= "at all.";
echo "Now \$b = ", $b, "<BR>";
?>
        </BODY>
</HTML>
```

The results of this example appear in Figure 2-5. (For more on strings, take a look at all the PHP string *functions* available in Chapter 3.)

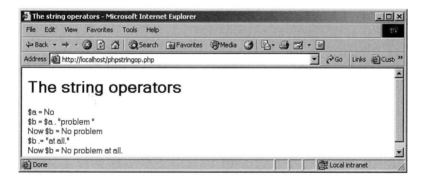

FIGURE 2-5   The string operators.

Bitwise Operators

PHP also comes with a set of operators that can work with the individual bits in an integer. You don't usually use the bitwise operators unless you've had some experience programming and want to work with individual bits in various values. If you don't know about bits, bytes, and so on, don't worry; you can skip this chunk without harm.

NOTE
Besides integers, you can also work with strings using these operators; in that case, the ASCII value of each character is used.

For example, the And operator, &, works on two operands like this: $a | $b. In the result, bits that are set (that is, equal to 1, not 0) in either $a or $b are set. So, for example, if $a equals 1 (which has the 0th bit set) and $b = 2 (which has the 1st bit set), then $a | $b will equal 1 | 2; both the 0th bit and the 1st bit are set in the result, so it equals 3.

You can see the bitwise operators and what they do in Table 2-2.

TABLE 2-2   The Bitwise Operators

Operator	Operation	Example	Result
$a & $b	And	$a & $b	Bits that are set in both $a and $b are set.
$a | $b	Or	$a | $b	Bits that are set in either $a or $b are set.
$a ^ $b	Xor	$a ^ $b	Bits that are set in $a or $b but not both are set.
~ $a	Not	~ $a	Bits that are set in $a are not set, and vice versa.
$a << $b	Shift left	$a << $b	Shift the bits of $a $b steps to the left (each step means "multiply by two").
$a >> $b	Shift right	$a >> $b	Shift the bits of $a $b steps to the right (each step means "divide by two").

Notice the *shift* operators here, which let you shift bits to the right or the left. For example, 4 << 1 means that we're shifting the bits in the value 4 left one place, which ends up giving you 8 (the same as multiplying by 2). Conversely, 4 >> 1 shifts the bits in 4 to the right one place, giving you 2 (the same as dividing by 2).

These operators are meant to work on the bits in individual integers, not on boolean values, and, as mentioned, this kind of work is usually only performed by programmers who have special needs to work with those bits. If you do need this kind of bit-by-bit functionality, however, it's available for you in PHP.

Using *if* Statements

Here's where you can start making choices based on your data: by using if statements. Just about all high-level programming languages, including PHP, have an if statement, and here's what it looks like formally:

```
if (expression)
    statement
```

Here, *expression* is an expression that can be evaluated to a boolean TRUE/FALSE value. For example, if *expression* were 5 > 2, then it would evaluate to TRUE because 5 is greater than 2. If *expression* is TRUE, then *statement* is executed; if *expression* is FALSE, *statement* is not executed.

The if statement is great because your script can make choices at run time, based on the run-time value of your data, which can include text the user has entered in a web page (such as a password), values retrieved from a database (such as inventory available), or even data fetched from another web site (such as stock prices).

Here's an example that tests whether the value in a variable named $temperature is less than 80 degrees:

```php
<?php
    $temperature = 75;
    if ($temperature < 80)
        echo "Nice day.";
?>
```

In this case, $temperature holds a value of 75, so the statement echo "Nice day."; is executed, and this is what you see:

```
Nice day.
```

But what if you have multiple statements you want to execute if a certain condition is true? That's no problem—a PHP statement can also be a *compound statement*, which means it can contain any number of simple statements, as long as you enclose them in curly braces.

For example, here are three simple statements made into one compound PHP statement just by enclosing them between { and }:

```php
{
    echo "Your time is up!<BR>";
    echo "Please put the phone down.";
    $hang_up_now = TRUE;
}
```

You can see how this new compound statement might appear inside an if statement in phpif.php, Example 2-5.

EXAMPLE 2-5   Using the *if* statement, phpif.php

```html
<HTML>
    <HEAD>
        <TITLE>Using the if statement</TITLE>
    </HEAD>

    <BODY>
        <H1>Using the if statement</H1>
        <?php
            $minutes= 4;
            if($minutes > 3) {
                echo "Your time is up!<BR>";
                echo "Please put the phone down.";
                $hang_up_now = TRUE;
            }
        ?>
    </BODY>
</HTML>
```

And you can see this new example at work in Figure 2-6.

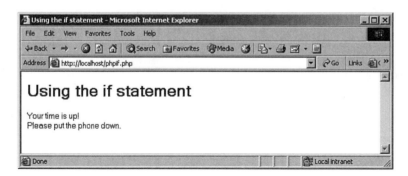

FIGURE 2-6   Using the *if* statement.

Here's another example. PHP has functions named is_int, is_float, is_array, and so on to return the type of a variable. Using them, you can test the type of a variable before using it, like this:

```php
if (is_int($variable))
    $variable = $variable + 10;
```

The if statement is a basic one that you'll use in practically all your scripts—and more on it is coming up in this chapter.

The Comparison Operators

There is an entire set of operators designed to be used with the `if` statement—the *comparison operators*. In the previous chunk's example, we used the greater-than (>) operator to check the value in `$minutes`:

```php
<?php
    $minutes= 4;
        if($minutes > 3) {
            echo "Your time is up!<BR>";
            echo "Please put the phone down.";
            $hang_up_now = TRUE;
    }
?>
```

Comparison operators let you compare two values like this. All the PHP comparison operators are shown in Table 2-3.

TABLE 2-3   The Comparison Operators

Operator	Operation	Example	Result
==	Equal	$a == $b	TRUE if $a is equal to $b.
===	Identical	$a === $b	TRUE if $a is equal to $b, and they are of the same type.
!=	Not equal	$a != $b	TRUE if $a is not equal to $b.
<>	Not equal	$a <> $b	TRUE if $a is not equal to $b.
!==	Not identical	$a !== $b	TRUE if $a is not equal to $b, or they are not of the same type.
<	Less than	$a < $b	TRUE if $a is strictly less than $b.
>	Greater than	$a > $b	TRUE if $a is strictly greater than $b.
<=	Less than or equal to	$a <= $b	TRUE if $a is less than or equal to $b.
>=	Greater than or equal to	$a >= $b	TRUE if $a is greater than or equal to $b.

For example, if you wanted to check whether the value in the variable `$temperature` was exactly 75 degrees, you could use ==, the equality operator:

```php
<?php
    $temperature = 75;
    if ($temperature == 75) {
        echo "75 degrees today, not too bad.";
    }
?>
```

Here's another example, this time using the not equal operator, !=, which returns TRUE if two values are not equal. In this case, we're checking to make sure that the temperature is not 75 degrees:

```php
<?php
    $temperature = 80;
    if ($temperature != 75) {
        echo "It's not 75 degrees today.";
    }
?>
```

The results:

```
It's not 75 degrees today.
```

Here's an important detail about floating point precision. Internally, floating point numbers are stored in binary, not decimal, format. That means the floating point number that you think is 8.00000000 is really stored internally as 7.99999999, which is very close, but separate enough to make an equality (==) test fail. Usually, decimal values such as 1.75 or 3.12 cannot be converted into exactly the same number in the internal binary format your computer uses, which means that you can't expect to rely on floating point values down to the last digit, or even the last couple of digits, for complete precision.

So how can you compare floating point numbers for equality? The easiest way is to compare them and make sure they are within a certain range. For example, say you have a value that you're using for pi: $value = 3.1415926535;. PHP comes with a built-in function named pi (see "The Math Functions" in this chapter) that will return the value of pi to fairly high precision (3.1415926535898), so we can check our value against that by checking their difference using the abs function to get the absolute value (also see "The Math Functions" in this chapter for the abs function):

```php
<?php
    $value = 3.1415926535;
    if (abs($value - pi()) < .0000001) {
    echo "Close enough";
}
?>
```

Logical Operators

There's more to the story than just the comparison operators, however. For example, what if you wanted to make sure the temperature was above 75 *and* below 80? You might do this by using nested if statements:

```
$temperature = 76;
if ($temperature > 75) {
    if ($temperature < 80) {
        echo "We're in the comfort zone.";
    }
}
```

There's a simpler way, though. You can use the && logical And operator to connect the conditions $temperature > 75 and $temperature < 80 together so that both must be true for the if statement to execute its internal statement. Here's what this looks like:

```
<?php
$temperature = 76;
if ($temperature > 75 && $temperature < 80) {
    echo "We're in the comfort zone.";
}
?>
```

Here, we're connecting the conditions $temperature > 75 and $temperature < 80 using the && operator, and both of them have to be true for the resulting overall expression to be true. You can see the complete list of the PHP logical operators in Table 2-4.

TABLE 2-4 The Logical Operators

Operator	Operation	Example	Result
and	And	$a and $b	TRUE if both $a and $b are TRUE.
or	Or	$a or $b	TRUE if either $a or $b is TRUE.
xor	Xor	$a xor $b	TRUE if either $a or $b is TRUE, but not both.
!	Not	! $a	TRUE if $a is not TRUE.
&&	And	$a && $b	TRUE if both $a and $b are TRUE.
||	Or	$a || $b	TRUE if either $a or $b is TRUE.

NOTE
Why are there two And operators and two Or operators? The && and || operators have higher precedence than the and and or operators; see Table 2-1.

Using *else* Statements

The if statement has more power built into it. You know that if the if statement's condition is true, the if statement's internal statement will be executed. But what if the if statement's condition is false? Does that mean you can't execute any code?

Nope. You can use an *else* statement (also called an else *clause*) to execute code when an if statement's condition is false. For example, take a look at this code; the if statement's condition is false, so the internal statement echo "We're in the comfort zone."; will not be executed:

```php
<?php
    $temperature = 26;

    if ($temperature > 75 && $temperature < 80) {
        echo "We're in the comfort zone.";
    }
    else {
        echo "We're outside the comfort zone.";
    }
?>
```

Because the if statement's condition is false, however, the internal statement in the else statement *will* be executed. In this case, that means you'll see this from the script:

```
We're outside the comfort zone.
```

Now you can handle if statements either way—whether the if statement's condition is true *or* false.

Here's another example; in this case, we'll check a student's grade on a test:

```php
<?php
    $score = 89;

    if ($score > 50) {
        echo "Whew, you passed.";
    }
    else {
        echo "Uh oh.";
    }
?>
```

The results:

```
Whew, you passed.
```

Using *elseif* Statements

In fact, even more is built into the `if` statement. You can also use *elseif* statements to check other conditions. Say, for example, that you want to tell students what their grades were on a recent test using a handy PHP script. If you were restricted to using `if` and `else` statements, your script might look like this, where you could only report whether a student got an A or not:

```php
<?php
    $test_score = 78;
    if ($test_score > 90) {
        echo "You got an A!";
    }
    else {
        echo "You didn't get an A.";
    }
?>
```

The `elseif` statement can come to the rescue here. This statement is much like an `else` statement because it's only executed if the main `if` condition was false—but you can include a new condition to test in each `elseif` statement. Here's how that would work for checking whether the student got an A, B, C, D, or...uh oh...:

```php
<?php
    $test_score = 78;
    if ($test_score > 90) {
        echo "You got an A!";
    }
    elseif ($test_score > 80) {
        echo "You got a B.";
    }
    elseif ($test_score > 70) {
        echo "You got a C.";
    }
    elseif ($test_score > 60) {
        echo "You got a D.";
    }
    else {
        echo "Uh oh.";
    }
?>
```

Here's what you'd see from this script:

```
You got a C.
```

Very cool—now you can test many conditions in the same `if` statement.

The Ternary Operator

Believe it or not, there's an operator that acts just like an if statement, the ternary operator. This operator has an unusual form; just ?:. Here's how you use it:

```
$result = condition ? expression1 : expression2;
```

If *condition* is true, then *expression1* is assigned to $result; otherwise, *expression2* is assigned to it instead. This can lead to some pretty compact statements. For example, take a look at this script from the previous "Using else Statements" section:

```
$temperature = 26;

if ($temperature > 75 && $temperature < 80) {
    echo "We're in the comfort zone.";
}
else {
    echo "We're outside the comfort zone.";
}
```

All six lines of the if statement can be condensed into a single line using the ternary operator (note that this statement is too long for a single line in the book, so I'm cutting it up onto two lines):

```
$temperature = 26;
echo $temperature > 75 && $temperature < 80 ? "We're in the comfort zone." :
    "We're outside the comfort zone.";
```

Here's another example, which finds the absolute value of numbers (note that this example uses the - negation operator to reverse the sign of numbers if needed):

```
<?php
    $value = -25;
    $abs_value = $value < 0 ? -$value : $value;
    echo $abs_value;
?>
```

The following example is a little more complex; it converts decimal numbers to hexadecimal (base 16) as long as they will fit into a single hexadecimal digit. It uses the PHP chr function (see Chapter 3) to convert numbers to ASCII characters:

```
<?php
    $value = 14;
    $output = $value < 10 ? "0x" . $value : "0x" . chr($value - 10 + 65);
    echo "In hexadecimal, $value = $output.";
?>
```

This script provides this result: In hexadecimal, 14 = 0xE.

Using *switch* Statements

If you have many conditions to test, even using elseif statements can become a little tedious. For those circumstances when you have plenty of conditions to check, you should consider a *switch* statement, which is built for testing multiple conditions.

A switch statement starts with the keyword switch; you indicate the item you're testing by placing it in parentheses. You create multiple tests using the *case* statement, specifying a value for each statement. If the switch's test value matches a case statement's value, the internal statements in the case statement are executed up to a *break* statement, which ends the case statement. If no case matches, the statements in a *default* statement, if present, are executed. Here's an example, which displays different text based on the temperature:

```php
<?php
$temperature = 70;
switch ($temperature){
    case 70:
        echo "Nice weather.";
        break;
    case 71:
        echo "Still nice weather.";
        break;
    case 72:
        echo "Getting warmer.";
        break;
    default:
        echo "Temperature outside the range.";
}
?>
```

In this case, you'd see:

```
Nice weather.
```

Pretty cool. Note that the values you specify in a case statement may only be integer or floating point numbers and strings.

What if you want to match multiple values in the same case statement? In that case, you can omit the break statement in various case statements, which means that execution will fall through to the next case statement. For example, to match temperature ranges such as 70-72, 73-75, and so on, take a look at phpswitch.php, Example 2-6.

EXAMPLE 2-6   Using the *switch* statement, phpswitch.php

```
<HTML>
    <HEAD>
        <TITLE>
            Using the switch statement
        </TITLE>
    </HEAD>

    <BODY>
        <H1>
            Using the switch statement
        </H1>
        <?php
            $temperature = 74;
            switch ($temperature) {
                case 70:
                case 71:
                case 72:
                    echo "Nice weather.";
                    break;
                case 73:
                case 74:
                case 75:
                    echo "Still nice weather.";
                    break;
                case 76:
                case 77:
                case 78:
                    echo "Getting warmer.";
                    break;
                default:
                    echo "Temperature outside the range.";
            }
        ?>
    </BODY>
</HTML>
```

The results appear in Figure 2-7.

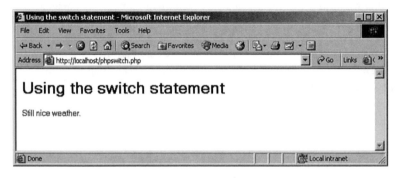

FIGURE 2-7   Using the *switch* statement.

Working with *for* Loops

One of the things that computers excel at is handling repetitive tasks. For example, say you have 10,000 student scores to average; adding them all up manually would take a lot of time—but it's no problem for a computer. Computers handle repetitive tasks such as this with *loops*, and the first loop we're going to take a look at is the *for* loop, which when repeated executes a statement (which can be a compound statement):

```
for (expression1; expression2; expression3) statement
```

In this statement, *expression1* lets you set up your loop, often by initializing a loop counter variable (also called a loop *index*) that will track how many times the loop has executed. This expression is executed before the loop's statement is run each time through the loop. The next expression, *expression2*, is the test expression—the loop will keep going while this expression remains true. You usually test the value in your loop counter here. The final expression, *expression3*, is executed after *statement* is executed, each time through the loop. You usually increment your loop counter variable in this expression.

Here's a simple example, phpfor.php, Example 2-7, to make this all clear. In this case, we'll use a for loop to display a line of text five times. The loop starts by setting a loop counter variable that we'll name $loop_counter to 0. The loop increments the counter each time after it runs and then tests to make sure that the loop counter doesn't exceed 5.

EXAMPLE 2-7   Using the *for* loop, phpfor.php

```
<HTML>
    <HEAD>
        <TITLE>
            Using the for loop
        </TITLE>
    </HEAD>

    <BODY>
        <H1>
            Using the for loop
        </H1>
        <?php
            for ($loop_counter = 0; $loop_counter < 5; $loop_counter++){
                echo "I'm going to do this five times.<BR>";
            }
        ?>
    </BODY>
</HTML>
```

The results appear in Figure 2-8, where, as you can see, the text is displayed five times.

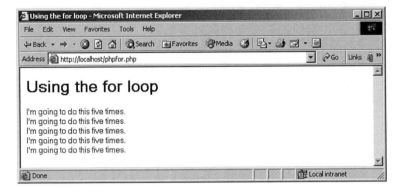

FIGURE 2-8 Using the *for* loop.

The expressions in a for loop can handle multiple indexes if you want, as long as you separate them with the comma operator. Here's an example that uses two loop indexes:

```php
<?php
for ($var1=2, $var2=2; $var1 < 5 && $var2 < 5; $var1++, $var2++){
    echo "$var1 x $var2 = ", $var1 * $var2, "<BR>";
}
?>
```

And here's what the result looks like in a browser:

```
2 x 2 = 4
3 x 3 = 9
4 x 4 = 16
```

You don't have to use a loop index at all in a for loop. This example uses some (fictitious) functions to connect to a data source over the Internet, process the received data, and move to the next data item as the loop progresses:

```
for (initialize_connection(); process_new_data() != "quit"; move_to_next_item()){
    echo "Getting more data....";
}
```

You can also *nest* for loops, one inside another, as we'll see when we work with arrays.

Working with *while* Loops

Another important type of loop is the `while` loop. Rather than using a loop index, this loop keeps going while a certain condition is true, executing its statement over and over:

`while (expression) statement`

Here, *statement* can be a compound statement, surrounded in curly braces. This loop will keep going as long as the condition *expression* remains true. As you can imagine, if you don't want the loop to keep going forever, you have to do something in *statement* eventually that will make *expression* false.

Example 2-8, phpwhile.php, shows a `while` loop. In this case, we'll display the value in a variable as long as it's less than 10—note that we double the value in the variable each time through the loop so that the loop will eventually stop, and we assign a value to the variable before beginning so it doesn't start off with a value of 0 (which would mean the loop would never stop).

EXAMPLE 2-8   Using the *while* loop, phpwhile.php

```
<HTML>
    <HEAD>
        <TITLE>
            Using the while loop
        </TITLE>
    </HEAD>

    <BODY>
        <H1>
            Using the while loop
        </H1>
        <?php
            $value =1;
            while ($value < 10){
                echo "New value:", $value, "<BR>";
                $value *=2;
            }
        ?>
    </BODY>
</HTML>
```

You can see the results in Figure 2-9; the `while` loop displays the current value of the variable, doubling it each time through, until that value exceeds 10. Perfect.

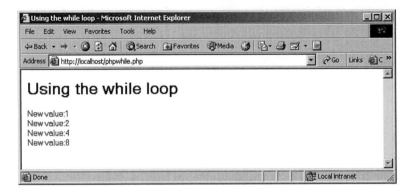

FIGURE 2-9 Using the *while* loop.

This kind of loop is often used when your loop doesn't have an explicit loop index. For example, when you're reading data from a file, you can use functions to test where you're at in the file whose data you're reading. Here's how it looks in outline—we open the file and test if we're at the end of the file (these are made-up functions):

```php
<?php
    open_file();
    while (not_at_end_of_file()){
        .
        .
        .

    }
?>
```

If we're not at the end of the file, we read and echo a line from the file. Then we test if we're at the end of the file again, and if so, we quit. Otherwise, we read another line:

```php
<?php
    open_file();
    while (not_at_end_of_file()){
        $data = read_one_line_from_file();
        echo $data;
    }
?>
```

Working with *do...while* Loops

Besides while loops, you can also use *do...while* loops in PHP. These loops are just like while loops, except that the condition is checked at the *end* of the loop, not the beginning:

```
do
    statement
while (expression)
```

Here's what the while loop example in the previous chunk would look like as a do...while loop instead:

```
<?php
    $value =1;
    do{
        echo $value, "<BR>";
        $value *=2;
    } while ($value < 10);
?>
```

The difference between while loops and do...while loops is where the condition is tested—at the beginning or the end of the loop. That can make a big difference. For example, if the condition is false before the loop even starts, a while loop wouldn't even execute once. Here's an example where the condition is false from the very beginning, so this script doesn't echo anything:

```
<?php
$value =20;
while ($value < 10){
    $value *=2;
    echo $value, "<BR>";
}
?>
```

However, in a do...while loop, the condition is tested at the end, so this script does echo 20 in a browser:

```
<?php
$value =20;
do{
    echo $value, "<BR>";
    $value *=2;
} while ($value < 10);

?>
```

Working with *foreach* Loops

There's a special loop, the *foreach* loop, that makes working with complex variables such as arrays easier. We'll get the details on foreach in the next chapter, but we'll take a quick look at it here. Arrays store multiple data items, and this loop lets you loop over arrays without using a loop index. Here's how you use it:

```
foreach (array_expression as $value) statement
foreach (array_expression as $key => $value) statement
```

You can see an example in phpforeach.php, Example 2-9, where foreach is looping over an array of fruits and echoing each to the browser window.

EXAMPLE 2-9   Using the *foreach* loop, phpforeach.php

```
<HTML>
    <HEAD><TITLE>Using the foreach loop</TITLE></HEAD>

    <BODY>
        <H1>Using the foreach loop</H1>
            <?php
                $arr = array("apples", "oranges", "bananas");
                foreach ($arr as $value) {
                    echo "Current fruit: $value<BR>";
                }
            ?>
    </BODY>
</HTML>
```

The results appear in Figure 2-10; the loop was able to loop over all the items in the array automatically. The specifics of this loop are coming up in Chapter 3.

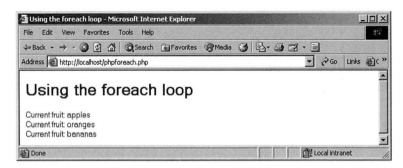

FIGURE 2-10   Using the *foreach* loop.

Breaking Out of Loops

In case you want to stop a loop or switch statement early, the *break* statement ends execution of the current for, foreach, while, do...while, or switch statement. You've already seen the break statement at work in the switch statement. Here, we're ending the code that should be executed in a case statement inside a switch statement:

```
$temperature = 70;
switch ($temperature):
    case 70:
        echo "Nice weather.";
        break;
        .
        .
        .
```

You can also end loop execution early with the break statement. For example, in this loop, execution will continue five times—unless we stop things early at, say, the third loop iteration:

```php
<?php
    for ($loop_counter = 0; $loop_counter < 5; $loop_counter++){
        echo "I'm going to do this five times unless stopped!<BR>";
        if ($loop_counter == 2) {
            .

            .

            .
        }
    }
?>
```

Here's how that might look using the break statement:

```php
<?php
    for ($loop_counter = 0; $loop_counter < 5; $loop_counter++){
        echo "I'm going to do this five times unless stopped!<BR>";
        if ($loop_counter == 2) {
            echo "Enough already, I'm quitting.<BR>";
            break;
        }
    }
?>
```

And this is what you see:

```
I'm going to do this five times unless stopped!
I'm going to do this five times unless stopped!
I'm going to do this five times unless stopped!
Enough already, I'm quitting.
```

Skipping Interactions with *continue*

Here's another tip: you can use the *continue* statement inside a loop to skip the rest of the current loop iteration and continue with the next iteration. That's useful in case you need to skip an iteration, as in phpcontinue.php, Example 2-10, which prints out reciprocals (one over a number, 1/n). In this case, we use *continue* to avoid trying to figure out 1/0 (which is infinite and would cause a math error).

EXAMPLE 2-10   Using the *continue* statement, phpcontinue.php

```
<HTML>
    <HEAD><TITLE>Using the continue statement</TITLE></HEAD>

    <BODY>
        <H1>Using the continue statement</H1>
        <?php
            for ($value = -2; $value < 2; $value++){
                if($value == 0){
                    continue;
                }
                echo "1/$value = ", 1 / $value, "<BR>";
            }
        ?>
    </BODY>
</HTML>
```

The results appear in Figure 2-11. Note that we skipped the problematic iteration!

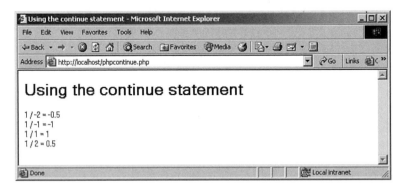

FIGURE 2-11   Using the *continue* statement.

Some Alternative Syntax

PHP also has some alternative syntax for if, while, for, foreach, and switch statements. In each case, the form of the alternate syntax changes the opening curly brace to a colon (:) and the closing brace to endif;, endwhile;, endfor;, endforeach;, or endswitch;, respectively.

Here's an example showing an if statement using alternate syntax:

```php
<?php
$value = 10;
if ($value == 1):
    echo "\$value holds 1";
elseif ($value == 10):
    echo "\$value holds 10.";
else:
    echo "\$value does not hold 1 or 10.";
endif;
?>
```

This example echoes: "$value holds 10.".

Here's an example of using a for loop and alternate syntax:

```php
<?php
    for ($loop_counter = 0; $loop_counter < 5; $loop_counter++) :
        echo "I'm going to do this five times.<BR>";
    endfor;
?>
```

That's it; now that we've got operators and loops under our belts, we're ready to tackle the next step—working with strings and arrays, coming up next in Chapter 3.

Summary

PHP allows you to take control of your code with operators and flow control. Operators give you a quick way to handle data in single statements, adding numbers, for example, or testing equality. Flow control statements are very powerful because they let you make decisions based on the data in your scripts. Here's a summary of the salient points:

- The five math operators, +, -, *, /, and %, give you basic math capabilities. The math functions, from abs to tanh, give you more math power.

- The assignment operators, =, +=, -=, *=, /=, .=, %=, &=, |=, ^=, <<=, and >>=, let you assign values to variables, even combining the assignment with other operators such as +, -, *, and so on.

- The ++ and -- operators let you increment and decrement values.

- The execution operator, ``, lets you execute system commands.

- The string operators, . and .=, let you concatenate strings.

- The bitwise operators, &, |, ^, ~, <<, and >>, let you work on the individual bits in values.

- The comparison operators, ==, ===, !=, <>, !==, <, >, <=, and >=, let you compare values.

- The logical operators, and, or, xor, !, &&, and ||, let you chain truth values together.

- The if statement lets you check the truth value of expressions and execute code depending on the results.

- The switch statement lets you test many conditions at once, sort of like an extended if statement.

- The for loop iterates over statements as needed while a test condition remains true. It has an initialization part, a part tested after every loop iteration, and a part that is executed after every loop iteration.

- The while loop keeps looping over a set of statements while a test condition remains true.

- Do...while loops are the same as while loops, except that the test condition is tested at the end of the loop.

- The foreach loop is designed to work with collections of data such as arrays.

CHAPTER 3

Handling Strings and Arrays

Two data types merit some special attention—strings and arrays. We've already seen strings at work, including single- and double-quoted strings (recall also that double-quoted strings allow variable interpolation). PHP also comes packed with more string power, and we're going to dig into that in this chapter—tons of functions are built into PHP that work with strings, from sorting strings to searching them, trimming extra spaces off of them, and getting their lengths. We'll get a handle on those functions in this chapter.

Besides strings, we're also going to get a handle on *arrays* in this chapter. We've seen how to store data in simple variables, but there's more to the story here. Arrays can hold multiple data items, assigning each one a numeric or text *index* (also called a *key*). For example, if you want to store some student test scores, you can store them in an array, and then you can access each score in the array via a numeric index. That's great as far as computers are concerned because you can work through all the elements in an array simply by steadily incrementing that index, as you might do with a loop. In that way, you can use your computer to iterate over all the elements in an array in order to print them out or find their average value, for example.

Arrays represent the first time we're associating data items together. Up to this point, we've only worked with simple variables, but working with arrays is fundamental to PHP for such tasks as reading the data that users enter in web pages. We'll get the details on strings and arrays in this chapter, and I'll start with the string functions.

Listing of String Functions

PHP has plenty of built-in string functions. Table 3-1 lists a selection of them.

TABLE 3-1   The String Functions

Function	Purpose
chr	Returns a specific character, given its ASCII code
chunk_split	Splits a string into smaller chunks
crypt	Supports one-way string encryption (hashing)
echo	Displays one or more strings
explode	Splits a string on a substring
html_entity_decode	Converts all HTML entities to their applicable characters
htmlentities	Converts all applicable characters to HTML entities
htmlspecialchars	Converts special characters to HTML entities
implode	Joins array elements with a string
ltrim	Strips whitespace from the beginning of a string
number_format	Formats a number with grouped thousand separators
ord	Returns the ASCII value of character
parse_str	Parses the string into variables
print	Displays a string
printf	Displays a formatted string
rtrim	Strips whitespace from the end of a string
setlocale	Sets locale information
similar_text	Calculates the similarity between two strings
sprintf	Returns a formatted string
sscanf	Parses input from a string according to a format
str_ireplace	Case-insensitive version of the str_replace function.
str_pad	Pads a string with another string
str_repeat	Repeats a string
str_replace	Replaces all occurrences of the search string with the replacement string

Function	Purpose
str_shuffle	Shuffles a string randomly
str_split	Converts a string to an array
str_word_count	Returns information about words used in a string
strcasecmp	Binary case-insensitive string comparison
strchr	Alias of the strstr function
strcmp	Binary-safe string comparison
strip_tags	Strips HTML and PHP tags from a string
stripos	Finds position of first occurrence of a case-insensitive string
stristr	Case-insensitive version of the strstr function
strlen	Gets a string's length
strnatcasecmp	Case-insensitive string comparisons
strnatcmp	String comparisons using a "natural order" algorithm
strncasecmp	Binary case-insensitive string comparison of the first n characters
strncmp	Binary-safe string comparison of the first n characters
strpos	Finds position of first occurrence of a string
strrchr	Finds the last occurrence of a character in a string
strrev	Reverses a string
strripos	Finds the position of last occurrence of a case-insensitive string
strrpos	Finds the position of last occurrence of a char in a string
strspn	Finds the length of initial segment matching mask
strstr	Finds the first occurrence of a string
strtolower	Converts a string to lowercase
strtoupper	Converts a string to uppercase
strtr	Translates certain characters
substr_compare	Binary-safe (optionally case-insensitive) comparison of two strings from an offset
substr_count	Counts the number of substring occurrences
substr_replace	Replaces text within part of a string
substr	Returns part of a string
trim	Strips whitespace from the beginning and end of a string

Using the String Functions

Here's an example that puts some of the useful string functions to work:

```php
<?php
    echo trim("     No worries."), "\n";
    echo substr("No worries.", 3, 7), "\n";
    echo "\"worries\" starts at position ", strpos("No worries.", "worries"), "\n";
    echo ucfirst("no worries."), "\n";
    echo "\"No worries.\" is ", strlen("No worries."), " characters long.\n";
    echo substr_replace("No worries.", "problems.", 3, 8), "\n";
    echo chr(65), chr(66), chr(67), "\n";
    echo strtoupper("No worries."), "\n";
?>
```

In this example, we're using trim to trim leading spaces from a string, substr to extract a substring from a string, strpos to search a string for a substring, ucfirst to convert the first character of a string to uppercase, strlen to determine a string's length, substr_replace to replace a substring with another string, chr to convert an ASCII code to a letter (ASCII 65 = "A", ASCII 66 = "B", and so on), and strtoupper to convert a string to uppercase.

Here are the results of this script, line by line:

```
No worries.
worries
"worries" starts at position 3
No worries.
"No worries." is 11 characters long.
No problems.
ABC
NO WORRIES.
```

This example shows some of the more powerful string functions at work. The list of string functions is a long one, but you'll usually find what you need in the table—and if not, you can often cobble together a solution using two or more of these functions.

Here's another tip: In PHP, you can also pick out the characters in a string by enclosing the place of the character you want in curly braces, like this:

```php
$string = 'No worries.';
$first_character = $string{0};
```

Formatting Strings

There's a pair of string functions that are particularly useful when you want to format data for display (such as when you're formatting numbers in string form): `printf` and `sprintf`. The `printf` function echoes text directly, and you assign the return value of `sprintf` to a string. Here's how you use these functions (items in square brackets, [and], in function specifications like this one are optional):

```
printf (format [, args])
sprintf (format [, args])
```

The `format` string is composed of zero or more *directives*: characters that are copied directly to the result, and *conversion specifications*. Each conversion specification consists of a percent sign (%), followed by one or more of these elements, in order:

- An optional *padding specifier* that indicates which character should be used to pad the results to the correct string size. This may be a space character or a 0 (zero character). The default is to pad with spaces.

- An optional *alignment specifier* that indicates whether the results should be left-justified or right-justified. The default is right-justified (a - character here will make it left-justified).

- An optional number, the *width specifier*, specifying how many characters (minimum) this conversion should result in.

- An optional *precision specifier* that indicates how many decimal digits should be displayed for floating-point numbers. (There is no effect for types other than `float`.)

- A *type specifier* that says what type the argument data should be treated as.

Here are the possible type specifiers:

%   A literal percent character. No argument is required.

b   The argument is treated as an integer, and presented as a binary number.

c   The argument is treated as an integer, and presented as the character with that ASCII value.

d   The argument is treated as an integer, and presented as a (signed) decimal number.

u   The argument is treated as an integer, and presented as an unsigned decimal number.

f   The argument is treated as a float, and presented as a floating-point number.

- The argument is treated as an integer, and presented as an octal number.

s   The argument is treated as and presented as a string.

x   The argument is treated as an integer and presented as a hexadecimal number (with lowercase letters).

X   The argument is treated as an integer and presented as a hexadecimal number (with uppercase letters).

These functions take a little getting used to, especially when you're formatting floating point values. For example, a format specifier of %6.2 means that a floating point number will be given six places in the display, with two places behind the decimal point. Here's an example that puts printf and sprintf to work:

```php
<?php
    printf("I have %s apples and %s oranges.\n", 4, 56);

    $year = 2005;
    $month = 4;
    $day = 28;
    printf("%04d-%02d-%02d\n", $year, $month, $day);

    $price = 5999.99;
    printf("\$%01.2f\n", $price);

    printf("%6.2f\n", 1.2);
    printf("%6.2f\n", 10.2);
    printf("%6.2f\n", 100.2);

    $string = sprintf("Now I have %s apples and %s oranges.\n", 3, 5);
    echo $string;
?>
```

In this example, we're formatting simple integers as strings, aligning floating-point numbers vertically so the decimal point lines up, and so on. Here's what you see when you run this script at the command line:

```
I have 4 apples and 56 oranges.
2005-04-28
$5999.99
  1.20
 10.20
100.20
Now I have 3 apples and 5 oranges.
```

NOTE
Another function useful for formatting numbers is number_format().

Converting to and from Strings

Converting between string format and other formats is a common task on the Internet because the data passed from the browser to the server and back in text strings. To convert to a string, you can use the (string) cast or the strval function; here's what this might look like:

```php
<?php
    $float = 1.2345;
    echo (string) $float, "\n";
    echo strval($float), "\n";
?>
```

A boolean TRUE value is converted to the string "1", and the FALSE value is represented as "" (empty string). An integer or floating point number (float) is converted to a string representing the number with its digits (including the exponent part for floating point numbers). The value NULL is always converted to an empty string.

You can also convert a string to a number. The string will be treated as a float if it contains any of the characters '.', 'e', or 'E'. Otherwise, it will be treated as an integer.

PHP determines the numeric value of a string from the *initial part* of the string. If the string starts with numeric data, it will use that. Otherwise, the value will be 0 (zero). Valid numeric data consists of an optional sign (+ or -), followed by one or more digits (including a decimal point if you're using it) and an optional exponent (the exponent part is an 'e' or 'E', followed by one or more digits).

PHP will do the right thing if you start using a string in a numeric context, as when you start adding values together. Here are some examples to make all this clearer:

```php
<?php
    $number = 1 + "14.5";
    echo "$number\n";
    $number = 1 + "-1.5e2";
    echo "$number\n";
    $text = "5.0";
    $number = (float) $text;
    echo $number / 2.0, "\n";
?>
```

And here's what you see when you run this script:

```
15.5
-149
2.5
```

Creating Arrays

It's time to take the next step up in PHP sophistication: arrays. Arrays are collections of values stored under a single name, and they're a big part of PHP work. You use arrays when you have a set of data to work with, such as the test scores of a set of students. Arrays are easy to handle in PHP because each data item, or *element*, can be accessed with an index value.

You can create arrays by assigning data to them, just as you do with other variables. You can give arrays the same names as you give to standard variables, and like variable names, array names begin with a $. PHP knows you're working with an array if you include [] after the name, like this:

```
$fruits[1] = "pineapple";
```

This creates an array named $fruits and sets the element at index 1 to "pineapple". From now on, you can refer to this element as you would any simple variable—you just include the index value to make sure that you reference the data you want, like this:

```
echo $fruits[1];
```

This statement echoes "pineapple". And you can add new values with different numeric indexes:

```
$fruits[2] = "pomegranate";
$fruits[3] = "tangerine";
```

Now you can refer to $fruits[1] (which is "pineapple"), $fruits[2] (which is "pomegranate"), and $fruits[3] (which is "tangerine"). In this case, we've stored strings using numeric indexes, but you can also use string indexes. Here's an example:

```
$apple_inventory["Pittsburgh"] = 2343;
$apple_inventory["Albany"] = 5778;
$apple_inventory["Houston"] = 18843;
```

You can refer to the values in this array by string, as $apple_inventory["Pittsburgh"] (which holds 2343), $apple_inventory["Albany"] (which holds 5778), and $apple_inventory["Houston"] (which holds 18843). Note that in PHP, the same array can have *both* numeric and text indexes, if you want to set things up that way.

There's also a shortcut for creating arrays—you can simply use [] after the array's name. Here's an example:

```
$fruits[] = "pineapple";
$fruits[] = "pomegranate";
$fruits[] = "tangerine";
```

In this case, $fruits[0] will end up holding "pineapple", $fruits[1] will hold "pomegranate", and $fruits[2] will hold "tangerine".

PHP starts numbering array elements with 0. If you wanted to loop over all the elements in this array, you'd start with 0, as in this for loop—note that you use the *count* function to find the number of elements in an array:

```
for ($index = 0; $index < count($fruits); $index++){
    echo $fruits[$index], "\n";}
```

Here's an even shorter shortcut for creating an array, using the PHP *array* function:

```
$fruits = array("pineapple", "pomegranate", "tangerine");
```

This also creates the same array, starting from an index value of 0. What if you wanted to start with an index value of 1? You could specify that with => like this:

```
$fruits = array(1 => "pineapple", "pomegranate", "tangerine");
```

Now the array would look like this:

```
$fruits[1] = "pineapple";
$fruits[2] = "pomegranate";
$fruits[3] = "tangerine";
```

You can create arrays with text as index values in the same way:

```
$apple_inventory = array("Pittsburgh" => 2343,
"Albany" => 5778, "Houston"] => 18843);
```

This creates the following array:

```
$apple_inventory["Pittsburgh"] = 2343;
$apple_inventory["Albany"] = 5778;
$apple_inventory["Houston"] = 18843;
```

The => operator lets you specify *key/value* pairs. For example, "Pittsburgh" is the key for the first element, and 2343 is the value.

NOTE

Here's another shortcut: if you have a well-defined range of data, you can automatically create array elements to match with the range function, such as the numbers 1 to 10 or characters "a" to "z" like this: $values = range("a", "z");.

Modifying Arrays

After you've created an array, what about modifying it? No problem—you can modify the values in arrays as easily as other variables. One way is to access an element in an array simply by referring to it by index. For example, say you have this array:

```
$fruits[1] = "pineapple";
$fruits[2] = "pomegranate";
$fruits[3] = "tangerine";
```

Now say you want to change the value of $fruits[2] to "watermelon". No problem at all:

```
$fruits[1] = "pineapple";
$fruits[2] = "pomegranate";
$fruits[3] = "tangerine";

$fruits[2] = "watermelon";
```

Then say you wanted to add a new element, "grapes", to the end of the array. You could do that by referring to $fruits[], which is PHP's shortcut for adding a new element:

```
$fruits[0] = "pineapple";
$fruits[1] = "pomegranate";
$fruits[2] = "tangerine";

$fruits[2] = "watermelon";

$fruits[] = "grapes";
```

All that's left is to loop over the array and display the array contents, as shown in Example 3-1, phparray.php.

EXAMPLE 3-1 Modifying an array's contents, phparray.php

```
<HTML>
    <HEAD>
        <TITLE>
            Modifying an array
        </TITLE>
    </HEAD>

    <BODY>
        <H1>
            Modifying an array
        </H1>

        <?php
            $fruits[0] = "pineapple";
            $fruits[1] = "pomegranate";
```

```
            $fruits[2] = "tangerine";

            $fruits[2] = "watermelon";

            $fruits[] = "grapes";

            for ($index = 0; $index < count($fruits); $index++){
                echo $fruits[$index], "<BR>";                    }
        ?>
    </BODY>
</HTML>
```

The results appear in Figure 3-1. As you can see, we not only were able to modify $fruits[2] successfully but were also able to add "grapes" to the end of the array.

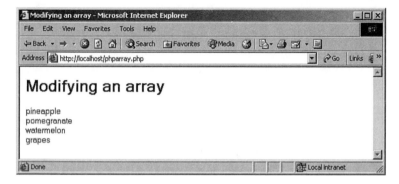

FIGURE 3-1 Modifying an array.

You can also copy a whole array at once if you just assign it to another array:

```
<?php
    $fruits[0] = "pineapple";
    $fruits[1] = "pomegranate";
    $fruits[2] = "tangerine";
    $fruits[2] = "watermelon";
    $fruits[] = "grapes";
    $produce = $fruits;
    echo $produce[2];
?>
```

This script gives you this output:

```
watermelon
```

Removing Array Elements

Another way of modifying arrays is to remove elements from them. To remove an element, you might try setting an array element to an empty string, "", like this:

```php
<?php
    $fruits[0] = "pineapple";
    $fruits[1] = "pomegranate";
    $fruits[2] = "tangerine";

    $fruits[1] = "";

    for ($index = 0; $index < count($fruits); $index++){
        echo $fruits[$index], "\n";
    }
?>
```

But that doesn't remove the element; it only stores a blank in it:

```
pineapple

tangerine
```

To remove an element from an array, use the *unset* function:

```
unset($values[3]);
```

This actually removes the element $values[3]. Here's how that might work in our example:

```php
<?php
    $fruits[0] = "pineapple";
    $fruits[1] = "pomegranate";
    $fruits[2] = "tangerine";

    unset($fruits[1]);

    for ($index = 0; $index < count($fruits); $index++){
        echo $fruits[$index], "\n";
    }
?>
```

Now when you try to display the element that's been unset, you'll get a warning:

```
pineapple
PHP Notice:  Undefined offset:  1 in C:\php\t.php on line 8
```

Looping Over Arrays

You already know you can loop over an array using a for loop and the count function, which determines how many elements an array contains:

```php
<?php
    $fruits[0] = "pineapple";
    $fruits[1] = "pomegranate";
    $fruits[2] = "tangerine";
    for ($index = 0; $index < count($fruits); $index++){
        echo $fruits[$index], "\n";
    }
?>
```

Here's what you get:

```
pineapple
pomegranate
tangerine
```

There's also a function for easily displaying the contents of an array, print_r:

```php
<?php
    $fruits[0] = "pineapple";
    $fruits[1] = "pomegranate";
    $fruits[2] = "tangerine";
    print_r($fruits);
?>
```

Here are the results:

```
Array
(
    [0] => pineapple
    [1] => pomegranate
    [2] => tangerine
)
```

The foreach statement was specially created to loop over collections such as arrays. This statement has two forms:

```
foreach (array_expression as $value) statement
foreach (array_expression as $key => $value) statement
```

The first form of this statement assigns a new element from the array to $value each time through the loop. The second form places the current element's key, another name for its index, in $key and its value in $value each time through the loop. For example, here's how you can display all the elements in an array using foreach:

```php
<?php
    $fruits = array("pineapple", "pomegranate", "tangerine");
    foreach ($fruits as $value) {
        echo "Value: $value\n";
    }
?>
```

Here are the results:

```
Value: pineapple
Value: pomegranate
Value: tangerine
```

And here's how you can display both the keys and values of an array:

```php
<?php
    $fruits = array("pineapple", "pomegranate", "tangerine");

    foreach ($fruits as $key => $value) {
        echo "Key: $key; Value: $value\n";
    }
?>
```

Here are the results:

```
Key: 0; Value: pineapple
Key: 1; Value: pomegranate
Key: 2; Value: tangerine
```

You can even use a while loop to loop over an array if you use a new function, *each*. The each function is meant to be used in loops over collections such as arrays; each time through the array, it returns the current element's key and value and then moves to the next element. To handle a multiple-item return value from an array, you can use the *list* function, which will assign the two return values from each to separate variables.

Here's what this looks like for our $fruits array:

```php
<?php
    $fruits = array("pineapple", "pomegranate", "tangerine");

    while (list($key, $value) = each ($fruits)) {
        echo "Key: $key; Value: $value\n";
    }
?>
```

Here's what you get from this script:

```
Key: 0; Value: pineapple
Key: 1; Value: pomegranate
Key: 2; Value: tangerine
```

Listing of the Array Functions

Just as it has many string functions, PHP also has many array functions. You can see a sample of them in Table 3-2.

TABLE 3-2 The Array Functions

Function Name	Purpose
array_chunk	Splits an array into chunks
array_combine	Creates an array by using one array for the keys and another for the values
array_count_values	Counts the values in an array
array_diff	Computes the difference of arrays
array_fill	Fills an array with values
array_intersect	Computes the intersection of arrays
array_key_exists	Checks whether the given key or index exists in the array
array_keys	Returns the keys in an array
array_merge	Merges two or more arrays
array_multisort	Sorts multiple or multidimensional arrays
array_pad	Pads array to the specified length with a value
array_pop	Pops the element off the end of an array
array_push	Pushes one or more elements onto the end of array
array_rand	Picks one or more random elements out of an array
array_reduce	Reduces the array to a single value with a callback function
array_reverse	Returns an array with elements in reverse order
array_search	Searches the array for a given value and returns the corresponding key
array_shift	Shifts an element off the beginning of array
array_slice	Extracts a slice of the array
array_sum	Calculates the sum of values in an array
array_unique	Removes duplicate elements from an array
array_unshift	Adds one or more elements to the beginning of an array
array_walk	Calls a user-supplied function on every member of an array
array	Creates an array
asort	Sorts an array and maintains index association
count	Counts the elements in an array

continues

TABLE 3-2 continued

Function Name	Purpose
current	Returns the current element in an array
each	Returns the current key and value pair from an array and advances the array cursor
in_array	Checks whether a value exists in an array
key	Gets a key from an associative array
krsort	Sorts an array by key in reverse order
ksort	Sorts an array by key
list	Assigns variables as if they were an array
natcasesort	Sorts an array using a case-insensitive "natural order" algorithm
natsort	Sorts an array using a "natural order" algorithm
pos	Alias of the current function
reset	Sets the pointer of an array to its first element
rsort	Sorts an array in reverse order
shuffle	Shuffles an array's elements
sizeof	Alias of the count function
sort	Sorts an array
usort	Sorts an array by values with a user-defined comparison function

We'll see a number of the most important array functions in this chapter, such as those that let you sort the contents of an array, which are coming up next.

Sorting Arrays

PHP offers all kinds of ways to sort the data in arrays, starting with the simple sort function, which you use on arrays with numeric indexes. In the following example, we create an array, display it, sort it, and then display it again:

```php
<?php
    $fruits[0] = "tangerine";
    $fruits[1] = "pineapple";
    $fruits[2] = "pomegranate";

    print_r($fruits);

    sort($fruits);

    print_r($fruits);
?>
```

Here are the results—as you can see, the new array is in sorted order; note also that the elements have been given new numeric indexes:

```
Array
(
    [0] => tangerine
    [1] => pineapple
    [2] => pomegranate
)
Array
(
    [0] => pineapple
    [1] => pomegranate
    [2] => tangerine
)
```

You can sort an array in reverse order if you use rsort instead:

```php
<?php
    $fruits[0] = "tangerine";
    $fruits[1] = "pineapple";
    $fruits[2] = "pomegranate";

    print_r($fruits);
    rsort($fruits);
    print_r($fruits);
?>
```

Here's what you get:

```
Array
(
    [0] => tangerine
    [1] => pineapple
    [2] => pomegranate
)
Array
(
    [0] => tangerine
    [1] => pomegranate
    [2] => pineapple
)
```

What if you have an array that uses text keys? Unfortunately, if you use sort or rsort, the keys are replaced by numbers. If you want to retain the keys, use asort instead, as in this example:

```
<?php
    $fruits["good"] = "tangerine";
    $fruits["better"] = "pineapple";
    $fruits["best"] = "pomegranate";

    print_r($fruits);

    asort($fruits);

    print_r($fruits);
?>
```

Here are the results:

```
Array
(
    [good] => tangerine
    [better] => pineapple
    [best] => pomegranate
)
Array
(
    [better] => pineapple
    [best] => pomegranate
    [good] => tangerine
)
```

You can use arsort to sort arrays such as this in reverse order. What if you wanted to sort an array such as this one based on keys, not values? Just use ksort instead. To sort by reverse by keys, use krsort. You can even define your own sorting operations with a custom sorting function you use with PHP's usort.

Navigating through Arrays

PHP also includes a number of functions for navigating through arrays. That navigation is done with an array *pointer*, which holds the current location in an array. Here's how it works. Say you have this array:

```
$vegetables[0] = "corn";
$vegetables[1] = "broccoli";
$vegetables[2] = "zucchini";

print_r($vegetables);
echo "<BR>";
```

You can get the current element in this array with the current function:

```
echo "Current: ", current($vegetables), "<BR>";
```

And you can move the pointer to the next element with the next function:

```
echo "Next: ", next($vegetables), "<BR>";
```

The prev function moves the pointer back:

```
echo "Prev: ", prev($vegetables), "<BR>";
```

The end function moves the pointer to the last element:

```
echo "End: ", end($vegetables), "<BR>";
```

Want to move back to the beginning of the array? Use reset:

```
reset($vegetables);
```

And we can display the new current element, which will be the beginning of the array, like this:

```
echo "Current: ", current($vegetables), "<BR>";
```

Let's put all this together in a web page, as you can see in Example 3-2, phpnavigate.php.

EXAMPLE 3-2   Navigating through an array, phpnavigate.php

```html
<HTML>
        <HEAD>
            <TITLE>
                Navigating through an array
            </TITLE>
        </HEAD>

        <BODY>
            <H1>
                Navigating through an array
            </H1>
        <?php

            $vegetables[0] = "corn";
            $vegetables[1] = "broccoli";
            $vegetables[2] = "zucchini";

            print_r($vegetables);
            echo "<BR>";

            echo "Current: ", current($vegetables), "<BR>";
            echo "Next: ", next($vegetables), "<BR>";
            echo "Prev: ", prev($vegetables), "<BR>";
            echo "End: ", end($vegetables), "<BR>";
            echo "Resetting the array.<BR>";
            reset($vegetables);
            echo "Current: ", current($vegetables), "<BR>";

        ?>
    </BODY>
</HTML>
```

This page appears in Figure 3-2, where we've used the array pointer to move through an array. Very nice.

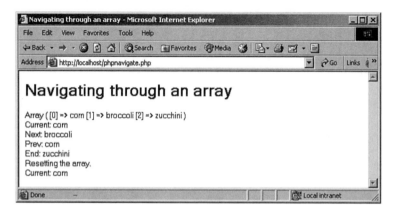

FIGURE 3-2   Navigating through an array.

Imploding and Exploding Arrays

You can also convert between strings and arrays by using the PHP *implode* and *explode* functions: implode implodes an array to a string, and explode explodes a string into an array.

For example, say you want to put an array's contents into a string. You can use implode, passing it the text you want to separate each element with in the output string (in this example, we use a comma) and the array to work on:

```php
<?php
    $vegetables[0] = "corn";
    $vegetables[1] = "broccoli";
    $vegetables[2] = "zucchini";
    $text = implode(",", $vegetables);
    echo $text;
?>
```

This gives you:

```
corn,broccoli,zucchini
```

There are no spaces between the items in this string, however, so we change the separator string from ", " to ", ":

```php
$text = implode(", ", $vegetables);
```

The result is:

```
corn, broccoli, zucchini
```

What about exploding a string into an array? To do that, you indicate the text that you want to split the string on, such as ", ", and pass that to explode. Here's an example:

```php
<?php
    $text = "corn, broccoli, zucchini";
    $vegetables = explode(", ", $text);
    print_r($vegetables);
?>
```

And here are the results. As you can see, we exploded the string into an array correctly:

```
Array
(
    [0] => corn
    [1] => broccoli
    [2] => zucchini
)
```

Extracting Variables from Arrays

The *extract* function is handy for copying the elements in arrays to variables if your array is set up with string index values. For example, take a look at this case, where we have an array with string indexes:

```
$fruits["good"] = "tangerine";
$fruits["better"] = "pineapple";
$fruits["best"] = "pomegranate";
        .
        .
        .
```

When you call the extract function on this array, it creates variables corresponding to the string indexes: $good, $better, and so on:

```
$fruits["good"] = "tangerine";
$fruits["better"] = "pineapple";
$fruits["best"] = "pomegranate";

extract($fruits);
        .
        .
        .
```

Take a look at how this works in Example 3-3, phpextract.php.

EXAMPLE 3-3   Extracting variables from an array, phpextract.php

```
<HTML>
        <HEAD>
            <TITLE>Extracting variables from an array</TITLE>
        </HEAD>

        <BODY>
            <H1>Extracting variables from an array</H1>
        <?php
            $fruits["good"] = "tangerine";
            $fruits["better"] = "pineapple";
            $fruits["best"] = "pomegranate";

            extract($fruits);

            echo "\$good = $good<BR>";
            echo "\$better = $better<BR>";
            echo "\$best = $best<BR>";
        ?>
        </BODY>
</HTML>
```

Now $good will hold "tangerine", $better will hold "pineapple", and $best will hold "pomegranate". You can see the results in Figure 3-3.

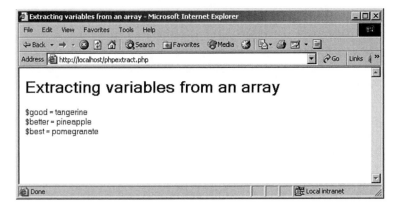

FIGURE 3-3 Filling variables from an array.

You can also use the PHP list function to get data from an array like this and store it in as many variables as you like. Here's an example:

```php
<?php
    $vegetables[0] = "corn";
    $vegetables[1] = "broccoli";
    $vegetables[2] = "zucchini";
    list($first, $second) = $vegetables;
    echo $first, "\n";
    echo $second;
?>
```

And here is the result:

```
corn
broccoli
```

Can you go the opposite way and copy variables into an array? Sure, just use the *compact* function. You pass this function the *names* of variables (with the $), and compact finds those variables and stores them all in an array:

```php
<?php
    $first_name = "Cary";
    $last_name = "Grant";
    $role = "Actor";
    $subarray = array("first_name", "last_name");
    $resultarray = compact("role", $subarray);
?>
```

Merging and Splitting Arrays

You can also cut up and merge arrays when needed. For example, say you have a three-item array of various fruits and want to get a subarray consisting of the last two items. You can do this with the `array_slice` function, passing it the array you want to get a section of, the *offset* at which to start, and the *length* of the array you want to create:

```php
<?php
    $fruits["good"] = "tangerine";
    $fruits["better"] = "pineapple";
    $fruits["best"] = "pomegranate";
    $subarray = array_slice($fruits, 1, 2);
    foreach ($subarray as $value) {
        echo "Fruit: $value\n";
    }
?>
```

Here are the results:

```
Fruit: pineapple
Fruit: pomegranate
```

If `offset` is negative, the sequence will be measured from the end of the array. If `length` is negative, the sequence will stop that many elements from the end of the array.

NOTE

If you don't give the length of the subarray you want, you'll get all the elements to the end (or the beginning, if you're going in the opposite direction) of the array.

You can also merge two or more arrays with `array_merge`:

```php
<?php
    $fruits = array("pineapple", "pomegranate", "tangerine");
    $vegetables = array("corn", "broccoli", "zucchini");

    $produce = array_merge($fruits, $vegetables);

    foreach ($produce as $value) {
        echo "Produce item: $value\n";
    }
?>
```

And here's what you get (see also "Using the Array Operators" in this chapter):

```
Produce item: pineapple
Produce item: pomegranate
Produce item: tangerine
Produce item: corn
Produce item: broccoli
Produce item: zucchini
```

Comparing Arrays

PHP also includes support for comparing arrays and determining which elements are the same—or which are different. For example, say you have these two arrays, where only the second element is the same:

```
$local_fruits = array("apple", "pomegranate", "orange");
$tropical_fruits = array("pineapple", "pomegranate", "papaya");
```

You can use the `array_diff` function to create a new array, which we'll call `$difference`, that holds the elements that are different between the two arrays:

```
<?php
    $local_fruits = array("apple", "pomegranate", "orange");
    $tropical_fruits = array("pineapple", "pomegranate", "papaya");

    $difference = array_diff($local_fruits, $tropical_fruits);

    foreach ($difference as $key => $value) {
        echo "Key: $key; Value: $value\n";
    }
?>
```

Here's what this script displays:

```
Key: 0; Value: apple
Key: 2; Value: orange
```

Now say you're working with two arrays that use text indexes, and you want to see which elements have either different keys or values when comparing the arrays:

```
    $local_fruits = array("fruit1" => "apple", "fruit2" => "pomegranate",
        "fruit3" => "orange");
    $tropical_fruits = array("fruit1" => "pineapple", "fruit_two" => "pomegranate",
        "fruit3" => "papaya");
```

You can determine which array elements have either different keys or values by using the `array_diff_assoc` function (arrays with text indexes are also called *associative arrays*, hence the name `array_diff_assoc`) this way:

```
<?php
    $local_fruits = array("fruit1" => "apple", "fruit2" => "pomegranate",
        "fruit3" => "orange");
    $tropical_fruits = array("fruit1" => "pineapple", "fruit_two" => "pomegranate",
        "fruit3" => "papaya");

    $difference = array_diff_assoc($local_fruits, $tropical_fruits);
```

```
        foreach ($difference as $key => $value) {
            echo "Key: $key; Value: $value\n";
        }
    ?>
```

And here's what you get—note that we've been able to find all array elements that differ in either key or value:

```
Key: fruit1; Value: apple
Key: fruit2; Value: pomegranate
Key: fruit3; Value: orange
```

What if you want to find all array elements that the arrays have in common instead? In that case, use array_intersect. Here's an example, where we're finding the elements in common between our two arrays:

```php
<?php
    $local_fruits = array("apple", "pomegranate", "orange");
    $tropical_fruits = array("pineapple", "pomegranate", "papaya");

    $common = array_intersect($local_fruits, $tropical_fruits);

    foreach ($common as $key => $value) {
        echo "Key: $key; Value: $value\n";
    }
?>
```

And this is what you get:

```
Key: 1; Value: pomegranate
```

You can also do the same with arrays that use text indexes if you use array_intersect_assoc:

```php
<?php
    $local_fruits = array("fruit1" => "apple", "fruit2" => "pomegranate",
        "fruit3" => "orange");
    $tropical_fruits = array("fruit1" => "pineapple", "fruit2" => "pomegranate",
        "fruit3" => "papaya");

    $common = array_intersect_assoc($local_fruits, $tropical_fruits);

    foreach ($common as $key => $value) {
        echo "Key: $key; Value: $value\n";
    }
?>
```

And here's what this script gives you:

```
Key: fruit2; Value: pomegranate
```

Comparing arrays in PHP? No problem at all.

Manipulating the Data in Arrays

You can do even more with the data in arrays. For example, if you want to delete duplicate elements, you can use array_unique:

```php
<?php
    $scores = array(65, 60, 70, 65, 65);
    print_r($scores);
    $scores = array_unique($scores);
    print_r($scores);
?>
```

Here's what this script looks like when you run it—note that the duplicate elements are removed:

```
Array
(
    [0] => 65
    [1] => 60
    [2] => 70
    [3] => 65
    [4] => 65
)
Array
(
    [0] => 65
    [1] => 60
    [2] => 70
)
```

Here's another useful array function—array_sum, which adds all the values in an array:

```php
<?php
    $scores = array(65, 60, 70, 64, 66);

    echo "Average score = ", array_sum($scores) / count($scores);
?>
```

In this case, we're finding the average student score from the $scores array:

```
Average score = 65
```

And here's another one—the array_flip function will flip an array's keys and values. You can see that at work in Example 3-4, phpflip.php.

EXAMPLE 3-4   Flipping an array, phpflip.php

```
<HTML>
        <HEAD>
            <TITLE>
                Flipping an array
            </TITLE>
        </HEAD>

        <BODY>
            <H1>
                Flipping an array
            </H1>
            <?php
                $local_fruits = array("fruit1" => "apple", "fruit2" =>
                    "pomegranate", "fruit3" => "orange");
                foreach ($local_fruits as $key => $value) {
                    echo "Key: $key; Value: $value<BR>";
                }

                echo "<BR>";

                $local_fruits = array_flip($local_fruits);

                foreach ($local_fruits as $key => $value) {
                    echo "Key: $key; Value: $value<BR>";
                }
            ?>
        </BODY>
</HTML>
```

The results appear in Figure 3-4—note that the keys and values were indeed flipped.

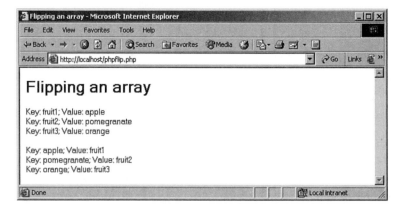

FIGURE 3-4   Flipping an array.

Creating Multidimensional Arrays

So far, we've been using only one-dimensional arrays, with only one set of keys. However, arrays with multiple sets of keys are also possible, and sometimes you need them. You might, for example, store test scores for various students like this:

```
$test_scores["Frank"] = 95;
$test_scores["Mary"] = 87;
```

But what if you gave a second test? You can add a second index to stand for the test number; here's what that might look like:

```php
<?php
    $test_scores["Frank"][1] = 95;
    $test_scores["Frank"][2] = 85;
    $test_scores["Mary"][1] = 87;
    $test_scores["Mary"][2] = 93;
    print_r($test_scores);
?>
```

Now $test_scores["Frank"][1] is Frank's test score on the first test, $test_scores["Frank"][2] is his score on the second test, and so on. This script displays the new multidimensional array with print_r:

```
    [Frank] => Array
        (
            [1] => 95
            [2] => 85
        )

    [Mary] => Array
        (
            [1] => 87
            [2] => 93
        )
```

You can access individual elements using both indexes, like this:

```
echo "Frank's first test score is ", $test_scores["Frank"][1], "\n";
```

Want to interpolate an array item in double quotes? Enclose it in curly braces (and use single quotes for any text keys to avoid conflict with the double quotes):

```
echo "Frank's first test score is {$test_scores['Frank'][1]}\n";
```

You can also use the flowing syntax to create multidimensional arrays—but note that this will start the arrays off at an index value of 0:

```php
<?php
    $test_scores["Frank"][] = 95;
    $test_scores["Frank"][] = 85;
    $test_scores["Mary"][] = 87;
    $test_scores["Mary"][] = 93;
    print_r($test_scores);
?>
```

In PHP, multidimensional arrays can be thought of as *arrays of arrays*. For example, a two-dimensional array may be considered as a single-dimensional array where each element is a single-dimensional array. Here's an example:

```php
<?php
    $test_scores = array("Frank" => array(95, 85), "Mary" => array(87, 93));
    print_r($test_scores);
?>
```

This is what the results look like:

```
[Frank] => Array
    (
        [0] => 95
        [1] => 85
    )

[Mary] => Array
    (
        [0] => 87
        [1] => 93
    )
```

What if you wanted to start the array at index 1 instead of 0? You could do this:

```php
<?php
    $test_scores = array("Frank" => array(1 => 95, 2 => 85),
        "Mary" => array(1 => 87, 2 => 93));
    print_r($test_scores);
?>
```

And here's what you would get:

```
[Frank] => Array
    (
        [1] => 95
        [2] => 85
    )

[Mary] => Array
    (
        [1] => 87
        [2] => 93
    )
```

Looping Over Multidimensional Arrays

So what about looping over multidimensional arrays? For example, what if your array contains two dimensions? Looping over it isn't a problem—just loop over the first index first and then the second index in an internal loop. You can do that by *nesting* a for loop inside another for loop:

```php
<?php
    $test_scores[0][] = 95;
    $test_scores[0][] = 85;
    $test_scores[1][] = 87;
    $test_scores[1][] = 93;
    for ($outer_index = 0; $outer_index < count($test_scores);
        $outer_index++){
        for($inner_index = 0; $inner_index < count($test_scores[$outer_index]);
            $inner_index++){
            echo "\$test_scores[$outer_index][$inner_index] = ",
                $test_scores[$outer_index][$inner_index], "\n";
        }
    }
?>
```

In this way, we can set the first index in the array, print out all elements by incrementing the second index, and then increment the first index to move on. Here's what you get, just as you should:

```
$test_scores[0][0] = 95
$test_scores[0][1] = 85
$test_scores[1][0] = 87
$test_scores[1][1] = 93
```

You can also use foreach loops—and in fact they're a better idea than for loops if you're using text indexes (which can't be incremented for iterating through a loop). In the following example, each time through the outer loop, we extract a new single-dimensional array to iterate over:

```php
<?php
    $test_scores["Frank"]["first"] = 95;
    $test_scores["Frank"]["second"] = 85;
    $test_scores["Mary"]["first"] = 87;
    $test_scores["Mary"]["second"] = 93;
    foreach ($test_scores as $outer_key => $single_array) {
        .
        .
        .
    }
?>
```

And we iterate over the single-dimensional array in the inner `foreach` loop, as you can see in phpmultidimensional.php, Example 3-5.

EXAMPLE 3-5 Looping over multidimensional arrays, phpmultidimensional.php

```
<HTML>
        <HEAD>
            <TITLE>
                Looping over multidimensional arrays
            </TITLE>
        </HEAD>

        <BODY>
            <H1>
                Looping over multidimensional arrays
            </H1>
            <?php
                $test_scores["Frank"]["first"] = 95;
                $test_scores["Frank"]["second"] = 85;
                $test_scores["Mary"]["first"] = 87;
                $test_scores["Mary"]["second"] = 93;
                foreach ($test_scores as $outer_key => $single_array) {
                    foreach ($single_array as $inner_key => $value) {
                        echo "\$test_scores[$outer_key][$inner_key] =
                            $value<BR>";
                    }
                }
            ?>
        </BODY>
</HTML>
```

The results appear in Figure 3-5. Very cool.

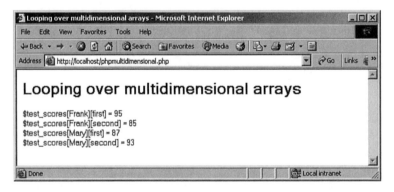

FIGURE 3-5 Looping over multidimensional arrays.

Using the Array Operators

Want more array power? Check out the array operators:

`$a + $b`	Union of $a and $b.
`$a == $b`	TRUE if $a and $b have the same elements.
`$a === $b`	TRUE if $a and $b have the same elements in the same order.
`$a != $b`	TRUE if $a is not equal to $b.
`$a <> $b`	TRUE if $a is not equal to $b.
`$a !== $b`	TRUE if $a is not identical to $b.

Most of these have to do with comparing arrays, but the + operator is designed to concatenate arrays. You can see an example in phparrayops.php, Example 3-6, where we put to work not only the + operator but also the == operator, checking to see if two arrays have the same elements (in this case, they don't).

EXAMPLE 3-6   Using array operators, phparrayops.php

```
<HTML>
        <HEAD>
            <TITLE>
                Using array operators
            </TITLE>
        </HEAD>

        <BODY>
            <H1>
                Using array operators
            </H1>
            <?php
                $fruits["apples"] = 3839;
                $fruits["oranges"] = 2289;
                $vegetables["broccoli"] = 1991;
                $vegetables["corn"] = 9195;
                echo "\$fruits: ";
                print_r($fruits);
                echo "<BR>";
                echo "\$vegetables: ";
                print_r($vegetables);
                echo "<BR>";
                $produce = $fruits + $vegetables;
                echo "\$produce: ";
                print_r($produce);
                echo "<BR>";
```

continues

EXAMPLE 3-6 continued

```
                    if ($fruits == $vegetables){
                        echo "\$fruits has the same elements as \$vegetables<BR>";
                    }
                    else {
                        echo "\$fruits does not have the same elements as
                            \$vegetables<BR>";
                    }
            ?>
        </BODY>
</HTML>
```

The results appear in Figure 3-6, where you can see that the + operator did indeed con-catenate the arrays we wanted it to, and the == operator did indeed compare the two arrays properly.

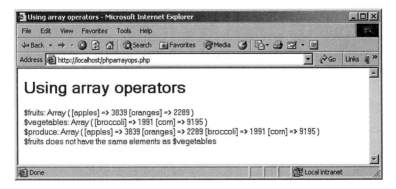

FIGURE 3-6 Using array operators.

Summary

PHP gives you some great ways of working with data in strings and arrays. Both have many different functions available. Here's a summary of the salient points in this chapter:

- The many string functions do everything from searching strings to formatting them for display. Take a look at Table 3-1 for a refresher.

- The `printf` and `sprintf` functions format strings for display.

- The `strstr` function searches a string for a `substring`.

- The `substr_compare` function lets you compare strings.

- You access the items in an array by using a numeric or string index.

- PHP knows you're working with an array if you include [] after a variable's name.

- The `unset` function removes items from arrays.

- The `foreach` statement provides a great way of looping over arrays.

- The array functions do everything from merging arrays to searching them.

- You can sort arrays with the `sort` function.

- You can convert between strings and arrays using the PHP `implode` and `explode` functions.

- You can use the `array_diff` function to create a new array that holds the elements that are different between two arrays.

- You can create multidimensional arrays simply by using two array indexes in square brackets, [and].

That's it for our coverage of strings and arrays for the moment, both of which we'll see again throughout the book. Now it's time to turn to working with and creating functions in Chapter 4, "Breaking It Up: Functions."

Breaking It Up: Functions

We've been making a lot of progress when it comes to handling data in the previous few chapters—we've dealt with simple variables, constants, arrays, and even multidimensional arrays. So how about getting more sophisticated at handling *code*?

You already know that PHP comes with many built-in functions that are ready to be used. In this chapter, we're going to create our own functions.

As your code gets longer, being able to create your own functions is an essential step because it breaks up that code into manageable sections. As you know, functions are sets of statements that can be called by name, which means that they're ideal for packaging your code into manageable chunks. When your scripts get longer than two dozen statements or so, you should consider breaking up things into functions.

Creating functions also facilitates script development—if you've got a problem in a script that is 2,000 lines long, imagine how hard it will be to find that error. But if you've broken up your code into functions, each of which is only two dozen lines or so, it'll be much easier—and when you know that a given function works as it should, you don't have to worry about it anymore.

Breaking up scripts as they get longer is also a good idea in terms of *scope*. Scope is the *visibility* of an item, such as a variable, in your script—for example, if you have a 2,000 line script, and you use a variable named $counter at the beginning, but then you forget that you've done so and use another variable with the same name near the end of the script, they're actually the same variable. Thus, you have an unintentional conflict because when you use $counter in one place, it'll set its value everywhere.

Restricting code to functions helps solve this unintentional problem—the variables you use in a function can be restricted to the scope of that function. Thus, you don't have to worry about those variables overlapping other variables with the same name by mistake—they cannot escape the scope of the function.

All this and more is coming up in this chapter as we create our own functions, an essential PHP skill.

Creating a Function

How do you create your own function? Here's how to do it formally:

```
function function_name([argument_list...])
{
    [statements;]
    [return return_value;]
}
```

What does all this mean? Let's take a look at an example. Say that all your web pages have a navigation bar with hyperlinks at the bottom. Instead of including all the code to send the needed HTML to the browser in each web page that features this bar, you could set up a function, which we'll call nav_bar, to do it for you:

```
function nav_bar()
{
    .
    .
    .
}
```

The statements in this function will be executed when you call it, so here's where we add the echo statements to send the HTML for the navigation bar and its hyperlinks back to the browser (" " inserts a space in HTML to separate the links):

```
function nav_bar()
{
    echo "<hr>";
    echo "<center>";
    echo "<a href='home.html'>Home</a>   ";
    echo "<a href='map.html'>Site Map</a>   ";
    echo "<a href='help.html'>Help</a>";
    echo "</center>";
}
```

Now when you call this function, the navigation bar is displayed. Centralizing the code to display your navigation bar also helps because if you want to change it, you only have to change it once, in the nav_bar function. You can see how this function might be called in phpnavbar.php, Example 4-1.

EXAMPLE 4-1 Calling a function, phpnavbar.php

```
<HTML>
        <HEAD>
            <TITLE>Using functions to create a navigation bar</TITLE>
        </HEAD>
```

```
<BODY>
    <H1>Using functions to create a navigation bar</H1>

<?php
    echo "<H3>Welcome to my web page!</H3>";
    echo "<br>";
    echo "How do you like it?";
    echo "<br>";
    echo "<br>";

    nav_bar();

    function nav_bar()
    {
        echo "<hr>";
        echo "<center>";
        echo "<a href='home.html'>Home</a>   ";
        echo "<a href='map.html'>Site Map</a>   ";
        echo "<a href='help.html'>Help</a>";
        echo "</center>";
    }
?>
</BODY>
</HTML>
```

You can see the navigation bar displayed at the bottom of the web page in Figure 4-1. Now to create that navigation bar, all you must do is call this new function.

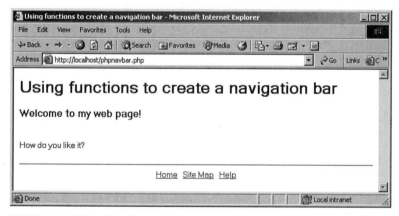

FIGURE 4-1 Using a function.

Here's something else to know about functions—the code in them doesn't run until the function is called. This is different from the standard code in a script, which is run when the web page loads. Being able to run code when you want gives you more control.

Passing Data to Functions

You can also send data to a function by using its *argument list*, which is a comma-separated list of variable names:

```
function function_name([argument_list...])
{
    [statements;]
    [return return_value;]
}
```

How does this work? Say for example that you wanted to customize the navigation bar we created in the previous chunk by adding some text and a copyright statement. You could do that by passing those two items to the nav_bar function. If you wanted to refer to those items as, say, $text and $copyright in the body of the function, you could set up the function like this:

```
function nav_bar($text, $copyright)
{
        .
        .
        .
}
```

Now you can refer to the data passed to the function by name, as $text and $copyright. Here's how we add their values to the navigation bar, displaying it in italics:

```
function nav_bar($text, $copyright)
{
        echo "<hr>";
        echo "<center>";
        echo "<a href='home.html'>Home</a>   ";
        echo "<a href='map.html'>Site Map</a>   ";
        echo "<a href='help.html'>Help</a>";
        echo "<hr>";
        echo "<FONT SIZE='1'><I>$text</I></FONT>";
        echo "<BR><FONT SIZE='1'><I>$copyright</I></FONT>";
        echo "</center>";
}
```

How do you call this new version of the function? Take a look at phpcustomnavbar.php, Example 4-2, where we're passing the text "SuperDuperBig Co." and "(c) 2005" to this function; these text items will be stored in the variables $text and $copyright, respectively.

EXAMPLE 4-2   Passing data to a function, phpcustomnavbar.php

```
<HTML>
        <HEAD>
            <TITLE>Passing data to customize a navigation bar</TITLE>
        </HEAD>
        <BODY>
            <H1>Passing data to customize a navigation bar</H1>
            <?php
                echo "<H3>Welcome to my web page!</H3>";
                echo "<br>";
                echo "How do you like it?";
                echo "<br><br>";

                nav_bar("SuperDuperBig Co.", "(c) 2005");

                function nav_bar($text, $copyright)
                {
                    echo "<hr>";
                    echo "<center>";
                    echo "<a href='home.html'>Home</a>   ";
                    echo "<a href='map.html'>Site Map</a>   ";
                    echo "<a href='help.html'>Help</a>";
                    echo "<hr>";
                    echo "<FONT SIZE='3'><I>$text</I></FONT>";
                    echo "<BR><FONT SIZE='3'><I>$copyright</I></FONT>";
                    echo "</center>";
                }
            ?>
        </BODY>
</HTML>
```

You can see the results in Figure 4-2, where the nav_bar function has been able to read the data we passed to it and has inserted it into the navigation bar.

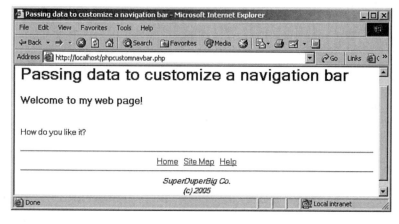

FIGURE 4-2   Passing data to a function.

Passing Arrays to Functions

Besides data such as simple variables, you can also pass arrays to functions with no extra work. Here's an example, where we're creating a function named array_echoer that simply echoes the contents of an array:

```php
<?php
    $fruits[0] = "pineapple";
    $fruits[1] = "pomegranate";
    $fruits[2] = "tangerine";
    $fruits[3] = "watermelon";
    array_echoer($fruits);

    function array_echoer($array)
    {
        for ($index = 0; $index < count($array); $index++){
            echo "Element $index: ", $array[$index], "\n";
        }
    }
?>
```

Here are the results:

```
Element 0: pineapple
Element 1: pomegranate
Element 2: tangerine
Element 3: watermelon
```

Here's another example where we're averaging student test scores that are held in an array:

```php
<?php
    $test_scores[0] = 98;
    $test_scores[1] = 36;
    $test_scores[2] = 54;
    $test_scores[3] = 64;
    array_averager($test_scores);

    function array_averager($scores)
    {
        $total = 0;
        for ($index = 0; $index < count($scores); $index++){
            $total += $scores[$index];
        }
        echo "Average score = ", $total / count($scores);
    }
?>
```

Here's what you see from this script:

```
Average score = 63
```

Setting Up Default Argument Values

We've seen how to pass data to functions, as in this example, where we're passing a greeting to echo:

```
greeting("No worries, your suite is waiting for you.");

function greeting($text)
{
    echo $text, "\n";
}
```

This is what you get from this script:

```
No worries, your suite is waiting for you.
```

But if you forget to pass an argument to this function and call it this way:

```
greeting();
```

You'll get this error:

```
PHP Warning:  Missing argument 1 for greeting() in C:\php\t.php on line 5
```

To avoid this issue, you can give function arguments a *default value* that is used if you don't supply a value. You do this with the = sign and the default value:

```
<?php
    greeting();

    function greeting($text = "Hi, I hope you have a nice day.")
    {
        echo $text, "\n";
    }
?>
```

Now if you call the greeting function with no arguments, you'll see this:

```
Hi, I hope you have a nice day.
```

If you do pass data to the function, the default value won't be used.

You can give default values to more than one argument, but once you start assigning default values, you have to give them to all arguments that follow as well so that PHP won't get confused if more than one argument is missing. Here's an example:

```
function greeting($text1, $text2 = "No ", $text = "worries.")
{
    echo $text1, $text2, $text3, "\n";
}
```

Here's another example, phpdefault.php, Example 4-3—the PHP Cruise Lines application, which lets users make reservations. The default reservation is for two passengers in an outside cabin, but other options are OK too, as shown in the script.

EXAMPLE 4-3 Using default values, phpdefault.php

```
<HTML>
        <HEAD>
            <TITLE>Using default values</TITLE>
        </HEAD>

        <BODY>
            <H1>Using default values</H1>
            <?php
                echo "<H1>Welcome to PHP Cruise Lines</H1>";
                book("Steve");
                book("Mary", 1);
                book("Ward", 4, FALSE);

                function book($name, $number = 2, $outside_cabin = TRUE)
                {
                    echo "Welcome, $name, you have a reservation for $number" .
                    " passengers";
                    if($outside_cabin)
                        echo " in an outside cabin.";
                    else
                        echo " in an inside cabin.";
                }
            ?>
        </BODY>
</HTML>
```

You can see the results in Figure 4-3.

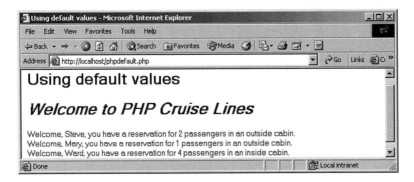

FIGURE 4-3 Using default values.

Passing Arguments by Reference

Here's something to know about functions—when you pass an argument to a function in PHP, it's passed *by value* by default. That means that a copy of the data is passed to the function, not the actual data itself.

But what if you wanted to modify the original value that you pass to a function? For example, what if you wanted to add a little more to a text string that you pass to a function? In this example, we're trying to concatenate "No" and "worries." using a function named add_text:

```php
<?php
    $string = "No ";

    add_text($string);
    echo $string;

    function add_text($text)
    {
        $text .= "worries.";
    }
?>
```

If you run this script, you just see:

No

However, you can fix this script with a single character. You simply preface an argument that you pass to a function with &, and PHP will pass that argument *by reference*:

```php
    $string = "No ";

    add_text($string);
    echo $string;

    function add_text(&$text)
    {
        $text .= "worries.";
    }
```

Now a *reference* to the original data ($string) is passed to the add_text function. That means you now have access to the original data in $string in the function. If you want to change that data, as we're doing here by appending "worries." to it, there's no problem. You can see what this looks like in a web page in phpbyref.php in Example 4-4.

EXAMPLE 4-4   Passing data by reference, phpbyref.php

```
<HTML>
        <HEAD>
            <TITLE>
                Passing data by reference
            </TITLE>
        </HEAD>

        <BODY>
            <H1>
                Passing data by reference
            </H1>
            <?php
                $string = "No ";

                add_text($string);
                echo $string;

                function add_text(&$text)
                {
                    $text .= "worries.";
                }
            ?>
        </BODY>
</HTML>
```

And you can see the results in Figure 4-4, where we were able to successfully modify the original data in $string that was passed to the function. Cool.

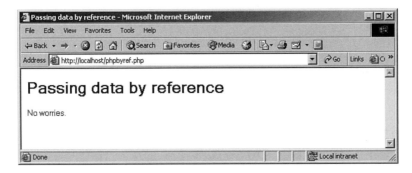

FIGURE 4-4   Passing data by reference.

But be careful when you pass data by reference—you can inadvertently alter the data in the original variable that was passed to you, thereby creating a bug that's very hard to track down (which is why passing by value is the default).

Creating Variable-Length Argument Lists

Here's another thing you can do with functions in PHP—you can pass a variable number of arguments to functions. This is not the same as setting up default arguments; in this case, you can call the same function with a different number of arguments, and you can retrieve all the arguments using special functions instead of giving each argument a default value. You can pass as many arguments as you want. For example, if you have a function named joiner that joins string together, you might call it like this:

```
joiner("No", "worries");
joiner("No", "worries", "here.");
joiner("Here's", "a", "longer", "string.");
```

In the joiner function, you can use three PHP functions to get the number of arguments passed to you, a single argument that you specify by number, and an array that holds all the arguments passed to you. Here are those functions:

- func_num_args. Returns the number of arguments passed

- func_get_arg. Returns a single argument

- func_get_args. Returns all arguments in an array

Here's what the joiner function might look like using func_num_args to get the number of arguments and func_get_args to get all the passed arguments in an array:

```
function joiner()
{
    $text = "";
    $arg_list = func_get_args();

    for ($loop_index = 0;$loop_index < func_num_args(); $loop_index++) {
        $text .= $arg_list[$loop_index] . " ";
    }
    echo $text;
}
```

Now you can call this function as shown in phpvariableargs.php, Example 4-5.

EXAMPLE 4-5   Passing data by reference, phpvariableargs.php

```
<HTML>
        <HEAD>
            <TITLE>Using variable-length argument lists</TITLE>
        </HEAD>

        <BODY>
```

continues

EXAMPLE 4-5 continued

```
            <H1>Using variable-length argument lists</H1>
            <?php

    echo "joiner(\"No\", \"worries\") =  ", joiner("No", "worries"),
        "<BR>";

    echo "joiner(\"No\", \"worries\", \"here.\") =  ", joiner("No",
        "worries", "here."), "<BR>";

    echo "joiner(\"Here's\", \"a\", \"longer\", \"string.\") =  ",
        joiner("Here's", "a", "longer", "string."), "<BR>";

    function joiner()
    {
        $text = "";
        $arg_list = func_get_args();

        for ($loop_index = 0;$loop_index < func_num_args();
            $loop_index++) {
            $text .= $arg_list[$loop_index] . " ";
        }
        echo $text;
    }
    ?>
        </BODY>
</HTML>
```

The results appear in Figure 4-5, where we've been able to get all the arguments passed to us—cool.

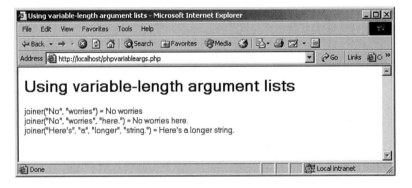

FIGURE 4-5 Creating functions with variable-length argument lists.

You can also use the func_get_arg function to get a single argument; just pass it the (0-based) position of the argument you want, and it will return that argument's value.

Returning Values from Functions

So far, so good with functions. But they're designed to return values, and although we've used built-in PHP functions that do that throughout the book already, we haven't written any of our own that do that.

To return a value from a function, you use the *return* statement. Here's how you use it:

```
return (value);
```

The parentheses (which make return look like a function even though it's actually statement) are optional. For instance, PHP doesn't come with a handy square function to square numbers, but you can create one using return like this:

```php
<?php
    function square($value)
    {
        return $value * $value;
    }
?>
```

Now you can call this function just as you would call and use a normal built-in PHP function:

```php
<?php
    echo "What's 16 x 16? Why, it's ", square(16), ".";

    function square($value)
    {
        return $value * $value;
    }
?>
```

And here's what you see in this case:

```
What's 16 x 16? Why, it's 256.
```

You can also return boolean values, just as you might return any other value. For instance, say you wanted to check whether it's a nice day outside with a function check_temperature. This function should return TRUE if it's a nice day and FALSE otherwise. Here's what that might look like:

```php
<?php
    $degrees = 67;

    if(check_temperature($degrees)){
        echo "Nice day.";
    }
```

```
    else {
        echo "Not so nice day.";
    }

    function check_temperature($temperature)
    {
        $return_value = FALSE;
        if($temperature > 65 && $temperature < 75){
            $return_value = TRUE;
        }
        return $return_value;
    }
?>
```

And here's what you get:

```
Nice day.
```

You're not restricted to a single return statement in a function; you can have as many as you like. Just bear in mind that when a return statement is executed, you leave the function and jump back to the code that called the function in the first place. For instance, here's what converting the previous example to using two return statements looks like:

```
<?php
    $degrees = 67;

    if(check_temperature($degrees)){
        echo "Nice day.";
    }
    else {
        echo "Not so nice day.";
    }

    function check_temperature($temperature)
    {
        if($temperature > 65 && $temperature < 75){
            return TRUE;
        }
        return FALSE;
    }
?>
```

And you get the same result as before:

```
Nice day.
```

The return statement is one of the things that really makes functions, well, functional. With this statement, you can use functions to process data and send the results back to the calling code. That's very useful when you're using functions to break up your code and want to have each function return the results of its internal work.

Returning Arrays from Functions

What about getting a function to return a whole array of values? No problem in PHP; the return statement can return arrays as easily as simple values.

For example, say you need a function that doubles the values in an array named array_doubler. You'd start by passing an array to this new function:

```
function array_doubler($arr)
{
    .
    .
    .
}
```

In the body of the function, you can loop over all elements, doubling them and storing them back in the array that's been passed to the function like this:

```
function array_doubler($arr)
{
    for($loop_index = 0; $loop_index < count($arr); $loop_index++){
        $arr[$loop_index] *= 2;
    }
    .
    .
    .
}
```

Finally, you just return the doubled array as you would any other value:

```
function array_doubler($arr)
{
    for($loop_index = 0; $loop_index < count($arr); $loop_index++){
        $arr[$loop_index] *= 2;
    }

    return $arr;
}
```

You can see how using this function works in Example 4-6, phpdoubler.php, where we're passing an array to a function—and returning the array with each element doubled as well.

EXAMPLE 4-6   Returning arrays from functions, phpdoubler.php

```
<HTML>
        <HEAD>
            <TITLE>
                Return arrays from functions
```

continues

EXAMPLE 4-6 continued

```
            </TITLE>
        </HEAD>

        <BODY>
            <H1>
                Return arrays from functions
            </H1>
            <?php
                $array = array(1, 2, 3, 4, 5, 6);

                $array = array_doubler($array);

                echo "Here are the doubled values;<BR>";

                foreach ($array as $value) {
                    echo "Value: $value<BR>";
                }

                function array_doubler($arr)
                {
                    for($loop_index = 0; $loop_index < count($arr);
                        $loop_index++){
                        $arr[$loop_index] *= 2;
                    }
                    return $arr;
                }
            ?>
        </BODY>
</HTML>
```

In phpdoubler.php, we're passing an array with the elements 1, 2, 3, 4, 5, and 6; `doubler` doubles each element and returns the array, as you see in Figure 4-6.

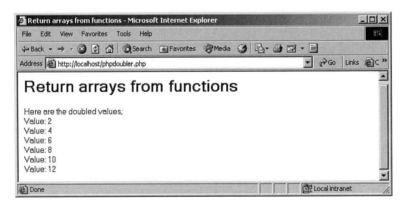

FIGURE 4-6 Returning arrays from functions.

Returning Lists from Functions

Returning arrays from functions is one way to return multiple values from a single function call, but there's another—you can return a *list*. This is a handy way of returning multiple values from a single function call. We can use the same function, `array_doubler`, as in the previous chunk:

```
function array_doubler($arr)
{
    for($loop_index = 0; $loop_index < count($arr); $loop_index++){
        $arr[$loop_index] *= 2;
    }

    return $arr;
}
```

This function is passed an array. It doubles each element's value in the array and returns that array. When that array is returned, you can assign it to a list of variables like this:

```
list($first, $second, $third, $fourth, $fifth, $sixth) = array_doubler($array);
```

This assigns the first element of the array to `$first`, the second element to `$second`, and so on. All that's left is to echo the values of `$first`, `$second`, and so on, as you see in phplist.php, Example 4-7.

EXAMPLE 4-7 Returning lists from functions, phplist.php

```
<HTML>
    <HEAD>
        <TITLE>
            Return lists from functions
        </TITLE>
    </HEAD>

    <BODY>
        <H1>
            Return lists from functions
        </H1>
        <?php
            $array = array(1, 2, 3, 4, 5, 6);

            list($first, $second, $third, $fourth, $fifth, $sixth) =
                array_doubler($array);

            echo "\$first: $first<BR>";
            echo "\$second: $second<BR>";
            echo "\$third: $third<BR>";
```

continues

EXAMPLE 4-7 continued

```
                      echo "\$fourth: $fourth<BR>";
                      echo "\$fifth: $fifth<BR>";
                      echo "\$sixth: $sixth<BR>";

                      function array_doubler($arr)
                      {
                          for($loop_index = 0; $loop_index < count($arr);
                              $loop_index++){
                              $arr[$loop_index] *= 2;
                          }
                          return $arr;
                      }
                ?>
        </BODY>
</HTML>
```

The results appear in Figure 4-7, where, as you see, we've been able to assign the various array elements to the variables $first, $second, $third, and so on.

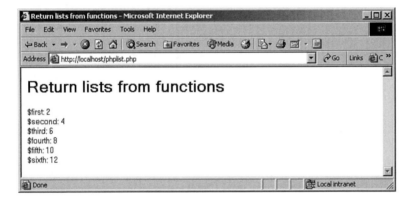

FIGURE 4-7 Returning lists from functions.

What if you only wanted, say, the first three elements of the returned array? You could do something like this, ignoring the last three elements:

```
list($first, $second, $third) = array_doubler($array);

echo "\$first: $first\n";
echo "\$second: $second\n";
echo "\$third: $third\n";
```

No problem at all. Note, however, that you can't *directly* return a list from a function like this:

```
return list($arr[0], $arr[1], $arr[2], $arr[3], $arr[4], $arr[5]);  //Won't work!
```

Returning References from Functions

Besides passing values by reference, you can also *return* references from functions, which you might want to do if you need to move references around your code while processing them. (This is not something you'll be using every day, so feel free to skip to the next chunk.) References point to the same location in memory. For example, if you set $value to 5, you could create a reference to that variable with this syntax:

```
$value = 5;
$ref = & $value;
```

Now $ref is a reference to $value, and it will point to the same data in memory as $value—changing one changes the other.

Here's how returning references from a function works. We'll create a function that will take a reference and just return that reference, like this:

```
function &return_a_reference(& $reference)
{
    return $reference;
}
```

Note the syntax here; this function returns a reference, so you use & in front of its name when creating it.

You also use & when getting the return value from a function that returns a reference, like the following, where we recover the reference to $value passed to the function and use it to increment the value in $value:

```
$value = 5;
echo "Old value: ", $value, "\n";

$ref =& return_a_reference($value);
$ref++;
echo "New value: ", $value, "\n";

function &return_a_reference(& $reference)
{
    return $reference;
}
```

And here's what you see—we were able to increment $value by incrementing the reference to that variable:

```
Old value: 5
New value: 6
```

Using Variable Scope

As already noted, the scope of a variable is the area of your code in which it's visible. Now that we're breaking our code into functions, scope becomes a more important issue. In simple scripts, everything's in the same scope. For example, if you use a variable named $count at one point in a script:

```php
<?php
    $count = 1;
    .
    .
    .
?>
```

Then it's the same variable when you refer to it later on as well:

```php
<?php
    $count = 1;
    .
    .
    .
    $count = 55;
    .
    .
    .
?>
```

As your scripts get larger, of course, you might introduce a new variable named $count in the same script, forgetting that you already have one with that name, which results in conflict—changing one will change the other because they're the same as far as PHP is concerned.

That's where functions come in—they break up your code and can resolve conflicts such as this one. If you use variables in functions, their scope is restricted to those functions by default. That means that the first echo statement here will echo 5, while the second will echo 100000, because $value within the function is in the function's scope:

```php
$value = 5;
echo "At script level, \$value = ", $value, "<BR>";

function local_scope()
{
    $value = 1000000;
    echo "But in the function, \$value = ", $value, "<BR>";
}
```

You can see how this works in Example 4-8, phpscope.php, where we're checking the same variable, $value, inside and outside a function.

EXAMPLE 4-8   Checking local scope in functions, phpscope.php

```
<HTML>
        <HEAD>
            <TITLE>
                Using local scope
            </TITLE>
        </HEAD>

        <BODY>
            <H1>Using local scope<H1>
            <?php
                $value = 5;
                echo "At script level, \$value = ", $value, "<BR>";
                local_scope();
                echo "At script level again, \$value still = ", $value, "<BR>";

                function local_scope()
                {
                    $value = 1000000;
                    echo "But in the function, \$value = ", $value, "<BR>";
                }
            ?>
    </BODY>
</HTML>
```

The results of this script appear in Figure 4-8.

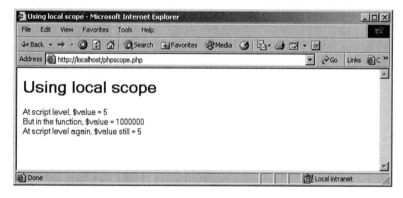

FIGURE 4-8   Checking function scope.

Note in particular that the local value of $value inside the function was *not* available outside the function. As you can see, local variables in functions are restricted to function scope.

Getting Global Access

You already know that variables inside a function have their own scope and don't mix with variables outside the function:

```
$value = 5;
echo "At script level, \$value = ", $value, "<BR>";
local_scope();
echo "At script level again, \$value still = ", $value, "<BR>";

function local_scope()
{
    $value = 1000000;
    echo "But in the function, \$value = ", $value, "<BR>";
}
```

But what if you actually wanted to access the value of a script-level variable, called a *global* variable, inside a function? For example, if you set $value to 5 at the script level, you might try to access its value inside a function like this:

```
$value = 5;

function global_scope()
{
    echo "\$value = ", $value, "<BR>";
}
```

However, this won't work (although it will in some languages) because PHP wants to prevent unintentional conflict between global and local variables. If you want to access a global variable in a function, you have to explicitly say so. One way of doing this is with the *global* keyword, as you see in phpglobal.php, Example 4-9.

EXAMPLE 4-9 Using global scope data in functions, phpglobal.php

```
<HTML>
    <HEAD>
        <TITLE>
            Using global and local scope
        </TITLE>
    </HEAD>

    <BODY>
        <H1>
            Using global and local scope
        </H1>
        <?php
            $value = 5;
            echo "At script level, \$value = ", $value, "<BR>";
```

```
                local_scope();
                global_scope();
                echo "At script level again, \$value still = ", $value, "<BR>";

                function local_scope()
                {
                    $value = 1000000;
                    echo "But in the function, \$value = ", $value, "<BR>";
                }

                function global_scope()
                {
                    global $value;
                    echo "Using the global scope, \$value = ", $value, "<BR>";
                }
            ?>
    </BODY>
</HTML>
```

After you indicate that you want access to the global value in $value, PHP gives it to you, as you can see in Figure 4-9.

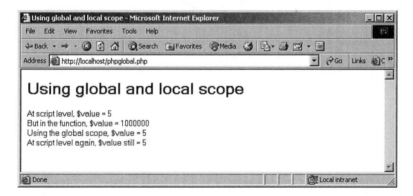

FIGURE 4-9   Using global and local scope.

You can also access global data by using the special PHP-defined $GLOBALS array. Here's how you would do that in this example:

```
function global_scope()
{
    echo "Using the global scope, \$value = ", $GLOBALS["value"], "<BR>";
}
```

Using Static Variables

It's important to know that local variables in functions are reset to their default values every time the function is called, unless you take special steps. For example, say you had a counter function that incremented a count held in an internal variable each time you called it, as in Example 4-10, phpstatic.php.

EXAMPLE 4-10   The problem with local variables, phpstatic.php

```
<HTML>
        <HEAD>
            <TITLE>Using static variables</TITLE>
        </HEAD>
        <BODY>
            <H1>Using static variables</H1>
            <?php
                echo "Current count: ", track_count(), "<BR>";
                echo "Current count: ", track_count(), "<BR>";
                echo "Current count: ", track_count(), "<BR>";
                echo "Current count: ", track_count(), "<BR>";
                echo "Current count: ", track_count(), "<BR>";

                function track_count()
                {
                    $counter = 0;
                    $counter++;
                    return $counter;
                }
            ?>
        </BODY>
</HTML>
```

Unfortunately, the $count local variable is set to 0 each time the function is called and then incremented to 1, so instead of incrementing the count, all you see each time this function is called is 1, as shown in Figure 4-10.

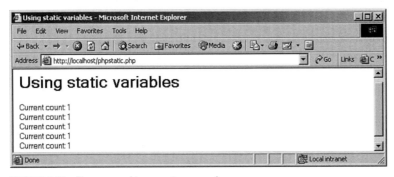

FIGURE 4-10   The non-working counter example.

The solution is to declare $count as *static*, which means it will retain its value between function calls. You can see this fix—just a single word!—at work in Example 4-11, phgpstatic.php.

EXAMPLE 4-11   Using global scope data in functions, phgpstatic.php

```
<HTML>
        <HEAD>
            <TITLE>Using static variables</TITLE>
        </HEAD>
        <BODY>
            <H1>Using static variables</H1>
            <?php
                echo "Current count: ", track_count(), "<BR>";
                echo "Current count: ", track_count(), "<BR>";
                echo "Current count: ", track_count(), "<BR>";
                echo "Current count: ", track_count(), "<BR>";
                echo "Current count: ", track_count(), "<BR>";

                function track_count()
                {
                    static $counter = 0;
                    $counter++;
                    return $counter;
                }
            ?>
    </BODY>
</HTML>
```

Now $count retains its values between function calls, as you see in Figure 4-11.

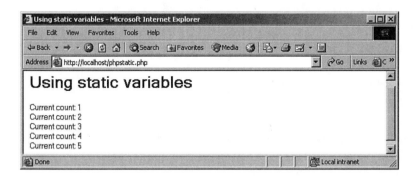

FIGURE 4-11   The working counter example.

Creating Variable Functions

PHP also supports *variable functions*. That means that a variable can hold the name of a function—and you can call the function just by including parentheses after the variable. This lets you determine which function is called at run time.

NOTE

Why would you want to determine which function is called at run time? There are a number of reasons, such as implementing *callback functions*, where you want some code to call you back—you can pass the name of your function to some other code, and the other code can call you back when something happens (such as an Internet connection being made). You can also create *dispatch tables* of function names, where the correct function to call can only be determined at run time, such as when you're waiting to see what a user wants you to do.

Here's an example; say you have a function named `apples`:

```
function apples()
{
    echo "In apples() now.<BR>";
    echo "We have plenty of apples.<BR><BR>";
}
```

To call it using function variables, just assign a variable (`$function_variable` in the following script) the text `"apples"` and then call that variable like a function:

```
$function_variable = "apples";
$function_variable();

function apples()
{
    echo "In apples() now.<BR>";
    echo "We have plenty of apples.<BR><BR>";
}
```

For that matter, you can pass arguments to these kinds of functions, and you can even set up default argument values, as you see in phpvarfunctions.php, Example 4-12.

EXAMPLE 4-12 Using variable functions, phpvarfunctions.php

```
<HTML>
    <HEAD>
        <TITLE>Using static variables</TITLE>
    </HEAD>
    <BODY>
        <H1>Using static variables</H1>
        <?php
```

```
                $function_variable = "apples";
                $function_variable();

                $function_variable = "oranges";
                $function_variable("In oranges() now.");

                $function_variable = "bananas";
                $function_variable("In bananas() now.");

                function apples()
                {
                    echo "In apples() now.<BR>";
                    echo "We have plenty of apples.<BR><BR>";
                }

                function oranges($argument)
                {
                    echo "$argument <BR>";
                    echo "We have plenty of oranges also.<BR><BR>";
                }

                function bananas($argument="")
                {
                    echo "$argument <BR>";
                    echo "Well stocked on bananas too.<BR><BR>";
                }
            ?>
    </BODY>
</HTML>
```

The results appear in Figure 4-12, where we've been able to pass data to variable functions without difficulty.

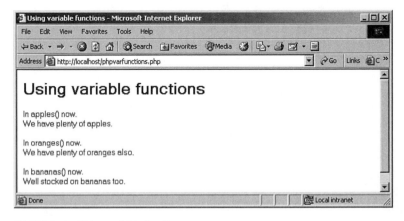

FIGURE 4-12 Using variable functions.

Creating Conditional Functions

PHP is an interpreted language, which means that functions declared inside conditional statements, such as if statements, can't be called until the PHP interpreter executes that conditional statement and sees those functions. For example, say you have a function like this:

```
function existing_function()
{
  echo "existing_function(): I'm ready to run as soon as the script
    starts.<BR>";
}
```

That function can be called as soon as your script starts to run:

```
existing_function();
```

But what if your function is declared inside an if statement?

```
if ($create_function) {
    function created_function()
    {
        echo "created_function(): I'm not ready until the if statement
            executes.<BR>";
    }
}
```

In this case, PHP will only be able to find the function after this if statement's body has executed—that is, if the variable $create_function here is TRUE. The interpreter will not have seen the function until it executes the if statement's body. So if you want to call the function, make sure that the $create_function variable is TRUE first, like this:

```
if ($create_function){
    created_function();
}
```

You can see all this in a working script in phpconditionalfunction.php, Example 4-13, where we're calling a conditional function—but only after the if statement containing this function executes.

EXAMPLE 4-13   Using variable functions, phpconditionalfunction.php

```
<HTML>
        <HEAD>
            <TITLE>
                Creating Conditional Functions
            </TITLE>
        </HEAD>
```

```
<BODY>

    <H1>
        Creating Conditional Functions
    </H1>

    <?php
        function existing_function()
        {
          echo "existing_function(): I'm ready to run as soon as the
                script starts.<BR>";
        }

        existing_function();

        $create_function = TRUE;

        if ($create_function) {
          function created_function()
          {
             echo "created_function(): I'm not ready until the if
                   statement executes.<BR>";
          }
        }

        if ($create_function){
           created_function();
        }
    ?>
    </BODY>
</HTML>
```

The results appear in Figure 4-13.

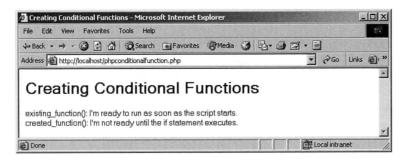

FIGURE 4-13   Using conditional functions.

Creating Functions within Functions

You can even nest functions in PHP. However, much as with conditional functions, the internal function isn't seen by PHP until the enclosing function is called. You can see an example in phpnestedfunction.php, Example 4-14, where we call a function within a function, but only after the enclosing function is called.

EXAMPLE 4-14 Using variable functions, phpnestedfunction.php

```
<HTML>
        <HEAD>
            <TITLE>Nesting Functions</TITLE>
        </HEAD>
        <BODY>
            <H1>Nesting Functions</H1>
            <?php
                function enclosing_function()
                {
                    echo "Hello from the enclosing function!<BR>";
                    function created_function()
                    {
                        echo "Hello from the nested function!<BR>";
                    }
                }

                enclosing_function();
                created_function();
            ?>
        </BODY>
</HTML>
```

The results appear in Figure 4-14, where you can see that both functions have run.

FIGURE 4-14 Nesting functions.

Using Include Files

As you know now, functions let you break up your code and reuse the same code over and over. However, there's another PHP mechanism that lets you break up and reuse your code as well—*include files*. An include file holds text that will be included in your script if you use the PHP `include` statement.

Here's an example. We'll define a few handy constants in an include file named constants.inc (PHP include files usually have the extension .inc, although you can use .php if you want to make it more difficult for the user to download your include files for security reasons), shown in Example 4-15. Note that this include file uses the `<?php ?>` syntax.

EXAMPLE 4-15   An include file, constants.inc

```
<?php
    define("pi", 3.14159);
    define("e", 2.71828);
?>
```

To include constants.inc in your script, use the statement `include("constants.inc");`, as in phpincludes.php, Example 4-16, and put the include file in the same directory as the script file. After you've included the include file, you're free to make use of the constants defined in it.

EXAMPLE 4-16   Using include files, phpincludes.php

```
<HTML>
    <HEAD><TITLE>Using include files</TITLE></HEAD>
    <BODY>
        <H1>Using include files</H1>
        <?php
            echo "Including constants.inc....<BR>";
            include("constants.inc");
            echo "Got this value for pi: ", pi, "<BR>";
            echo "Got this value for e: ", e, "<BR>";
        ?>
    </BODY>
</HTML>
```

The results, including the constants' values, appear in Figure 4-15.

You can also put code in include files, such as functions you might use frequently; you can even store entire libraries of functions this way. You can see a function, `included_function`, in function.inc in Example 4-17.

FIGURE 4-15　Using include files.

EXAMPLE 4-17　An include file with a function, function.inc

```php
<?php
    function included_function() {
        echo "Hello from the included function!<BR>";
    }
?>
```

We can call the included function in phpincludefunction.php, Example 4-18.

EXAMPLE 4-18　Using include files to include a function, phpincludefunction.php

```html
<HTML>
    <HEAD><TITLE>Using include files</TITLE></HEAD>
    <BODY>
        <H1>Using include files</H1>
        <?php
            echo "Including function.inc....<BR>";
            include("function.inc");

            included_function();          ?>
    </BODY>
</HTML>
```

The results appear in Figure 4-16. Very cool.

FIGURE 4-16　Using include files to include code.

Handling Errors Returned by Functions

Many times, if there's been an error in a function, that function returns a value of FALSE intentionally. Not only are many built-in PHP functions designed this way, but you can also write your own functions to do the same, as in this case where we're calculating reciprocals and return a value of FALSE if we're asked for the reciprocal of 0:

```
function reciprocal($value)
{
    if ($value != 0) {
        return 1 / $value;
    }
    else {
        return FALSE;
    }
}
```

One way of handling a value of FALSE returned from a function indicating there's an error is to use the PHP *die* function, the same as the PHP *exit* function. You pass this function a message, and it ends the script, displaying that message.

For example, the PHP fopen function opens files, as we discuss in Chapter 7, "Object-Oriented Programming and File Handling." If it can't open a file—as when the file can't be found—it returns a value of FALSE. You can use the PHP operator to try to open the file or quit using the die (or exit) function this way:

```
<?php
    $filename = "nonexistent_data_file";
    $file = fopen($filename, "r")
        or die("Cannot open file $filename. Does it exist?");
?>
```

Here's what you see when you try to open a non-existing file—first you see PHP's warning, and then the text echoed by the die function:

```
PHP Warning:  fopen(nonexistent_data_file): failed to open stream: No such file or
    directory in C:\php\t.php on line 3
Cannot open file nonexistent_data_file. Does it exist?
```

That's it for our coverage of functions in this chapter. In the next chapter, we're going to start bringing everything together by creating web pages into which the user can enter data that we can read. For many developers, this is the very heart of PHP.

Summary

Functions let you break up your code into manageable chunks, which is great for limiting the scope of possible conflicts between variables. You can pass data to functions and have functions return values as well. The whole idea here is to compartmentalize what's going on in your scripts so that you're dealing with only a dozen or so lines of code at a time instead of thousands. Here's a summary of the salient points in this chapter:

- You use the `function` statement to create a function.

- You call a function simply by using its name.

- You pass data to functions using an argument list enclosed in parentheses after the function's name. Inside the function's body, you can access the value of the arguments you've passed to the function using the name you gave each argument in the argument list.

- You can pass arrays to functions with no extra work.

- If you give an argument a default value, that value will be used if you don't supply a value for the argument when calling the associated function.

- If you prefix a function argument with &, that argument is passed by reference, which gives you direct access to the argument's data.

- Using the `func_get_args()` function, you can create functions with variable-length argument lists.

- Declaring variables as `static` inside a function preserves their value between function calls.

CHAPTER 5

Handling HTML Controls in Web Pages

This chapter discusses what brings many people to PHP—working with HTML controls, such as text fields, checkboxes, radio buttons, listboxes, and others. This is where your web pages come alive—they start getting interactive as we begin reading data sent to us from the user, such as the user's name, credit card number, and so on. They will be able to select pizza toppings, shoe sizes, and shipping dates—and you'll be able to handle that data back on the server, accessing it in your code. The HTML controls that we're going to embed in web pages appear in Table 5-1.

TABLE 5-1 The HTML controls

Control	Description
Buttons	Customizable buttons created with `<BUTTON>`.
Checkboxes	A checkbox, created with the `<INPUT TYPE=CHECKBOX>` element.
Hidden controls	Controls that contain text but do not appear in the web page. Created with the `<INPUT TYPE=HIDDEN>` element.
Image maps	Clickable image maps created with `<INPUT TYPE=IMAGE>`.
Lists	A multi-line list control, created with the `<SELECT>` element.
Password	Creates a password control using `<INPUT TYPE=PASSWORD">`.
Radio buttons	A radio button, created with the `<INPUT TYPE=RADIO>` element.
Reset	A reset button created with `<INPUT TYPE=RESET>`.
Select controls	Lists that let you select one or more items; uses `<SELECT>`, `<OPTION>`, and `<OPTGROUP>`.
Submit	A submit button created with `<INPUT TYPE=SUBMIT>`.
Text areas	A multi-line text control, created with the `<TEXTAREA>` element.
Text fields	A one-line text control, created with the `<INPUT TYPE=TEXT>` element.

Handling User Data with Web Forms

To read data from HTML controls using PHP, you need to place those controls in HTML forms in your Web pages, using the HTML <FORM> element. Here are the important attributes of this element:

- ACTION. This attribute provides the URL that will handle the form data. Note that you can omit this attribute, in which case its default is the URL of the current document.

- METHOD. Specifies the method or protocol for sending data to the target action URL. If you set it to GET (the default), this method sends all form name/value pair information in a URL that looks like: URL?name=value&name=value&name=value. If you use the POST method, the contents of the form are encoded as with the GET method, but they are sent in hidden environment variables.

- TARGET. Indicates a named frame for the browser to display the form results in.

For example, say that you wanted to read data that the user entered into the controls in a web page using a PHP script named phpreader.php in the same directory as phpreader.html. In that case, you could set the form's ACTION attribute to "phpreader.php" as here (if phpreader.php were not in the same directory, you'd have to give its URL, either relative to the current page or absolutely, such as http://some_isp.com/steve/phpreader.php):

```
<HTML>
    <HEAD>
        <TITLE>
            An HTML Form
        </TITLE>
    </HEAD>

    <BODY>
        <H1>
            Using HTML Forms
        </H1>
        <FORM METHOD="POST" ACTION="phpreader.php">
            .
            .
            .
        </FORM>
    </BODY>
</HTML>
```

Now you can stock your HTML form with controls such as text fields, radio buttons, and so on, and when the user puts data into those controls, all that data will be sent back to phpreader.php when the user clicks the Submit button. Forms like this one come standard with a Submit button, and you can add one to the form like this:

```
<HTML><HEAD><TITLE>An HTML Form</TITLE></HEAD>
    <BODY><H1>Using HTML Forms</H1>
        <FORM METHOD="GET" ACTION="phpreader.php">
            .
            .
            .
            <INPUT TYPE="SUBMIT" VALUE="Submit">
        </FORM>
    </BODY>
</HTML>
```

This displays the clickable Submit button that you see in web pages. Note that the caption of this button doesn't have to be "Submit"; you can set it to whatever you want, using the VALUE attribute. Here's how to create a Submit button with the caption "Sign me up!"

```
<INPUT TYPE="SUBMIT" VALUE="Sign me up!">
```

Besides Submit buttons, you can also display Reset buttons, which, when clicked, will reset the data in a form's controls back to their default (usually blank) values. Here's what a Reset button would look like—note that you can use any caption here, as with Submit buttons:

```
<FORM METHOD="GET" ACTION="phpreader.php">
            .
            .
            .
    <INPUT TYPE="SUBMIT" VALUE="Submit">
    <INPUT TYPE="RESET" VALUE="Reset">
</FORM>
```

So how do you actually access the data that's sent to you in your PHP scripts? If you've used the POST method, you can find that data in the $_POST array, as we're going to see in the next chunk on retrieving data from text fields. If you've used the GET method, you use the $_GET array. These arrays are *superglobal* arrays, which means that they're available to you without having to use the global keyword. Also, the $_REQUEST array holds data from both $_GET and $_POST.

Creating Text Fields

Text fields are those controls into which the user can enter single-line text, and they're very common in web pages. To create an HTML text field in a form, use the <INPUT TYPE="TEXT"> element enclosed in an HTML <FORM> element.

In this case, we'll use two web documents—an HTML page that displays a text field, and a PHP script that will read what the user entered and will display that text in a new web page. In the HTML page, we're going to need an HTML form to send the text in the text field to a PHP script named phptext.php:

```
<HTML>
    <HEAD>
        <TITLE>
            Using Text Fields
        </TITLE>
    </HEAD>

    <BODY>
        <CENTER>
            <H1>
                Using Text Fields
            </H1>
            <FORM METHOD="POST" ACTION="phptext.php">
                .
                .
                .
            </FORM>
        </CENTER>
    </BODY>
</HTML>
```

In this example, we'll ask for the user's name. We'll call the text field "Name" using the text field's NAME attribute so that we can refer to it in PHP code in order to recover the data the user entered into the text field. You can see how that looks in Example 5-1, phptext.html.

EXAMPLE 5-1 A text field, phptext.html

```
<HTML>
    <HEAD>
        <TITLE>
            Using Text Fields
        </TITLE>
    </HEAD>

    <BODY>
        <CENTER>
```

```
<H1>
    Using Text Fields
</H1>

<FORM METHOD="POST" ACTION="phptext.php">
    What's your name?

    <INPUT NAME="Name" TYPE="TEXT">

    <BR>
    <BR>

    <INPUT TYPE="SUBMIT" VALUE="Submit">
</FORM>

    </CENTER>
  </BODY>
</HTML>
```

That completes phptext.html; navigate to this web page (http://localhost/phptext.html if
you're using a local server), as shown in Figure 5-1. You can see the prompt to the user
here, the text field, and the Submit button.

FIGURE 5-1   Asking for the user's name.

To use this page, the user enters his or her name and then clicks the Submit button. The
user's name is sent to our PHP script. And in that script, we're going to extract the user's
name and echo it back in a new web page. See the next chunk for the details.

Retrieving Data from Text Fields

In the previous chunk, we created a web page with an HTML text field in a form that will send the contents of the text field to phptext.php when the user clicks the Submit button. So how can you retrieve the data from that text field?

We'll embed the user's name in a web page starting with the text "Your name is":

```
<HTML>
    <HEAD>
        <TITLE>
            Using Text Fields
        </TITLE>
    </HEAD>
    <BODY>
        <CENTER>
            <H1>
                Retrieving Data From Text Fields
            </H1>
            Your name is
            .
            .
            .
        </CENTER>
    </BODY>
</HTML>
```

To retrieve data from the web page, we'll use the $_REQUEST array, which holds the combined data of the $_POST and $_GET arrays, which means that you can use $_REQUEST with web pages that send you data using either the GET or POST methods. In the HTML page, phptext.html, we named the text field "Name" with the HTML NAME attribute, so to recover the value in that text field in the PHP script, you just use $_REQUEST["Name"], as shown in phptext.php, Example 5-2.

EXAMPLE 5-2   Reading data from a text field, phptext.php

```
<HTML>
    <HEAD>
        <TITLE>
            Using Text Fields
        </TITLE>
    </HEAD>

    <BODY>
        <CENTER>

            <H1>
                Retrieving Data From Text Fields
```

```
            </H1>
            Your name is
            <?php
                    echo $_REQUEST["Name"];
            ?>
        </CENTER>
    </BODY>
</HTML>
```

That's all it takes; now we're able to read the data the user entered into a text field. You can see the results in Figure 5-2, where we've gotten the user's name and displayed it. Now we're interacting with and accepting input from the user. Very cool.

FIGURE 5-2 Reading data from a text field.

That's how it works in PHP—you recover data from HTML controls like this: $_REQUEST["*ControlName*"], which will handle both GET and POST requests. If you prefer, you can use the $_GET or $_POST arrays instead; for example, if you've used the POST method:

```
<FORM METHOD="POST" ACTION="phptext.php">
    What's your name?

    <INPUT NAME="Name" TYPE="TEXT">
    <BR>
    <BR>
    <INPUT TYPE="SUBMIT" VALUE="Submit">
</FORM>
```

Then you could use $_POST to recover data with:

```
Your name is
<?php
    echo $_POST["Name"];
?>
```

Creating Text Areas

Text areas act like multi-line text fields, and you create them with the HTML <TEXTAREA> element. You can see an example, phptextarea.html, in Example 5-3, where we're asking the user to list his or her friends in a text area named "Friends". When the user clicks the Submit button here, that data will be sent to a PHP script, phptextarea.php, and we'll echo that data in a new web page.

EXAMPLE 5-3   A text area, phptextarea.html

```
<HTML>
    <HEAD>
        <TITLE>Using Text Areas</TITLE>
    </HEAD>

    <BODY>
        <CENTER>
        <H1>Using Text Areas</H1>
            <FORM METHOD="POST" ACTION="phptextarea.php">
                Please list your best friends:
                <BR>
                <TEXTAREA NAME="Friends" COLS="50" ROWS="5">
1.
2.
3.
4.

                </TEXTAREA>
                <BR>
                <BR>
                <INPUT TYPE="SUBMIT">
            </FORM>
        </CENTER>
    <BODY>
</HTML>
```

This web page, textarea.html, appears in Figure 5-3, with some user data.

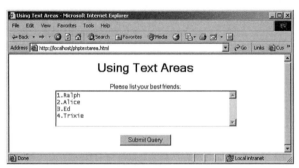

FIGURE 5-3   Using a text area.

To recover data from the text area in the PHP script phptextarea.php, you can use $_REQUEST["Friends"], as you see in Example 5-4.

EXAMPLE 5-4   A text area, phptextarea.php

```
<HTML>
    <HEAD>
        <TITLE>
            Using Text Areas
        </TITLE>
    </HEAD>

    <BODY>
        <CENTER>
            <H1>
                Retrieving Data From Text Areas
            </H1>

            Your best friends are:
            <?php
                echo $_REQUEST["Friends"];
            ?>

        </CENTER>
    </BODY>
</HTML>
```

You can see the results in Figure 5-4, where we've read the text the user entered into the text area. No problem.

FIGURE 5-4   Reading data from a text area.

Creating Checkboxes

Another fundamental control is the checkbox control, which is created with the HTML
`<INPUT TYPE="CHECKBOX">` element. You can see an example in checkboxes.html, Example
5-5, where we're asking the user if he or she wants some cash back.

EXAMPLE 5-5   Checkboxes, phpcheckboxes.html

```
<HTML>
    <HEAD>
        <TITLE>Using Checkboxes</TITLE>
    </HEAD>

    <BODY>
        <CENTER>
        <H1>Using Checkboxes</H1>
        <FORM METHOD="POST" ACTION="checkboxes.php">
            Do you want cash back?
            <INPUT NAME="Check1" TYPE="CHECKBOX" VALUE="Yes">
            Yes
            <INPUT NAME="Check2" TYPE="CHECKBOX" VALUE="No">
            No
            <BR>
            <BR>
            <INPUT TYPE="SUBMIT" VALUE="Submit">
        </FORM>
        </CENTER>
    </BODY>
</HTML>
```

You can see the two checkboxes in a browser in Figure 5-5.

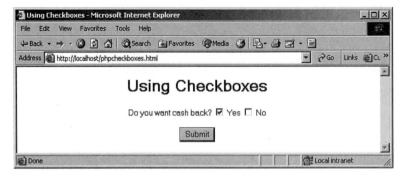

FIGURE 5-5   Creating checkboxes.

You can determine which checkbox the user checked in your code using
$_REQUEST["Check1"] and $_REQUEST["Check2"]. But what if the user only checked Check1
but not Check2? Asking for $_REQUEST["Check2"] will cause an error because it doesn't
exist. To check if it exists first, you can use the PHP *isset* function, which returns TRUE if
a variable has been set and FALSE otherwise. You can see what that looks like in the PHP
script that reads the checkbox settings, checkboxes.php, Example 5-6.

EXAMPLE 5-6   Reading data from checkboxes, phpcheckboxes.php

```
<HTML>
    <HEAD>
        <TITLE>
            Using Checkboxes
        </TITLE>
    </HEAD>

    <BODY>
        <CENTER>
            <H1>Retrieving Data From Checkboxes</H1>
            You checked
            <?php
                if (isset($_REQUEST["Check1"]))
                    echo $_REQUEST["Check1"], "<BR>";
                if (isset($_REQUEST["Check2"]))
                    echo $_REQUEST["Check2"], "<BR>";
            ?>
        </CENTER>
    </BODY>
</HTML>
```

As you can see in Figure 5-6, we have indeed been able to determine which checkbox the
user checked. Nothing to it.

FIGURE 5-6   Reading data from checkboxes.

Creating Radio Buttons

Users can check as many checkboxes as they want at once, but if you use radio buttons instead, the user can select only one of them at a time. That's useful if you want to present a set of exclusive options, such as the current day of the week or whether the user is ordering a pizza, sandwich, or calzone.

You group radio buttons together by giving two or more the same name, as you see in phpradio.html, Example 5-7.

EXAMPLE 5-7   Radio buttons, phpradio.html

```
<HTML>
    <HEAD>
        <TITLE>Using Radio Buttons</TITLE>
    </HEAD>
    <BODY>
        <CENTER>
            <H1>Using Radio Buttons</H1>
            <FORM METHOD="POST" ACTION="radio.php">
                Would you like cash back?
                <INPUT NAME="Radio1" TYPE="RADIO" VALUE="Yes">
                Yes
                <INPUT NAME="Radio1" TYPE="RADIO" VALUE="No">
                No
                <BR>
                <BR>
                <INPUT TYPE="SUBMIT" VALUE="Submit">
            </FORM>
        </CENTER>
    </BODY>
</HTML>
```

And you can see phpradio.html at work in Figure 5-7.

FIGURE 5-7   Creating radio buttons.

To recover the radio button that was selected in the radio button group, you use the name of the group with $_REQUEST, instead of having to work with each individual control as we did with checkboxes. You can see how this works in radio.php, Example 5-8.

EXAMPLE 5-8   Reading data from radio buttons, phpradio.php

```
<HTML>
    <HEAD>
        <TITLE>Using Radio Buttons</TITLE>
    </HEAD>
    <BODY>
        <CENTER>
            <H1>Retrieving Data From Radio Buttons</H1>
            <?php
                echo "You selected ", $_REQUEST["Radio1"];
            ?>
        </CENTER>
    </BODY>
</HTML>
```

The results appear in Figure 5-8, where we have indeed determined which radio button in the group the user selected.

FIGURE 5-8   Reading data from radio buttons.

What if you want multiple sets of radio buttons? No problem—just give each set of radio buttons its own name with the NAME attribute.

Creating Listboxes

Unlike the HTML controls we've already seen, HTML listboxes, created with <SELECT> controls, can support multiple selections. For example, take a look at phplistbox.html, Example 5-9, where we're letting the user select his or her favorite fruits.

EXAMPLE 5-9   Listboxes, phplistbox.html

```
<HTML>
    <HEAD>
        <TITLE>Using Lists</TITLE>
    </HEAD>

    <BODY>
        <CENTER>
            <H1>Using Lists</H1>
            <FORM METHOD="GET" ACTION="listbox.php">
                Select your favorite fruit(s):
                <BR>
                <BR>
                <SELECT NAME="Food[]" MULTIPLE="TRUE">
                    <OPTION>Apple</OPTION>
                    <OPTION>Orange</OPTION>
                    <OPTION>Pear</OPTION>
                    <OPTION>Pomegranate</OPTION>
                </SELECT>
                <BR>
                <BR>
                <INPUT TYPE="SUBMIT" VALUE="Submit">
            </FORM>
        </CENTER>
    </BODY>
</HTML>
```

The user can select multiple listbox items, as you see in Figure 5-9.

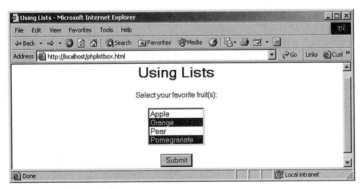

FIGURE 5-9   Using listboxes.

We've named the listbox "Food" here, but because multiple selections are possible, we can't just recover the selections using $_REQUEST["Food"]. Instead, we can refer to the first selection, if there is one, as $_REQUEST["Food"][0], the second, if there is one, as $_REQUEST["Food"][1], and so on. To catch them all, we'll use a foreach loop as you see in listbox.php, Example 5-10.

EXAMPLE 5-10 Retrieving data from lists, listbox.php

```html
<HTML>
    <HEAD>
        <TITLE>Using Lists</TITLE>
    </HEAD>

    <BODY>
        <CENTER>
            <H1>Retrieving Data From Lists</H1>
            You selected:
            <BR>
            <?php
            foreach($_REQUEST["Food"] as $fruit){
                echo $fruit, "<BR>";
            }
            ?>
        </CENTER>
    </BODY>
</HTML>
```

The results appear in Figure 5-10, where, as you can see, we're retrieving the selections the user made in a multi-user listbox. Not bad.

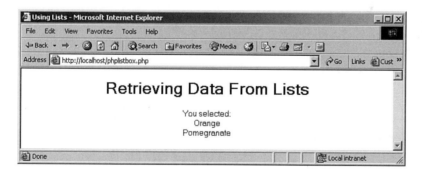

FIGURE 5-10 Reading data from listboxes.

Creating Hidden Controls

Another handy control type in PHP is the hidden control, which lets you store hidden text data in web pages. This is useful when you want to store data about a user and the user doesn't allow cookies to be stored, for instance.

Here's an example, phphidden.html, Example 5-11, which contains the text "No worries." in a hidden control named "Hidden".

EXAMPLE 5-11   Creating hidden data, phphidden.html

```
<HTML>
    <HEAD>
        <TITLE>
            Using Hidden Controls
        </TITLE>
    </HEAD>

    <BODY>
        <CENTER>
            <H1>
                Using Hidden Controls
            </H1>

            <FORM METHOD="POST" ACTION="phphidden.php">
                Click the button to see the hidden data.
                <INPUT NAME="Hidden" TYPE="HIDDEN" VALUE="No worries.">
                <BR>
                <BR>
                <INPUT TYPE="SUBMIT" VALUE="Click Me">
            </FORM>
        </CENTER>
    </BODY>
</HTML>
```

You can see this page, phphidden.html, in Figure 5-11. The data in the hidden control isn't visible—obviously—but when you click the button, the PHP script phphidden.php will retrieve that data and display it.

You can retrieve the data from a hidden control as you'd expect—by name, using $_GET or $_POST as appropriate, or by using $_REQUEST. You can see how that works in phphidden.php, Example 5-12, where we're recovering the data in the hidden control as $_REQUEST["Hidden"].

FIGURE 5-11 Using hidden controls.

EXAMPLE 5-12 Retrieving data from hidden controls, phphidden.php

```
<HTML>
    <HEAD>
        <TITLE>
            Retrieving Hidden Data
        </TITLE>
    </HEAD>

    <BODY>
        <CENTER>
            <H1>Retrieving Hidden Data</H1>
            The hidden data was:
            <BR>
            <?php
                echo $_REQUEST["Hidden"];
            ?>
        </CENTER>
    </BODY>
</HTML>
```

The results appear in Figure 5-12, where we've been able to read the data from the hidden control and echo it in a web page.

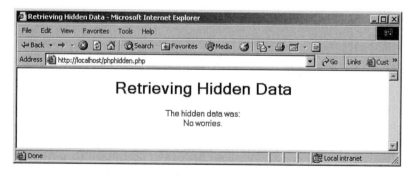

FIGURE 5-12 Reading data from hidden controls.

Creating Password Controls

Here's another useful type of HTML control—password controls. From a PHP point of view, these controls work just like text fields; but they're different from the user's point of view. The user sees only asterisks (*) each time he or she types a key instead of letters, so this control is handy for reading passwords and other sensitive data.

You can see an example, phppassword.html, in Example 5-13. This example asks the user what the password is by using a password control.

EXAMPLE 5-13 Using password controls, phppassword.html

```
<HTML>
    <HEAD>
        <TITLE>
            Using Password Controls
        </TITLE>
    </HEAD>

    <BODY>

        <CENTER>

            <H1>
                Using Password Controls
            </H1>

            <FORM METHOD="POST" ACTION="phppassword.php">
            What's the password?

                <INPUT NAME="Password" TYPE="PASSWORD">

                <BR>
                <BR>

                <INPUT TYPE="SUBMIT" VALUE=Submit>
            </FORM>

        </CENTER>

    </BODY>
</HTML>
```

You can see what this page looks like in Figure 5-13, where the user has already typed in a password (which in this case is "Open sesame") into a password control named Password.

Although you can't read the password when you type it in, the password is available to your PHP code. Use $_REQUEST["Password"], as you see in phppassword.php, Example 5-14.

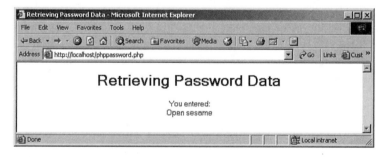

FIGURE 5-13   Using a password control.

EXAMPLE 5-14   Retrieving data from password controls, phppassword.php

```
<HTML>
    <HEAD>
        <TITLE>
            Retrieving Password Data
        </TITLE>
    </HEAD>

    <BODY>
        <CENTER>
            <H1>
                Retrieving Password Data
            </H1>
            You entered:
            <BR>
            <?php
                echo $_REQUEST["Password"];
            ?>
        </CENTER>
    </BODY>
</HTML>
```

The result appears in Figure 5-14, where we've been successful in reading the data from the password control. As you'd expect, in a real application, you'd want to check the password against a password list and deny access unless it checks out.

FIGURE 5-14   Reading data from a password control.

Creating Image Maps

PHP also supports HTML-based image maps, which are clickable images full of hot spots, although you work with them a little differently in PHP.

Here's an example, phpimap.html, Example 5-15, which displays an image (imap.jpg) and lets the user click it. To create an image map this way, you use the HTML `<INPUT TYPE="IMAGE">` element, setting the SRC attribute to the location of the image.

EXAMPLE 5-15 Creating an image map, phpimap.html

```
<HTML>
    <HEAD>
        <TITLE>
            Using Image Maps
        </TITLE>
    </HEAD>

    <BODY>
        <CENTER>

            <H1>
                Using Image Maps
            </H1>

            <FORM METHOD="POST" ACTION="phpimap.php">
                Click the image:
                <BR>

                <INPUT NAME="imap" TYPE="IMAGE" SRC="imap.jpg">

            </FORM>

        </CENTER>
    </BODY>
</HTML>
```

You can see what the image map looks like in Figure 5-15.

When the user clicks the map, the mouse location is sent to your PHP script. We've given the map the name "imap" using the HTML NAME attribute, and in other languages, you'd refer to the X and Y locations of the mouse as imap.x and imap.y. However, those aren't legal PHP names, so in PHP, you use imap_x and imap_y, as shown in phpimap.php, Example 5-16.

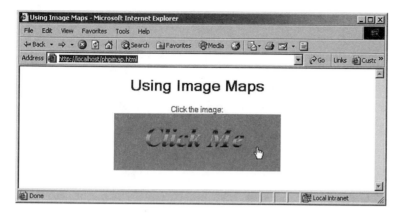

FIGURE 5-15   Using an image map.

EXAMPLE 5-16   Retrieving data from an image map, phpimap.php

```
<HTML>
    <HEAD>
        <TITLE>Retrieving Image Map Data</TITLE>
    </HEAD>

    <BODY>
        <CENTER>
            <H1>Retrieving Image Map Data</H1>
            <BR>
            You clicked at location (
            <?php
                echo $_REQUEST["imap_x"], ", ", $_REQUEST["imap_y"];
            ?>
            ).
        </CENTER>
    </BODY>
</HTML>
```

That's all it takes—now your script can detect the mouse location of image map clicks, as shown in Figure 5-16. When you know where the map was clicked, you know what action the user wants you to take.

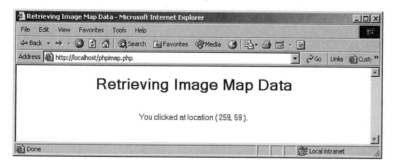

FIGURE 5-16   Reading data from an image map.

Uploading Files

HTML forms also let you upload files, and PHP is up to the task. For example, say that you want to upload a file named message.txtand make this text available to your code:

```
No
worries.
PHP
can
handle
this
too.
```

To upload files, you have to use a *multipart form*. How do you create one? You use the HTML <FORM> element's ENCTYPE attribute:

```
<FORM
    ENCTYPE="multipart/form-data"
        .
        .
        .

</FORM>
```

Now you're free to specify the name of the script to send the file to, as usual:

```
<FORM
    ENCTYPE="multipart/form-data"
    ACTION="phpfile.php" method="POST">
        .
        .
        .

</FORM>
```

To actually do the uploading, use an HTML file control, created with an <INPUT TYPE="file"> element:

```
<FORM
    ENCTYPE="multipart/form-data"
    ACTION="phpfile.php" method="POST">
    Upload this file: <INPUT NAME="userfile" TYPE="FILE">
        .
        .
        .

</FORM>
```

Note that in this case we're naming the control "userfile", which will be how we refer to the uploaded file—but not using the $_GET, $_POST, or $_REQUEST arrays. Instead, you use a superglobal (i.e., available to all code) array named $_FILES, which we'll do in the next chunk; our goal will be to display the contents of the uploaded file.

All that's left now is to add a Submit button, as shown in phpfile.html, Example 5-17.

EXAMPLE 5-17   A file upload control example, phpfile.html

```
<HTML>
    <HEAD>
        <TITLE>
            Uploading Files
        </TITLE>
    </HEAD>

    <BODY>
        <CENTER>
            <H1>
                Uploading Files
            </H1>

            <FORM
                ENCTYPE="multipart/form-data"
                ACTION="phpfile.php" method="POST">
                Upload this file: <INPUT NAME="userfile" TYPE="FILE" />
                <BR>
                <BR>
                <INPUT TYPE="SUBMIT" VALUE="Send File" />
            </FORM>
        </CENTER>
    </BODY>
</HTML>
```

The file upload control appears in Figure 5-17; browse to the file you want to upload, which is message.txt in this example, and click the Send File button.

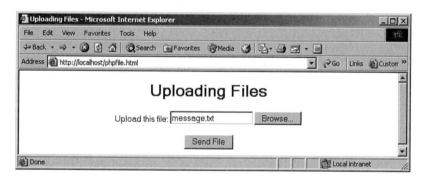

FIGURE 5-17   An HTML upload control.

Reading Uploaded Files

After you upload a file, you can access it using PHP, but it takes a little extra work. You use the superglobal array $_FILES to handle uploaded files; here are the specific elements you can use and what they mean. Note that the first index is the name of the file upload control, which is "userfile" in the previous chunk:

$_FILES['userfile']['name']. The original name of the file on the user's machine.

$_FILES['userfile']['type']. The MIME type of the file. For example, this could be "image/gif" or "text/plain".

$_FILES['userfile']['size']. The size of the uploaded file, in bytes.

$_FILES['userfile']['tmp_name']. The temporary filename of the file in which the uploaded file was stored on the server.

. The error code associated with this file upload.

When a file has been uploaded, it is stored as a temporary file on the server, and you can access that file as $_FILES['userfile']['tmp_name']. We're going to work with files in more depth in Chapter 6, "Creating Web Forms and Validating User Input," but we'll get a preview of how to do that now. You start by using the fopen function to open the temporary file:

```php
<?php
    $handle = fopen($_FILES['userfile']['tmp_name'], "r");
        .
        .
        .

?>
```

You can loop over the lines of text in the file in a while loop that ends when we've reached the end of the file, which we can test with the *feof* function:

```php
<?php
    $handle = fopen($_FILES['userfile']['tmp_name'], "r");
    while (!feof($handle)){
        .
        .
        .

    }
?>
```

To read lines of text from the file, use the *fgets* function like this, where we also display the text:

```php
<?php
    $handle = fopen($_FILES['userfile']['tmp_name'], "r");
    while (!feof($handle)){
        $text = fgets($handle);
        echo $text, "<BR>";
    }
?>
```

All that's left is to close the temporary file with *fclose*, as shown in phpupload.php, Example 5-18.

EXAMPLE 5-18   Reading an uploaded file, phpupload.php

```
<HTML>
    <HEAD>
        <TITLE>Retrieving File Data</TITLE>
    </HEAD>
    <BODY>
        <CENTER>
            <H1>Retrieving File Data</H1>
            <BR>
            Here are the contents of the file:
            <BR>
            <?php
                $handle = fopen($_FILES['userfile']['tmp_name'], "r");
                while (!feof($handle)){
                    $text = fgets($handle);
                    echo $text, "<BR>";
                }
                fclose($handle);
            ?>
        </CENTER>
    </BODY>
</HTML>
```

The results appear in Figure 5-18, where we've successfully uploaded the file. Very cool.

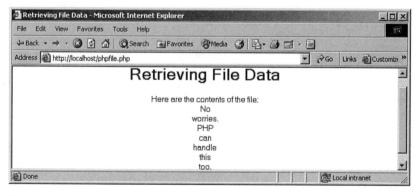

FIGURE 5-18   Reading text from an uploaded file.

Creating Buttons: Take 1

Another control you'll see often in web pages is the HTML button. Buttons are different from other controls, however, because when clicked, they don't *stay* clicked, which means that when the form is sent to your script, the button has long since popped up. So how do you determine which button the user clicked from PHP? One way is with a mix of JavaScript and a hidden control, as shown in phpbuttons.html, Example 5-19. When the user clicks a button, the JavaScript in this example stores the button name in a hidden HTML control named "Button" and then uses the submit function to post the results to a PHP script, phpbuttons.php.

EXAMPLE 5-19   Using buttons, phpbuttons.html

```
<HTML>
    <HEAD>
        <TITLE>Using Buttons</TITLE>
    </HEAD>
    <BODY>
        <H1>Using Buttons</H1>
        <FORM NAME="form1" ACTION="phpbuttons.php" METHOD="POST">
            <INPUT TYPE="HIDDEN" NAME="Button">
            <INPUT TYPE="BUTTON" VALUE="Button 1" ONCLICK="button1()">
            <INPUT TYPE="BUTTON" VALUE="Button 2" ONCLICK="button2()">
            <INPUT TYPE="BUTTON" VALUE="Button 3" ONCLICK="button3()">
        </FORM>
        <SCRIPT LANGUAGE="JavaScript">
            <!--
                function button1()
                {
                    document.form1.Button.value = "button 1"
                    form1.submit()
                }
                function button2()
                {
                    document.form1.Button.value = "button 2"
                    form1.submit()
                }
                function button3()
                {
                    document.form1.Button.value = "button 3"
                    form1.submit()
                }
            // -->
        </SCRIPT>
    </BODY>
</HTML>
```

You can see what this page looks like in a browser in Figure 5-19.

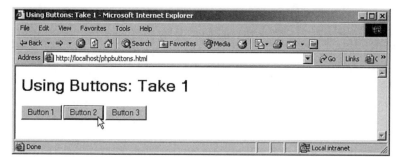

FIGURE 5-19 A set of clickable buttons.

Just click a button, and then you can read the name of the clicked button in the hidden field "Button" in your PHP script, as shown in phpbuttons.php, Example 5-20.

EXAMPLE 5-20 Reading buttons, phpbuttons.php

```
<HTML>
    <HEAD>
        <TITLE>Using Buttons</TITLE>
    </HEAD>
    <BODY>
        <CENTER>
        <H1>Using Buttons</H1>
        You clicked
        <?php
            if (isset($_REQUEST["Button"]))
                echo $_REQUEST["Button"], "<BR>";
        ?>
        </CENTER>
    </BODY>
</HTML>
```

You can see the results in Figure 5-20, where we've determined which button was clicked.

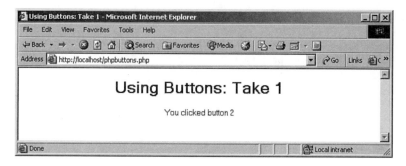

FIGURE 5-20 Determining which button was clicked.

Creating Buttons: Take 2

In the previous chunk, we used a mixture of JavaScript and a hidden control to determine which button of a set of three a user clicked in a web page. However, you can do the same thing without any JavaScript if you use three Submit buttons as your buttons.

To do that, you use three different HTML forms in your web page, each with its own Submit button. To the user, it looks as if you have three simple push buttons in your page, but when the user clicks one of the buttons, that form's data is sent back to your PHP script:

```
<FORM NAME="form1" ACTION="phpbuttons.php" METHOD="POST">
    <INPUT TYPE="SUBMIT" VALUE="Button 1">
</FORM>
```

To send some data back to the PHP script, we'll add a hidden control to each of the three forms, containing the name of the clicked button, as shown in phpbuttons2.html, Example 5-21.

EXAMPLE 5-21   Using buttons: take 2, phpbuttons2.html

```
<HTML>
    <HEAD>
        <TITLE>Using Buttons: Take 2</TITLE>
    </HEAD>

    <BODY>
        <H1>Using Buttons: Take 2</H1>
        <FORM NAME="form1" ACTION="phpbuttons.php" METHOD="POST">
            <INPUT TYPE="HIDDEN" NAME="Button" VALUE="button 1">
            <INPUT TYPE="SUBMIT" VALUE="Button 1">
        </FORM>
        <FORM NAME="form2" ACTION="phpbuttons.php" METHOD="POST">
            <INPUT TYPE="HIDDEN" NAME="Button" VALUE="button 2">
            <INPUT TYPE="SUBMIT" VALUE="Button 2">
        </FORM>
        <FORM NAME="form3" ACTION="phpbuttons.php" METHOD="POST">
            <INPUT TYPE="HIDDEN" NAME="Button" VALUE="button 3">
            <INPUT TYPE="SUBMIT" VALUE="Button 3">
        </FORM>
        </SCRIPT>
    </BODY>
</HTML>
```

This page appears in Figure 5-21, where you can see the three Submit buttons masquerading as three simple push buttons.

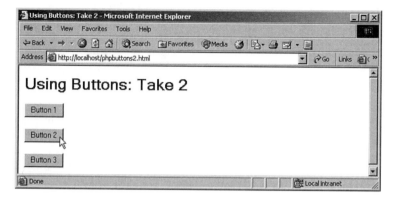

FIGURE 5-21   Determining which button was clicked, Take 2.

To read the name of the clicked button in phpbuttons2.php, Example 5-22, just extract the text from the hidden control, "Button".

EXAMPLE 5-22   Reading buttons: take 2, phpbuttons2.php

```
<HTML>
    <HEAD><TITLE>Using Buttons: Take 2</TITLE></HEAD>
    <BODY><CENTER>
        <H1>Using Buttons: Take 2</H1>
        You clicked
        <?php
            if (isset($_REQUEST["Button"]))
                echo $_REQUEST["Button"], "<BR>";
        ?>
    </CENTER></BODY>
</HTML>
```

The results appear in Figure 5-22, where we've been able to determine the clicked button.

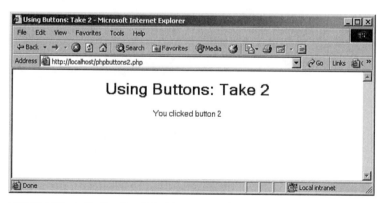

FIGURE 5-22   Indicating the clicked button, Take 2.

Here we've used hidden controls to store our data, but in fact there's an even simpler technique where you don't need them at all.

Creating Buttons: Take 3

We've seen two ways to handle push buttons in web pages, but there's a third way; you can pass data back to a PHP script using the VALUE attribute of Submit buttons, which can be read in a PHP script. This technique avoids having to use a hidden control to send data back to your script.

To do this, just give each Submit button the same name, "Button" in this next example, and assign the name of the button to the VALUE attribute in each of the three forms:

```
<FORM NAME="form1" ACTION="phpbuttons3.php" METHOD="POST">
    <INPUT TYPE="SUBMIT" NAME="Button" VALUE="button 1">
</FORM>
```

You can see how this looks in a web page in phpbuttons3.html, Example 5-23.

EXAMPLE 5-23   Using buttons: take 3, phpbuttons3.html

```
<HTML>
    <HEAD>
        <TITLE>Using Buttons: Take 3</TITLE>
    </HEAD>

    <BODY>
        <H1>Using Buttons: Take 3</H1>
        <FORM NAME="form1" ACTION="phpbuttons3.php" METHOD="POST">
            <INPUT TYPE="SUBMIT" NAME="Button" VALUE="button 1">
        </FORM>

        <FORM NAME="form2" ACTION="phpbuttons3.php" METHOD="POST">
            <INPUT TYPE="SUBMIT" NAME="Button" VALUE="button 2">
        </FORM>

        <FORM NAME="form3" ACTION="phpbuttons3.php" METHOD="POST">
            <INPUT TYPE="SUBMIT" NAME="Button" VALUE="button 3">
        </FORM>
        </SCRIPT>
    </BODY>
</HTML>
```

As you see in Figure 5-23, all three buttons are visible, as before, in the browser.

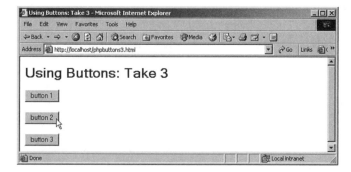

FIGURE 5-23   A set of buttons, Take 3.

In the PHP script, phpbuttons3.php, Example 5-24, all you need to do is the check value of the control named "Button"—which this time is a Submit button, not a hidden field.

EXAMPLE 5-24   Reading buttons: take 3, phpbuttons3.php

```
<HTML>
    <HEAD>
        <TITLE>Using Buttons: Take 3</TITLE>
    </HEAD>

    <BODY>
        <CENTER>
        <H1>Using Buttons: Take 3</H1>
        You clicked
        <?php
            if (isset($_REQUEST["Button"]))
                echo $_REQUEST["Button"], "<BR>";
        ?>
        </CENTER>
    </BODY>
</HTML>
```

As before, the PHP script can determine which button was clicked, as you see in Figure 5-24. Presto.

FIGURE 5-24   Indicating the clicked button, Take 3.

Summary

This chapter started our work with HTML controls. You saw how to retrieve user data from a variety of user controls, such as text fields and text areas. Here's a summary of the salient points in this chapter:

- In web forms, the `ACTION` attribute gives the URL that will handle the form data. You can omit this attribute, in which case it defaults to the URL of the current document.

- In web forms, the `METHOD` attribute specifies the method or protocol for sending data to the target action URL.

- In web forms, the `TARGET` attribute indicates a named frame for the browser to display the form results in.

- To retrieve data from a web page, you can use the `$_POST` array with web pages that were sent with the `POST` method, `$_GET` for those sent with the `GET` method, and the `$_REQUEST` array, which holds the combined data of the `$_POST` and `$_GET` arrays. Just use the name of the control whose data you want as an index in these arrays.

- To create an HTML text field in a form, use the `<INPUT TYPE="TEXT">` element enclosed in an HTML `<FORM>` element.

- Text areas act like multi-line text fields, and you create them with the HTML `<TEXTAREA>` element.

- You can also use checkbox controls, which are created with the HTML `<INPUT TYPE="CHECKBOX">` element.

- You can create HTML listboxes with `<SELECT>` controls.

- You create hidden controls with `<INPUT NAME="Hidden" TYPE="HIDDEN" VALUE="data">` elements.

- You create passwords with `<INPUT NAME="Password" TYPE="PASSWORD">` elements.

- To create image maps, you use the HTML `<INPUT TYPE="IMAGE">` element.

- To upload files, you have to use a multipart form, created with the HTML `<FORM>` element's `ENCTYPE` attribute. To do the uploading, use an HTML file control created with an `<INPUT TYPE="file">` element.

- You can create buttons with the `<INPUT TYPE="BUTTON" VALUE="Button 1">` element.

CHAPTER 6

Creating Web Forms and Validating User Input

In this chapter, we're going to develop web applications. The previous chapter gave us the basics of working with HTML controls such as text fields, list boxes, text areas, and so on, but more than that is involved in creating a web application. For example, part of the process often involves validating the data the user sent you to make sure it's in reasonable form before trying to use it.

In this chapter, we'll learn how to determine which browser the user has, validate the data they send us and report errors we want them to fix, redirect users to different URLs, see how to pack an entire web application into one form, and more.

For example, we're going to try to validate the data the user sent by checking whether values that should be integers are truly integers and whether strings hold the data they should with a function named validate_data. The validate_data function will place any errors it finds in a global array that we'll name $errors—and if there are errors, we'll display the errors and ask the user to reenter his or her data. If no errors occurred, we can process the data the user entered. The whole thing will look something like this:

```
validate_data();

if(count($errors) != 0){
    display_errors();
    display_welcome();
}
else {
    process_data();
}
```

Being able to validate data and ask the user to correct any errors like this is an invaluable part of any real web application.

Displaying All a Form's Data At Once

We'll start this chapter with a quick one—displaying all the data a form sends to your web application. When you're creating a web application and things aren't going right, you can use a PHP page like the one we'll develop here to see what's actually being sent to your code. As an example, we'll stock an HTML page with a number of controls, as you see in phpformdata.html, Example 6-1. You can see what this sample page looks like in Figure 6-1.

EXAMPLE 6-1   Submitting data in a form, phpformdata.html

```
<HTML>
    <HEAD><TITLE>Reading All Form Data</TITLE></HEAD>
    <BODY>
    <CENTER><H1>Reading All Form Data</H1>
        <FORM METHOD="POST" ACTION="phpformdata.php">
        What's your name?<INPUT NAME="Name" TYPE="TEXT">
        <BR><BR>
        Select your favorite fruit(s):
        <SELECT NAME="Food[]" MULTIPLE>
            <OPTION>Apple</OPTION>
            <OPTION>Orange</OPTION>
            <OPTION>Pear</OPTION>
            <OPTION>Pomegranate</OPTION>
        </SELECT>
        <BR><BR>
        <INPUT TYPE="SUBMIT" VALUE="Submit">
        </FORM>
    </CENTER>
    </BODY>
</HTML>
```

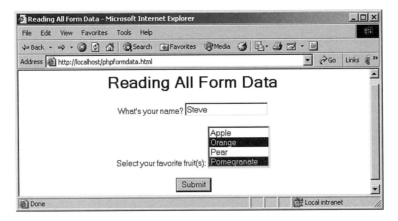

FIGURE 6-1   Submitting form data.

To read the data sent by the user, just use a foreach loop over $_REQUEST. If a particular data item is itself an array, we'll use a nested foreach to display its data, as you see in phpformdata.php, Example 6-2.

EXAMPLE 6-2   Displaying all the data in a form, phpformdata.html

```
<HTML>
    <HEAD><TITLE>Retrieving Data From Forms</TITLE></HEAD>
    <BODY><CENTER>
        <H1>Retrieving Data From Forms</H1>
        Here is the data from the form:<BR>
        <?php
            foreach($_REQUEST as $key => $value){
                if(is_array($value)){
                    foreach($value as $item){
                        echo $key, " => ", $item, "<BR>";
                    }
                }
                else {
                    echo $key, " => ", $value, "<BR>";
                }
            }
        ?>
    </CENTER></BODY>
</HTML>
```

You can see the results in Figure 6-2, where all form data is displayed.

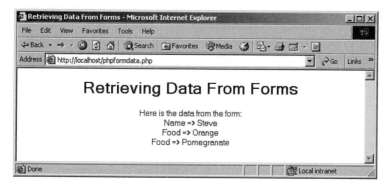

FIGURE 6-2   Reading data from forms.

Useful Server Variables

There's a special superglobal array, $_SERVER, that contains a great deal of information about what's going on with your web application. For example, $_SERVER['PHP_SELF'] holds the name of the current script, $_SERVER['REQUEST_METHOD'] holds the request method that was used ("GET", "POST", and so on), $_SERVER['HTTP_USER_AGENT'] holds the type of the user's browser, and so on. You can see a sampling of the most useful server variables available in $_SERVER in Table 6-1.

> **NOTE**
> The $HTTP_SERVER_VARS array contains the same information as shown in Tables 6-1 and 6-2 but is not a superglobal.

TABLE 6-1 The General Server Variables

Server variable	Description
'AUTH_TYPE'	When running under Apache as module doing HTTP authentication, this variable holds the authentication type.
'DOCUMENT_ROOT'	The document root directory under which the script is executing, as defined in the server's configuration file.
'GATEWAY_INTERFACE'	The revision of the CGI specification that the server is using, such as 'CGI/1.1'.
'PATH_TRANSLATED'	File system–based path to the current script.
'PHP_AUTH_PW'	When running under Apache as module doing HTTP authentication, this variable holds the password provided by the user.
'PHP_AUTH_USER'	When running under Apache as module doing HTTP authentication, this variable holds the username provided by the user.
'PHP_SELF'	The filename of the currently executing script, relative to the document root.
'QUERY_STRING'	The query string, if any, with which the page was accessed.
'REMOTE_ADDR'	The IP address from which the user is viewing the current page.
'REMOTE_HOST'	The Host name from which the user is viewing the current page.
'REMOTE_PORT'	The port being used on the user's machine to communicate with the web server.
'REQUEST_METHOD'	Specifies which request method was used to access the page; such as 'GET', 'HEAD', 'POST', 'PUT'.
'REQUEST_URI'	The URI that was given in order to access this page, such as '/index.html'.

Server variable	Description
`'SCRIPT_FILENAME'`	The absolute pathname of the currently executing script.
`'SCRIPT_NAME'`	Contains the current script's path. This is useful for pages that need to point to themselves.
`'SERVER_ADMIN'`	The value given to the SERVER_ADMIN directive (for Apache) in the web server configuration file.
`'SERVER_NAME'`	The name of the server host under which the script is executing.
`'SERVER_PORT'`	The port on the server machine being used by the web server for communication. By default setups, this is `'80'`.
`'SERVER_PROTOCOL'`	Name and revision of the information protocol through which the page was requested; such as `'HTTP/1.0'`.
`'SERVER_SIGNATURE'`	String containing the server version and virtual host name, which are added to server-generated pages.
`'SERVER_SOFTWARE'`	The server identification string.

These server variables are great because they give you a little more information—such as the name of the script that's running in this example, phpidentifier.php:

```
<HTML>
    <HEAD><TITLE>The Self Identifier Script</TITLE></HEAD>
    <BODY>
        <H1>The Self Identifier Script</H1>
        <?php
            echo "Welcome to ", $_SERVER["PHP_SELF"];
        ?>
    </BODY>
</HTML>
```

Here's what you see when you run this script:

```
Welcome to /phpindentifier.php
```

Useful HTTP Headers

In addition to the selection of $_SERVER variables in Table 6-1, a number of HTTP headers are built into the $_SERVER array as well. These are sent by the browser, and they contain information primarily about the browser.

For example, $_SERVER['HTTP_USER_AGENT'] holds the type of the user's browser, and we're going to put that information to use in the next chunk. You can see the HTTP headers that are accessible by your script using the $_SERVER array in Table 6-2.

> **NOTE**
> The $HTTP_SERVER_VARS array contains the same information as shown in Tables 6-1 and 6-2 but is not a superglobal.

TABLE 6-2 The HTTP Server Variables

HTTP variable	Description
'HTTP_ACCEPT'	Text in the Accept: header from the current request, if there is one.
'HTTP_ACCEPT_CHARSET'	Text in the Accept-Charset: header from the current request, if there is one, such as: '*, utf-8'.
'HTTP_ACCEPT_ENCODING'	Text in the Accept-Encoding: header from the current request, if there is one, such as: 'zip'.
'HTTP_ACCEPT_LANGUAGE'	Text in the Accept-Language: header from the current request, if there is one, such as 'en' for English.
'HTTP_CONNECTION'	Text in the Connection: header from the current request, if there is one, such as: 'Keep-Alive'.
'HTTP_HOST'	Text in the Host: header from the current request, if there is one.
'HTTP_REFERER'	The address of the page (if any) that referred the user agent to the current page. The browser sets this.
'HTTP_USER_AGENT'	Text in the User-Agent: header from the current request, if there is one. This is a string denoting the browser that is accessing the page.

These headers are great for learning more about the user's browser, such as what languages it can deal with, what character sets the browser can handle, and more. The most important piece of data here is the browser type, 'HTTP_USER_AGENT', and we'll put that to work in the next chunk.

Determining Browser Type with HTTP Headers

Now that you're creating web applications, it's often important to understand the environment you're working in—and that includes the browser the user has, which is responsible for displaying what you send it. Different browsers have different capabilities; for example, Internet Explorer has a <MARQUEE> element that no other browser has. And if you don't know whether the user has Internet Explorer, you won't be able to use the <MARQUEE> element. So how can you check what browser the user is using? Check $_SERVER["HTTP_USER_AGENT"]. For example, if the string in this array element contains the text "MSIE" (which you can check with the PHP string function strpos), the user has Internet Explorer. Here's an example, starting with the simple form you see in Example 6-3, phpbrowser.html.

EXAMPLE 6-3   A simple submittable form, phpbrowser.html

```
<HTML>
    <HEAD>
        <TITLE>Determining Browser Type</TITLE>
    </HEAD>
    <BODY>
        <CENTER>
        <H1>Determining Browser Type</H1>
        <FORM METHOD="POST" ACTION="phpbrowser.php">
        Click the button....
        <INPUT TYPE="SUBMIT" VALUE="Submit">
        </FORM>
        </CENTER>
    </BODY>
</HTML>
```

You can see this HTML page in Figure 6-3. When the user clicks the button, the browser sends all the standard HTTP headers to the server.

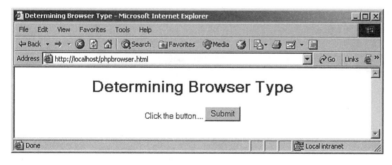

FIGURE 6-3   A submittable form.

In phpbrowser.php, Example 6-4, we check whether the user has Internet Explorer; if so, we display a <MARQUEE> element, and if not, a simple <H1> header.

EXAMPLE 6-4   Determining browser type, phpbrowser.php

```
<HTML>
    <HEAD>
        <TITLE>Determining Browser Type</TITLE>
    </HEAD>
    <BODY>
        <CENTER>
            <H1>Determining Browser Type</H1>
            <BR>
            <?php
                if(strpos($_SERVER["HTTP_USER_AGENT"], "MSIE")){
                    echo("<MARQUEE><H1>You're using the Internet
                        Explorer</H1></MARQUEE>");
                }
                else {
                    echo("<CENTER><H1>You are not using the Internet
                        Explorer</H1></CENTER>");
                }
            ?>
        </CENTER>
    </BODY>
</HTML>
```

The results appear in Figure 6-4, where the marquee text, "You're using the Internet Explorer" is scrolling across the screen.

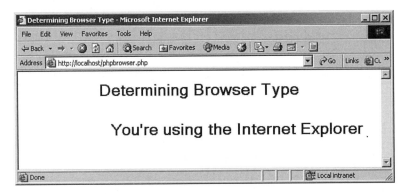

FIGURE 6-4   Determining browser type.

Redirecting Users with HTTP Headers

Besides reading HTTP headers, you can also create your own HTTP headers to send back to the browser. Probably the most useful of these is the location header, which tells the user's browser where to go.

To create an HTTP header, use the `header` function. For instance, to create a redirection header that tells the browser where you want it to go, call `header("Location: URL")`.

For example, we can display a set of three buttons that let the user navigate to one of the examples from the previous chapter: phpbuttons, phplists, or phptextarea. To do that, we'll use three different buttons, each in its own form, and we'll pass the name of the example in the button's VALUE attribute:

```
<FORM NAME="form1" ACTION="phpredirect.php" METHOD="POST">
    <INPUT TYPE="SUBMIT" NAME="Button" VALUE="phpbuttons">
</FORM>
```

You can see the HTML for these three buttons in phpredirect.html, Example 6-5.

EXAMPLE 6-5 Letting the user decide where to go, phpredirect.html

```
<HTML>
    <HEAD>
        <TITLE>Redirecting the user</TITLE>
    </HEAD>

    <BODY>
        <H1>Redirecting the user</H1>

        Which script would you like to see?
        <FORM NAME="form1" ACTION="phpredirect.php" METHOD="POST">
            <INPUT TYPE="SUBMIT" NAME="Button" VALUE="phpbuttons">
        </FORM>
        <FORM NAME="form2" ACTION="phpredirect.php" METHOD="POST">
            <INPUT TYPE="SUBMIT" NAME="Button" VALUE="phplistbox">
        </FORM>
        <FORM NAME="form3" ACTION="phpredirect.php" METHOD="POST">
            <INPUT TYPE="SUBMIT" NAME="Button" VALUE="phptextarea">
        </FORM>
        </SCRIPT>
    </BODY>
</HTML>
```

When the user clicks one of the buttons in this page, Figure 6-5, the name of his or her selection is passed back to our PHP script, phpredirect.php, Example 6-6.

FIGURE 6-5 Redirecting the user.

To perform the redirection, all our PHP script has to do is to use the header function, as you see in phpredirect.php, Example 6-6.

EXAMPLE 6-6 Redirecting a browser, phpredirect.php

```php
<?php
    $redirect = "Location: " . $_REQUEST['Button'] . ".html";
    echo header($redirect);
?>
```

For example, if you click the phplistbox button, you'll be redirected to the phplistbox example, as shown in Figure 6-6.

FIGURE 6-6 Navigating to the Lists example.

Redirecting is particularly good for creating hot spots in image maps, as here, where we're testing the mouse location and navigating to a new URL as required:

```php
<?php
    if($REQUEST["imap_x"] > 50 && $REQUEST["imap_x"] < 70){
        if($REQUEST["imap_y"] > 30 && $REQUEST["imap_y"] < 90){
            $redirect = "Location: www.php.net";
            echo header($redirect);
        }
    }
?>
```

Receiving Form Data in Custom Arrays

Here's a useful tidbit: PHP lets you organize the data you get from a form in your own custom arrays. For example, say you wanted to ask for the user's name and favorite color and would like to have that data stored as $text['name'] and $text['color']. You tell PHP how to do that by giving each text field control a name with square brackets, such as textdata[name], as you see in Example 6-7, phptextarray.html.

EXAMPLE 6-7   HTML for custom arrays example, phptextarray.html

```
<HTML>
    <HEAD>
        <TITLE>
            Using Text Fields
        </TITLE>
    </HEAD>
    <BODY>
        <CENTER>
            <H1>Using Text Fields</H1>
            <FORM METHOD="POST" ACTION="phptextarray.php">
                What's your name?
                <INPUT NAME="textdata[name]" TYPE="TEXT">
                <BR>
                <BR>
                What's your favorite color?
                <INPUT NAME="textdata[color]" TYPE="TEXT">
                <BR>
                <BR>
                <INPUT TYPE=SUBMIT VALUE=Submit>
            </FORM>
        </CENTER>
    </BODY>
</HTML>
```

This page appears in Figure 6-7.

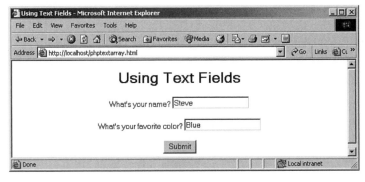

FIGURE 6-7   A custom array example.

To store this data in an array that we'll call $text, you simply use "textdata" as a key in the $_REQUEST array, as shown in Example 6-8, phptextarray.php.

EXAMPLE 6-8   Using custom arrays, phptextarray.php

```
<HTML>
    <HEAD>
        <TITLE>
            Using Text Field Arrays
        </TITLE>
    </HEAD>
    <BODY>
        <CENTER>
            <H1>Retrieving Data From Text Field Arrays</H1>
            Your name is
            <?php
                $text = $_REQUEST['textdata'];
                echo $text['name'], "<BR>";
            ?>
            Your favorite color is
            <?php
                $text = $_REQUEST['textdata'];
                echo $text['color'], "<BR>";
            ?>
        </CENTER>
    </BODY>
</HTML>
```

The results appear in Figure 6-8, where, as you can see, we've let PHP organize our data into a custom array to make things easier for us.

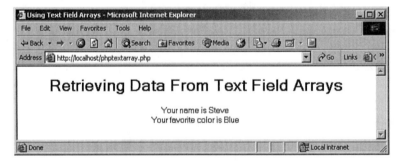

FIGURE 6-8   Getting data from custom arrays.

Web Applications Using a Single PHP Page

Up to this point, our web applications have involved two documents—an HTML opening page that gathers data from the user, and a PHP page that interprets and handles that data. However, many web applications that use PHP are written in a single PHP page. For example, say that you wanted to ask for the user's name and then display that name, all using the same PHP script. To wrap everything into one page, you'll need to be able to determine if this is the first time the user has seen the page, and if so, then you need to display the data-gathering page, sometimes called the *welcome page*. If the user has already entered his or her data, on the other hand, you need to read that data. This means you can determine what you're supposed to be doing by checking whether any data is ready for you to read. We'll use a text field named "Name" to hold the name of the user, so if it holds some data, we should display the name this way:

```php
<?php
    if(isset($_REQUEST["Name"])){
?>
    <H1>Using Text Fields</H1>
    Your name is
<?php
    echo $_REQUEST["Name"];
    }
```

On the other hand, if no data is waiting for you, you should display the text field and a prompt for the user to enter his or her name, as shown in phpsingle.php, Example 6-9.

EXAMPLE 6-9 Using one PHP document, phpsingle.php

```
<HTML>
    <HEAD>
        <TITLE>Using Text Fields</TITLE>
    </HEAD>
    <BODY>
        <CENTER><H1>Using Text Fields</H1>
        <?php
            if(isset($_REQUEST["Name"])){
        ?>
            <H1>Using Text Fields</H1>
            Your name is
        <?php
            echo $_REQUEST["Name"];
            }
            else {
        ?>
            <FORM METHOD="POST" ACTION="phptext.php">
                What's your name?
```

continues

EXAMPLE 6-9   continued

```
                    <INPUT NAME="Name" TYPE="TEXT">
                    <BR><BR>
                    <INPUT TYPE=SUBMIT VALUE=Submit>
                </FORM>
            <?php
                    }
            ?>
            </CENTER>
        </BODY>
</HTML>
```

Note that we're setting the ACTION attribute to the name of the current script (that's actually unnecessary; if you omit the ACTION attribute, the form's data will be sent back to the current PHP document). You can see the results of all this in Figure 6-9, where the PHP script is displaying the welcome page.

FIGURE 6-9   Putting everything into one PHP document.

When you click Submit, the script displays the user's name, as shown in Figure 6-10.

FIGURE 6-10   The results page.

Being able to wrap everything into one page like this is very handy.

Validating User Data

It's important to check the data that your user has entered by validating it and reporting any errors. To do that, we're going to develop some code over the next few chunks. In the previous chunk, we checked if there was some data waiting in a text field to determine whether we should display the welcome page, but sometimes that's not a good technique because you might not require data to be entered in that text field. Instead, developers often use a hidden field, and we'll name ours "seen_already". If this field is *not* present, the user hasn't seen the welcome page already, and we'll display it like this:

```
if(isset($_REQUEST["seen_already"])){
.
.
.
}
else {
    display_welcome();
}
```

If the user *has* already seen the welcome page, then we should try to validate the data he or she sent us. We'll do that with a function named validate_data, which adds error messages to a global array named $errors. After the call to validate_data, you can check if there were any errors by checking the length of the $errors array with count($errors); if errors occurred, we should display the errors and the welcome page so that the user can re-enter his or her data. If no errors occurred, we can process the data that the user sent to us:

```
$errors = array();

if(isset($_REQUEST["seen_already"])){

    validate_data();
    if(count($errors) != 0){
        display_errors();
        display_welcome();
    }
    else {
        process_data();
    }
}
else {
    display_welcome();
}
```

We'll implement the various functions used here on a case-by-case basis. The validate_data function will be different, for example, depending on whether you're checking for required data entry, whether a number is indeed an integer, and so on:

```
function validate_data()
{
    .
    .
    .
}
```

The display_errors function will just display the error messages we've collected:

```
function display_errors()
{
    global $errors;
    foreach ($errors as $err){
        echo $err, "<BR>";
    }
}
```

The process_data function is also dependent on what kind of data you're working with; we'll see a variety of ways to implement this function in the coming chunks:

```
function process_data()
{
    .
    .
    .
}
```

And we'll also implement the display_welcome function on a case-by-case basis. This function displays the controls the user should use. However, for all these cases, we want to make sure to create the hidden field "seen_already" here:

```
    function display_welcome()
    {
        echo "<FORM METHOD='POST' ACTION='phpvalidator.php'>";
        .
        .
        .
        echo "<INPUT TYPE='SUBMIT' VALUE='Submit'>";
        echo "<INPUT TYPE='HIDDEN' NAME='seen_already'
            VALUE='hidden_data'>";
        echo "</FORM>";
    }
?>
</CENTER></BODY></HTML>
```

OK, we've got our data-validating framework; now let's put it to work.

Validating Data: Requiring Data Entry

One of the most common types of data validation is to make sure that the user entered some required data. For example, say your application has a text field called "Name" that you want the user to enter his or her name in, as shown in Figure 6-11. If the user entered his or her name, that name is displayed, as you see in Figure 6-12.

FIGURE 6-11 Validating data.   **FIGURE 6-12** Handling correct data.

But what if the user didn't enter anything in the text field? We'll check that when we validate the form in our `validate_data` function. If there's no text in the "Name" text field, we'll add an error to our $errors array like this, using red text in HTML:

```php
function validate_data()
{
    global $errors;

    if($_REQUEST["Name"] == "") {
        $errors[] = "<FONT COLOR='RED'>Please enter your
            name</FONT>";
    }
}
```

All that's left is to customize the code in the `process_data` function to display the name the user entered and the code in the `display_welcome` function to display the text field and prompt "What's your name?" to the user. You can see how that works in the entire web application, phpvalidate.php, Example 6-10.

EXAMPLE 6-10 Requiring text entry, phpvalidate.php

```html
<HTML><HEAD><TITLE>Using Text Fields</TITLE></HEAD>
    <BODY><CENTER>
                <H1>Using Text Fields</H1>
        <?php
            $errors = array();

            if(isset($_REQUEST["seen_already"])){
```

continues

EXAMPLE 6-10   continued

```
                    validate_data();
                    if(count($errors) != 0){
                         display_errors();
                         display_welcome();
                    }
                    else {
                         process_data();
                    }
               }
               else {
                    display_welcome();
               }
          .
          .
          .

          function display_welcome()
          {
               echo "<FORM METHOD='POST' ACTION='phpvalidate.php'>";
               echo "What's your name?";
               echo "<BR>";
               echo "<INPUT NAME='Name' TYPE='TEXT'>";
               echo "<BR>";
               echo "<BR>";
               echo "<INPUT TYPE='SUBMIT' VALUE='Submit'>";
               echo "<INPUT TYPE='HIDDEN' NAME='seen_already'
                    VALUE='hidden_data'>";
               echo "</FORM>";
          }
     ?>
     </CENTER></BODY></HTML>
```

Now if the user doesn't enter anything in the text field, he or she will see an error message in red (shown in glorious black and white in the figure, though) in Figure 6-13.

FIGURE 6-13 Handling a validation error.

Validating Data: Checking for Numbers

One easy way to check if the user has entered a number is to convert the submitted text to a number (using PHP functions such as intval or floatval) and then back to a string (with the strval function), and compare the result with the original text. If the two are equal, the original text held a number. Here's what that might look like (the strcmp function returns a non-zero value if the strings you're comparing are different):

```
function validate_data()
{
    global $errors;

    if(strcmp($_REQUEST["Number"],
        strval(intval($_REQUEST["Number"])))) {
        $errors[] = "<FONT COLOR='RED'>Please enter an integer</FONT>";
    }
}
```

All that's left is to display any errors and create the welcome page, as shown in phpinteger.php, Example 6-11.

EXAMPLE 6-11   Requiring integer input, phpinteger.php

```
<HTML><HEAD><TITLE>Checking for Integers</TITLE></HEAD>
    <BODY><CENTER><H1>Checking for Integers</H1>
        <?php
            $errors = array();
            if(isset($_REQUEST["seen_already"])){
                validate_data();
                if(count($errors) != 0){
                    display_errors();
                    display_welcome();
                }
                else {_data();}
            }
            else {
                display_welcome();
            }
            function validate_data()
            {
                global $errors;
                if(strcmp($_REQUEST["Number"],
                    strval(intval($_REQUEST["Number"])))) {
                    $errors[] = "<FONT COLOR='RED'>Please enter an
                        integer</FONT>";
                }
            }
            function display_errors()
```

continues

EXAMPLE 6-11 continued

```
        {
            global $errors;
            foreach ($errors as $err){echo $err, "<BR>";}
        }
        function process_data()
        {
            echo "Your integer is ";
            echo $_REQUEST["Number"];
        }
        function display_welcome()
        {
            echo "<FORM METHOD='POST' ACTION='phpinteger.php'>";
            echo "Please enter an integer.";
            echo "<BR>";
            echo "<INPUT NAME='Number' TYPE='TEXT'>";
            echo "<BR>";
            echo "<BR>";
            echo "<INPUT TYPE='SUBMIT' VALUE='Submit'>";
            echo "<INPUT TYPE='HIDDEN' NAME='seen_already'
                VALUE='hidden_data'>";
            echo "</FORM>";
        }?>
</CENTER></BODY></HTML>
```

You can see an example where the user didn't enter an integer in Figure 6-14.

FIGURE 6-14 Checking for numbers.

Validating Data: Checking for Strings

PHP supports *regular expressions*, which let you check text for matches. For instance, in this next example, we'll insist that the text the user enters contains the string "PHP" using the case-insensitive regular expression '/php/i'. (We don't have the space here to cover regular expressions in detail, but they're great for checking text for matches—take a look at http://www.perldoc.com/perl5.6/pod/perlre.html for more on how to create them.) In PHP, you can use the *preg_match* function to use regular expressions; here's how you can insist that the user-entered text contains "PHP":

```
function validate_data()
{
    global $errors;
    if(!preg_match('/php/i', $_REQUEST["Text"])){
        $errors[] = "<FONT COLOR='RED'>Please include \"PHP\" in your
        text.</FONT>";
    }
}
```

The whole application, phpregularexpressions.php, appears in Example 6-12.

EXAMPLE 6-12   Requiring string input, phpregularexpressions.php

```
<HTML>
    <HEAD><TITLE>Using Regular Expressions</TITLE></HEAD>
    <BODY>
        <CENTER>
                <H1>Using Regular Expressions</H1>
        <?php
            $errors = array();
            if(isset($_REQUEST["seen_already"])){
                validate_data();
                if(count($errors) != 0){
                    display_errors();
                    display_welcome();
                }
                else {
                    process_data();
                }
            }
            else {
                display_welcome();
            }
            function validate_data()
            {
                global $errors;

                if(!preg_match('/php/i', $_REQUEST["Text"])){
```

continues

EXAMPLE 6-12   continued

```
                    $errors[] = "<FONT COLOR='RED'>Please include \"PHP\" in
                    your text.</FONT>";
            }
        }
        function display_errors()
        {
            global $errors;
            foreach ($errors as $err){
                echo $err, "<BR>";
            }
        }
        function process_data()
        {
            echo "You said: ";
            echo $_REQUEST["Text"];
        }
        function display_welcome()
        {
            echo "<FORM METHOD='POST'
                ACTION='phpregularexpressions.php'>";
            echo "Say something about PHP:";
            echo "<BR>";
            echo "<INPUT NAME='Text' TYPE='TEXT'>";
            echo "<BR>";
            echo "<BR>";
            echo "<INPUT TYPE='SUBMIT' VALUE='Submit'>";
            echo "<INPUT TYPE='HIDDEN' NAME='seen_already'
                VALUE='hidden_data'>";
            echo "</FORM>";
        }
    ?>
    </CENTER>
    </BODY>
</HTML>
```

You can see the results if you omit "PHP" somewhere in your text in Figure 6-15.

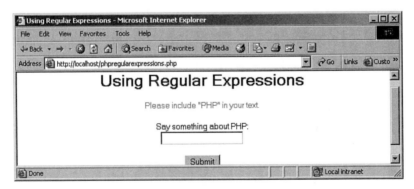

FIGURE 6-15   Searching for "PHP" in text data.

Removing HTML Tags

When you're validating data, here's something to watch out for—HTML in a user's text, especially if you're going to display that text. Malicious users can put some nasty HTML (including JavaScript) into submitted text, which would be executed if you display that text in a browser. You can use the PHP *strip_tags* function to remove all HTML tags from text, as shown in phpstrip.php, Example 6-13.

EXAMPLE 6-13   Removing HTML tags, phpstrip.php

```
<HTML><HEAD><TITLE>Using Text Fields</TITLE></HEAD>
    <BODY><CENTER><H1>Using Text Fields</H1>
        <?php
            $errors = array();
            if(isset($_REQUEST["seen_already"])){
                validate_data();
                if(count($errors) != 0){
                    display_errors();
                    display_welcome();
                }
                else {process_data();}
            }
            else {
                display_welcome();
            }
            function validate_data()
            {
                global $errors;
                if($_REQUEST["Name"] == "") {
                    $errors[] = "<FONT COLOR='RED'>Please enter your
                        name</FONT>";}
            }
            function display_errors()
            {
                global $errors;
                foreach ($errors as $err){
                    echo $err, "<BR>";}
            }
            function process_data()
            {
                echo "Your name is ";
                $ok_text = strip_tags($_REQUEST["Name"]);
                echo $ok_text;
            }
            function display_welcome()
            {
                echo "<FORM METHOD='POST' ACTION='phpstrip.php'>";
                echo "What's your name?<BR>";
```

continues

EXAMPLE 6-13   continued

```
        echo "<INPUT NAME='Name' TYPE='TEXT'>";
        echo "<BR><BR>";
        echo "<INPUT TYPE='SUBMIT' VALUE='Submit'>";
        echo "<INPUT TYPE='HIDDEN' NAME='seen_already'
            VALUE='hidden_data'>";
        echo "</FORM>";
    }
?></CENTER></BODY></HTML>
```

Now if the user enters text with HTML tags, as in Figure 6-16, those tags will be removed automatically and the text made safe, as you see in Figure 6-17.

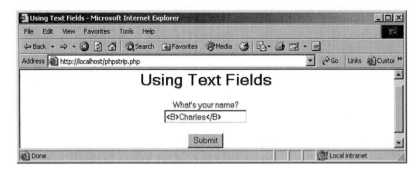

FIGURE 6-16   Text input with HTML tags.

FIGURE 6-17   Stripping HTML tags.

Encoding HTML Tags

What if you don't want to strip HTML tags, but you still want to render them harmless? You can use the *htmlentities* function instead, which encodes HTML tags. For example, <B>Charles</B> would be converted to <B>Charles</B>, which a browser will display as the text "<B>Charles</B>". You can see this at work in phpencode.php, Example 6-14.

EXAMPLE 6-14   Encoding HTML tags, phpencode.php

```
<HTML>
    <HEAD><TITLE>Using Text Fields</TITLE></HEAD>
    <BODY><CENTER><H1>Using Text Fields</H1>
        <?php
            $errors = array();
            if(isset($_REQUEST["seen_already"])){
                validate_data();
                if(count($errors) != 0){
                    display_errors();
                    display_welcome();
                }
                else {
                    process_data();
                }
            }
            else {
                display_welcome();
            }
            function validate_data()
            {
                global $errors;
                if($_REQUEST["Name"] == "") {
                    $errors[] = "<FONT COLOR='RED'>Please enter your
                        name</FONT>";
                }
            }
            function display_errors()
            {
                global $errors;

                foreach ($errors as $err){
                    echo $err, "<BR>";
                }
            }
            function process_data()
            {
                echo "Your name is ";
                $ok_text = htmlentities($_REQUEST["Name"]);
```

continues

EXAMPLE 6-14 continued

```
                echo $ok_text;
        }
        function display_welcome()
        {
                echo "<FORM METHOD='POST' ACTION='phpencode.php'>";
                echo "What's your name?<BR>";
                echo "<INPUT NAME='Name' TYPE='TEXT'>";
                echo "<BR><BR>";
                echo "<INPUT TYPE='SUBMIT' VALUE='Submit'>";
                echo "<INPUT TYPE='HIDDEN' NAME='seen_already'
                    VALUE='hidden_data'>";
                echo "</FORM>";
        }
    ?>
    </CENTER></BODY>
</HTML>
```

Now if the user enters data with HTML tags, as in Figure 6-18, the echoed text displays those HTML tags as in Figure 6-19—but they're just text, not HTML.

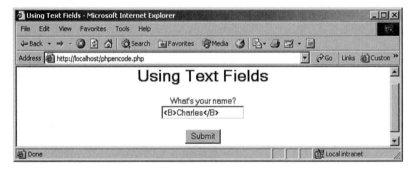

FIGURE 6-18 Text with HTML tags.

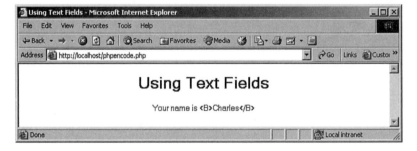

FIGURE 6-19 Encoding HTML tags.

Preserving Data

When your web application contains multiple controls, and you must tell the user there's a problem with the data in one of them, it's considerate if you preserve the data in the others if it checked out OK. For example, phprestore.php, Example 6-15, asks for the user's first name and last name. If the user omits one name, the web page still displays the name that the user entered, so no retyping is needed, but it also asks the user to add the missing data.

EXAMPLE 6-15   Preserving user-entered data, phprestore.php

```
<HTML>
    <HEAD><TITLE>Preserving Data</TITLE></HEAD>
    <BODY>
        <CENTER><H1>Preserving Data</H1>
        <?php
            $errors = array();
            if(isset($_REQUEST["seen_already"])){
                validate_data();
                if(count($errors) != 0){
                    display_errors();
                    display_welcome();
                } else {
                    process_data();
                }
            } else {
                display_welcome();
            }
            function validate_data()
            {
                global $errors;
                if($_REQUEST["FirstName"] == "") {
                    $errors[] = "<FONT COLOR='RED'>Please enter your first
                        name</FONT>";
                }
                if($_REQUEST["LastName"] == "") {
                    $errors[] = "<FONT COLOR='RED'>Please enter your last
                        name</FONT>";
                }
            }
            function display_errors()
            {
                global $errors;

                foreach ($errors as $err){
                    echo $err, "<BR>";
                }
            }
            function process_data()
```

continues

EXAMPLE 6-15 continued

```
            {
                echo "Your first name is ";
                echo $_REQUEST["FirstName"];
                echo "<BR>Your last name is ";
                echo $_REQUEST["LastName"];
            }
            function display_welcome()
            {
                $first_name = isset($_REQUEST["FirstName"]) ?
                    $_REQUEST["FirstName"] : "";
                $last_name = isset($_REQUEST["LastName"]) ?
                    $_REQUEST["LastName"] : "";
                echo "<FORM METHOD='POST' ACTION='phprestore.php'>";
                echo "What's your first name?";
                echo "<INPUT NAME='FirstName' TYPE='TEXT' VALUE='",
                    $first_name, "'>";
                echo "<BR>";
                echo "What's your last name?";
                echo "<INPUT NAME='LastName' TYPE='TEXT' VALUE='",
                    $last_name, "'>";
                echo "<BR>";
                echo "<INPUT TYPE='SUBMIT' VALUE='Submit'>";
                echo "<INPUT TYPE='HIDDEN' NAME='seen_already'
                    VALUE='hidden_data'>";
                echo "</FORM>";
            }
        ?>
        </CENTER></BODY>
</HTML>
```

You can see how this works in Figure 6-20, where the user omitted his last name, so we're asking him to fix it while still preserving the data he did enter. Cool.

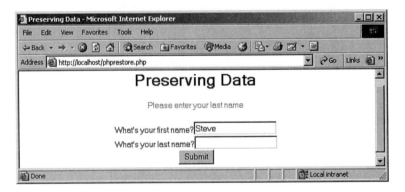

FIGURE 6-20   Preserving data despite errors.

Using JavaScript to Validate Data

Here's another option to consider when validating user data—JavaScript. Using JavaScript lets you check user data in the browser before it has to be sent back to the server to be checked. You save time by not requiring a roundtrip to the server, and you save demand on the server. This isn't a PHP topic, but it's worth a look. (Note that you might also validate on the server as well, in case the user has JavaScript turned off.)

Here's an example, where we'll check if a date the user is submitting is in the format 12/31/05 or 12/31/2005—and if not, we'll display an error, stopping the form from being submitted until it's fixed. To check the data, we'll write a JavaScript function named checker. When the form is submitted, we'll have JavaScript call that function:

```
<FORM NAME="form1" ACTION="somepage.php" METHOD="POST"
    ONSUBMIT="return checker()">
    Please enter a date:
    <INPUT TYPE="TEXT" NAME="text1">
    <INPUT TYPE="SUBMIT" value="Submit">
</FORM>
```

JavaScript can handle regular expressions, so the checker function will use them to check the format of the submitted date, as you see in phpjavascript.html, Example 6-16. You don't have to use regular expressions, of course; you could check numerical ranges, whether or not the user entered any data at all, and so on.

EXAMPLE 6-16   A JavaScript example, phpjavascript.html

```
<HTML>
    <HEAD>
        <TITLE>Verifying User Data</TITLE>
        <SCRIPT LANGUAGE="JavaScript">
            <!--
            function checker()
            {
                var regExp1 = /^(\d{1,2})\/(\d{1,2})\/(\d{2})$/
                var regExp2 = /^(\d{1,2})\/(\d{1,2})\/(\d{4})$/
                var result1 = document.form1.text1.value.match(regExp1)
                var result2 = document.form1.text1.value.match(regExp2)
                if (result1 == null && result2 == null) {
                    alert("Sorry, that's not a valid date.")
                    document.form1.text1.value = ""
                    return false
                } else {
                    document.form1.submit()
                }
            }
            //-->
```

continues

EXAMPLE 6-16   continued

```
        </SCRIPT>
    </HEAD>

    <BODY>
        <H1>Verifying User Data</H1>
        <FORM NAME="form1" ACTION="somepage.php" METHOD="POST"
            ONSUBMIT="return checker()">
            Please enter a date:
            <INPUT TYPE="TEXT" NAME="text1">
            <INPUT TYPE="SUBMIT" value="Submit">
        </FORM>
    </BODY>
<HTML>
```

You can see how this works in Figure 6-21, where the user has entered a date that's not formatted the way we want it.

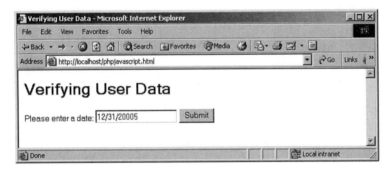

FIGURE 6-21   Checking user data.

When the user clicks the Submit button, he or she will see the error message box in Figure 6-22.

FIGURE 6-22   Giving error feedback.

Using HTTP Authentication

Here's a final topic for this chapter—determining whether the user has logged in. Most servers allow you to restrict access to sections of your web site by supporting usernames and passwords, which you add to configuration files in the server. When you try to access a restricted part of a web site, you'll get a dialog box that asks for your username and password, as shown in Figure 6-23.

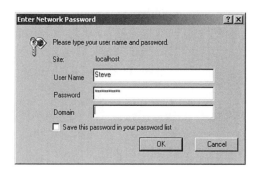

FIGURE 6-23   Entering username and password.

PHP allows you to determine whether the user has been authorized by checking the "PHP_AUTH_USER" key in $_SERVER. Here's an example—if $_SERVER['PHP_AUTH_USER'] has been set, we welcome the user by name—otherwise, we terminate the current script with the PHP exit function:

```php
<?php
    if (!isset($_SERVER['PHP_AUTH_USER'])) {
        header('WWW-Authenticate: Basic realm="workgroup"');
        header('HTTP/1.0 401 Unauthorized');
        echo 'Sorry, you are not authorized.';
        exit;
    }
    else {
        echo "Welcome, {$_SERVER['PHP_AUTH_USER']}.";
    }
?>
```

That completes our work with web applications for the moment. In the next chapter, we're going to add still more PHP power to our arsenal by doing some object-oriented programming and by working with files.

Summary

This chapter was all about web forms and validating user input. There's a lot more to creating web forms than simply creating HTML controls, and here are some of the salient points in this chapter:

- The special superglobal array, $_SERVER, contains a great deal of information about what's going on with your web application. $_SERVER['PHP_SELF'] holds the name of the current script, $_SERVER['REQUEST_METHOD'] holds the request method that was used ("GET", "POST", and so on), $_SERVER['HTTP_USER_AGENT'] holds the type of the user's browser, and so on. See Tables 6-1 and 6-2 for the details.

- In web forms, you can redirect the browser with the header method like this: echo header("Location: new_url.html");.

- You can combine web forms into one by checking if a user variable is set with the isset function; if so, data is waiting to be processed.

- PHP provides a variety of ways to validate the data the user sent you, such as using regular expressions on text data.

- To strip HTML tags, you can use the htmlentities function, which encodes HTML tags.

CHAPTER 7

Object-Oriented Programming and File Handling

I n this chapter, we're going to take a look at two important PHP topics—object-oriented programming (OOP) and file handling. You don't absolutely need object-oriented programming to make your pages work in PHP. However, if you're going to be sticking with PHP for the long term, or if you're building substantial web applications, then OOP holds some gems for you.

OOP was first introduced to handle larger programming tasks. As we've seen, functions let you break up your programs into smaller sections, which is a great help. OOP takes the next step, letting you wrap both functions and data into *objects*. This lets you divide up your scripts even further because an object can contain not only a group of functions, but also the data those functions may need. For example, think of what goes on inside a refrigerator: pumps, thermostats, fans, and more are all working together. If you had to work them all by hand, it would be a disaster, but if you wrap them all into a convenient object—a refrigerator—all you must remember is that the refrigerator cools food; the details are internal.

In the same way, wrapping functions and data together lets you break up long scripts. For example, one object might handle the screen display, another might validate data, another might work with a database, and so on.

Working with Classes and Objects

So how does this work in practice? First, you create a *class*, from which to create objects. A class is an object's *type*, just as integer might be a variable's type, and you can create your own classes. You might create a class named Animal, using the PHP class statement. This class might store the name of the animal internally, and it might have two functions (inside a class, functions are called *methods*) built into it: set_name and get_name. Here's what the class named Animal looks like (we'll dissect what's going on here in the first couple of chunks in this chapter). Note that this class stores the name data in an internal variable (called a *property* in OOP) called name:

```
class Animal
{
    var $name;

    function set_name($text)
    {
        $this->name = $text;
    }
    function get_name()
    {
        return $this->name;
    }
}
```

Now you can create objects of this new class with the *new* statement—for example, you might want to create an object named $lion. Objects such as these are stored in variables in PHP. After you create that object, you can access the get_name and set_name methods using the arrow operator, ->. Here's what that looks like:

```
<?php
    class Animal
    {
        var $name;

        function set_name($text)
        {
            $this->name = $text;
        }
        function get_name()
        {
            return $this->name;
        }
    }
```

```
    $lion = new Animal;
    $lion->set_name("Leo");
    echo "The name of your new lion is ", $lion->get_name(), ".";
?>
```

When you run this code, you get:

```
The name of your new lion is Leo.
```

We're going to take this apart in the pages to come to understand exactly what's going on here.

Besides OOP, this chapter also focuses on working with *files*. Being able to work with files on the server is one of the great things about PHP. For example, you might want to create a guest book page on your web site; you could do that by storing the guest book's details in a file. We'll see how to create, open, write to, and read from files in this chapter. Being able to store data on the server is one of the main reasons people turn to server scripts in the first place, and PHP gives you a lot of power here.

Creating a Class

A class is a collection of variables and functions—in OOP terms, properties and methods. A class is a type, and you create objects of that type and store them in PHP variables. We've already seen an example, the Animal class, which we'll dissect here in more detail. You start creating the Animal class with the class statement, giving the new name of this class like this:

```
class Animal
{
        .
        .
        .
}
```

This class is supposed to store the name of the animal, so we'll *declare* an internal variable, called a property in OOP, using the var statement—although the variable is called $name, the property is actually referred to simply as name:

```
class Animal
{
    var $name;
        .
        .
        .
}
```

As anywhere else in PHP, you don't have to declare variables you use in a class before you use them. However, when you're working with properties inside a class, you should declare them like this with the var statement, which helps make them accessible from objects you create of this class. Now the data in the name property is available to all the methods in the Animal class, such as the set_name method, which we'll use to set the animal's name:

```
class Animal
{
    var $name;

    function set_name($text)
    {
        .
        .
        .
    }
        .
        .
        .
}
```

How do you store the name passed to set_name in the name property? To access the
$name property, you use the $this built-in variable, which points to the current class. You
use $this with the arrow operator, ->, so that you can refer to the data in the name prop-
erty this way (note this is $this->name for the name property, not $this->$name):

```
class Animal
{
    var $name;

    function set_name($text)
    {
        $this->name = $text;
    }

        .
        .
        .

}
```

Now we've stored the name passed to the set_name method in the name property, we can
recover it using the get_name method:

```
class Animal
{
    var $name;

    function set_name($text)
    {
        $this->name = $text;
    }

    function get_name()
    {
        return $this->name;
    }
}
```

That's it; we've created the Animal class, which we'll put to work in the next chunk. Note
that you can assign simple, constant values to properties when you declare them in a
class, but not any kind of computed value:

```
class Animal
{
    var $name = "Leo";   // OK.
    var $name = "L" . "e" . "o";   // No good!
```

Note also that you can't intermingle the definition of a class with HTML; the entire class
definition must be inside the same <?php...?> script. In addition, because PHP has some
built-in methods that start with _ _ (two underscores), you shouldn't start any method
names with_ _.

Creating an Object

In the previous chunk, we created a class named Animal, but not much is going to happen with that class unless we create an object of that class. The simple variables we've seen in previous chapters can also have types—for example, integer, float, and so on. A class is an object's type, but you don't usually work with types directly—you create variables using them.

It's the same thing with classes and objects. You can use the new statement to create a variable, called an object, of a certain class. You don't have to use the new statement when creating simple variables of the built-in types such as integer or float, but you do when you want to create a variable that holds an object of a class.

For example, to create an object of the Animal class in a variable named $lion, you'd do this:

```php
<?php
    class Animal
    {
        var $name;
        function set_name($text)
        {
            $this->name = $text;
        }
        function get_name()
        {
            return $this->name;
        }
    }

    $lion = new Animal;
?>
```

Now you've got an object of the Animal class named $lion. You can access the methods of the Animal class using the arrow operator, like this, where we're setting the name of the Animal to Leo:

```php
$lion = new Animal;
$lion->set_name("Leo");
        .
        .
        .
```

This stores "Leo" in the object's name property. To access that name from outside the object, you can use the get_name method, as we've already done:

```
$lion = new Animal;
$lion->set_name("Leo");
echo "The name of your new lion is ", $lion->get_name(), ".";
```

When you run this code, you get:

```
The name of your new lion is Leo.
```

Interestingly, you can access properties from outside an object using the -> operator just as you can use it to access methods. For example, what if you wanted to read the $lion object's name property directly?

To read the name property directly from the $lion object without using the get_name method, you can simply use the expression $lion->name. That's all it takes; here's what it looks like in code:

```php
<?php
    class Animal
    {
        var $name;
        function set_name($text)
        {
            $this->name = $text;
        }

        function get_name()
        {
            return $this->name;
        }
    }

    $lion = new Animal;
    $lion->set_name("Leo");

    echo "The name of your new lion is ", $lion->name, ".";
?>
```

Just as before, when you run this code, you get:

```
The name of your new lion is Leo.
```

Using the -> operator, you can access both the methods of an object and its properties. Often it's a good idea to use methods, called *accessor methods*, to set property values, because you can restrict the type of data you want to store in a property, as here, where we're making sure that the name stored in the Animal class isn't too long:

```php
function set_name($text)
{
    if (strlen($text) <= 128){
        $this->name = $text;
    }
}
```

Restricting Access to Properties and Methods

You can access the methods and properties of an object by default, but sometimes that's not a good idea. For example, consider the accessor method set_name from the previous chunk, which restricts access to the name property:

```
function set_name($text)
{
    if (strlen($text) <= 128){
        $this->name = $text;
    }
}
```

It would be a good idea to make sure that no one can access the name property directly from outside the object. Currently, it's no problem to do that, using this syntax:

```
$lion = new Animal;
$lion->set_name("Leo");

echo "The name of your new lion is ", $lion->name, ".";
```

But it turns out that you can make the name property *private* to the Animal class if you want. You do that with the PHP access modifiers:

- public. Means "Accessible to all"

- private. Means "Accessible in the same class"

- protected. Means "Accessible in the same class and classes derived from that class"

By default, all methods and properties are declared public, which means there's no restriction on accessing them from outside an object. But if you declare the name property as private, using the private keyword, that property can't be accessed from code outside the class itself:

```
<?php
    class Animal
    {
        private $name;

        function set_name($text)
        {$this->name = $text;}
        function get_name()
        {return $this->name;}
    }

    $lion = new Animal;
    $lion->set_name("Leo");
```

```
        echo "The name of your new lion is ", $lion->name, ".";
?>
```

Now when you try to access this private property as $lion->name, you'll get an error:

```
The name of your new lion is PHP Fatal error:  Cannot access private property
Animal::$name in lion.php on line 20
```

Can you make methods private too? You sure can, as when you want to make a method entirely internal to a class. Here's how we make the get_name method private and then try to use it:

```
<?php
    class Animal
    {
        var $name;
        function set_name($text)
        {$this->name = $text;}
        private function get_name()
        {
            return $this->name;
        }
    }

    $lion = new Animal;
    $lion->set_name("Leo");

        echo "The name of your new lion is ", $lion->get_name(), ".";
?>
```

And here's what you see:

```
The name of your new lion is PHP Fatal error:

Call to private method Animal::get_name() from context '' in C:\php\t.php
on line 21
```

By default, everything in a class is public, which means it's accessible from outside the object (you can also use the public keyword to make that explicit). The protected keyword is used when one class is used as a base class of another, as we're going to see later in this chapter. Properties and methods made protected in a base class may only be used in that class and in any class *derived* from that class. More on how that works in a few pages.

Initializing Objects with Constructors

As we've already seen, you can use methods such as set_name to assign values to the internal data in an object:

```
var $name;
        .
        .
        .
function set_name($text)
{
    $this->name = $text;
}
```

However, there's an easy, built-in way to initialize the data in an object when you create that object—you can use a *constructor*. In PHP, a constructor is a special method with the name _ _construct (that's two underscores followed by construct), and when you create an object, you can use special syntax to pass data to the constructor.

Here's an example; in this case, we'll add a constructor to the Animal class to set the animal's name, just as the set_name method does. Here's what the constructor looks like:

```
function _ _construct($text)
{
    $this->name = $text;
}
```

Now when you create the $lion object, you can pass the name of the lion to the Animal class's constructor by using parentheses after the name of the class, like this:

```
$lion = new Animal("Leo");
```

That's all you need; now the text "Leo" is passed to the new Animal class constructor, which stores that text in the name property. You can see this code in context in phpconstructor.php.

EXAMPLE 7-1   Using an object constructor, phpconstructor.php

```
<HTML>
    <HEAD>
        <TITLE>
            Reading All Form Data
        </TITLE>
    </HEAD>

    <BODY>
        <CENTER>
            <H1>
```

```
                    Using constructors with objects
            </H1>
            <?php
                class Animal
                {
                    var $name;

                    function _ _construct($text)
                    {
                        $this->name = $text;
                    }
                    function set_name($text)
                    {
                        $this->name = $text;
                    }

                    function get_name()
                    {
                        return $this->name;
                    }
                }
                $lion = new Animal("Leo");
                echo "The name of your new lion is ", $lion->get_name(), ".";
            ?>
        </CENTER>
    </BODY>
</HTML>
```

The results appear in Figure 7-1, where, as you can see, the data we passed to the constructor was indeed put to work, as we wanted.

FIGURE 7-1 Using a constructor.

Want to dispose of an object? Use the unset statement like this: unset $object;.

Basing One Class on Another: Inheritance

It's often useful to base one class on another. For example, say that you've spent a lot of time developing a class named Vehicle that has all kinds of built-in methods that a vehicle might perform, such as start, run, steer, and stop. Now say that you want to create some other classes that are specific types of vehicles—Car, Truck, Helicopter, Oceanliner, and more.

You could rewrite the Vehicle class's start, run, steer, and stop methods in each of these new classes, or you could base those new classes on the Vehicle class through a process called *inheritance*. Using inheritance, the properties and methods of the base class (Animal) also become the properties and methods of the derived class(es) (Car, Truck, Helicopter, Oceanliner, and so on). Then you can customize the derived class(es) by adding your own properties and methods.

Here's an example; in this case, we'll derive a new class, Lion, from the Animal class. The Lion class will inherit all the properties and methods of the Animal class—and to customize the Lion class, we'll add a new method: roar. Obviously, the roar method wouldn't fit some types of Animals (goldfish don't roar), but it's an appropriate method to add to a class named Lion.

To derive one class from another, you use the *extends* keyword when declaring the derived class, indicating which case class you're extending. You can see this at work in phpinheritance.php, Example 7-2, where we're creating the Lion class by extending Animal and adding the roar method.

After creating an object of the new Lion class, we can use not only its roar method, but also the set_name method it inherited from the Animal class. It's all shown in Example 7-2.

EXAMPLE 7-2   Using inheritance, phpinheritance.php

```
<HTML>
    <HEAD>
        <TITLE>Using constructors to initialize objects</TITLE>
    </HEAD>

    <BODY>
        <CENTER>
            <H1>
                Using constructors to initialize objects
            </H1>
            <?php
                class Animal
                {
                    var $name;
```

```
                    function set_name($text)
                    {
                         $this->name = $text;
                    }

                    function get_name()
                    {
                         return $this->name;
                    }
               }
               class Lion extends Animal
               {
                    var $name;

                    function roar()
                    {
                         echo $this->name, " is roaring!<BR>";
                    }
               }

               echo "Creating your new lion...<BR>";
               $lion = new Lion;
               $lion->set_name("Leo");
               $lion->roar();
          ?>
     </CENTER>
 </BODY>
</HTML>
```

The results appear in Figure 7-2. Very cool.

FIGURE 7-2   Class inheritance.

Using inheritance, you can reuse the functionality of one class in others—very useful.

Using Protected Inheritance

You've seen that public properties and methods are available outside an object, and that private properties and methods are not. But when you make properties or methods *protected*, they're restricted to the current class, or any classes derived from the current class. For example, if you were to make the Animal class's set_name method protected and then tried to call it from a Lion object, it wouldn't work because it's protected:

```
class animal
{
    var $name;
    protected function set_name($text)
    {
        $this->name = $text;
    }
    function get_name()
    {
        return $this->name;
    }
}

echo "Creating your new lion...<BR>";
$lion = new Lion;
$lion->set_name("Leo");                         // Won't work!
$lion->roar();
```

Here's the error you get:

```
PHP Fatal error: Call to protected method animal::set_name() from context in
phpprotected.php on line 48
```

On the other hand, the protected set_name method *is* available in the code for both the Animal and Lion classes, so if you simply make the Lion class's constructor call this method to set the name, there'll be no problem, as you see in phpprotected.php, Example 7-3.

EXAMPLE 7-3   Using protected inheritance, phpprotected.php

```
<HTML>
    <HEAD>
        <TITLE>Using protected inheritance</TITLE>
    </HEAD>
    <BODY>
        <CENTER>
            <H1>Using protected inheritance</H1>
            <?php
                class animal
                {
                    var $name;
                    protected function set_name($text)
```

```
            {
                $this->name = $text;
            }

            function get_name()
            {
                return $this->name;
            }
        }
        class Lion extends Animal
        {
            var $name;

            function roar()
            {
                echo $this->name, " is roaring!<BR>";
            }

            function _ _construct($text)
            {
                $this->set_name($text);
            }
        }
        echo "Creating your new lion...<BR>";
        $lion = new Lion("Leo");
        $lion->roar();
    ?>
    </CENTER>
    </BODY>
</HTML>
```

You can see the results in Figure 7-3.

FIGURE 7-3 Using protected inheritance.

Overriding Methods

What if you're deriving a new class from a base class and happen to create a method in the new class with the same name as a method in the base class? In that case, you *override* the base class's method, and objects of the new class use the new method instead of the base class's method.

For example, here's the set_name method in the Animal class:

```
function set_name($text)
{
    $this->name = $text;
}
```

Now that we've created a new Lion class, we might decide it would be more befitting a lion's status to have its name in all capital letters. Thus, we might add a new method, also called set_name, to the Lion class, which converts the name you pass it to all capital letters using the strtoupper method:

```
function set_name($text)
{
    $this->name = strtoupper($text);
}
```

Now when you call set_name using an object of the Lion class, the Lion class's version of the set_name method is called, not the base class's version. You can see that at work in phpoverride.php, Example 7-4.

EXAMPLE 7-4   Overriding methods, phpoverride.php

```
<HTML>
    <HEAD>
        <TITLE>
            Overriding methods
        </TITLE>
    </HEAD>

    <BODY>
        <CENTER>
            <H1>
                Overriding methods
            </H1>
            <?php
                class animal
                {
                    var $name;

                    function set_name($text)
```

```
                {
                    $this->name = $text;
                }
                function get_name()
                {
                    return $this->name;
                }
            }
            class Lion extends Animal
            {
                var $name;

                function roar()
                {
                    echo $this->name, " is roaring!<BR>";
                }

                function set_name($text)
                {
                    $this->name = strtoupper($text);
                }
            }

            echo "Creating your new lion...<BR>";
            $lion = new Lion;
            $lion->set_name("Leo");
            $lion->roar();
        ?>
        </CENTER>
    </BODY>
</HTML>
```

The results appear in Figure 7-4—note that the overridden version of the method was indeed executed.

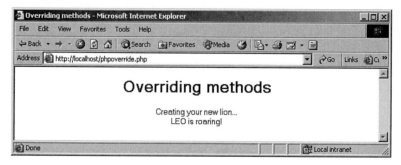

FIGURE 7-4 Overriding methods.

Accessing Base Class Methods

When you're using inheritance, you might want to access the base class's version of a method. For example, the set_name method looks like this in the Animal class:

```
function set_name($text)
{
    $this->name = $text;
}
```

If you override set_name in the derived Lion class, how can you reach the Animal class's version of this method? You just preface the name of the method with Animal:: like this:

```
function set_name($text)
{
    Animal::set_name($text);
}
```

You can see what this looks like in phpbasemethods.php, Example 7-5, where we're accessing the base class method Animal::set_name from the new version of this method in the derived class.

EXAMPLE 7-5   Accessing base class methods, phpbasemethods.php

```
<HTML>
    <HEAD>
        <TITLE>
            Accessing base class methods
        </TITLE>
    </HEAD>

    <BODY>
        <CENTER>
            <H1>
                Accessing base class methods
            </H1>
            <?php
                class Animal
                {
                    var $name;

                    function set_name($text)
                    {
                        $this->name = $text;
                    }

                    function get_name()
                    {
                        return $this->name;
```

```
            }
        }

        class Lion extends Animal
        {
            var $name;

            function roar()
            {
                echo $this->name, " is roaring!<BR>";
            }

            function set_name($text)
            {
                Animal::set_name($text);
            }
        }

        echo "Creating your new lion...<BR>";
        $lion = new Lion;
        $lion->set_name("Leo");
        $lion->roar();
    ?>
    </CENTER>
    </BODY>
</HTML>
```

You can see the results in Figure 7-5.

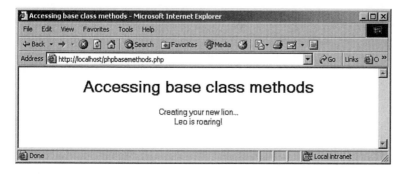

FIGURE 7-5 Overriding methods.

Using :: lets you specify the name of the class where PHP should search for a method, but there's a shortcut if you just want to refer to the current class's parent class—you can use the keyword parent like this: parent::set_name($text).

Opening a File: *fopen*

Being able to store and access data using files is a big advantage in PHP, and PHP comes with a set of file-handling functions built-in, as we're going to see in the remainder of this chapter. It all starts with the fopen function, which opens a file for reading or writing. Here's how you use this function in general:

```
fopen (string filename, string mode [, int use_include_path [, resource zcontext]])
```

In this function call, *filename* is the name of the file you're opening, *mode* indicates how you want to open the file (for example, to read from it or to write to it), *use_include_path* may be set to 1 or TRUE to specify that you want to search for the file in the PHP include path, and *zcontext* holds an optional file context (contexts modify or enhance the behavior of the data streams from and to files, and we're not going to deal with them in this book).

The mode parameter specifies the type of access you require to the stream. It may be any of the following:

'r'	Open for reading only.
'r+'	Open for reading and writing.
'w'	Open for writing only and truncate the file to zero length. If the file does not exist, attempt to create it.
'w+'	Open for reading and writing and truncate the file to zero length. If the file does not exist, attempt to create it.
'a'	Open for appending only. If the file does not exist, attempt to create it.
'a+'	Open for reading and writing, starting at the end of the file. If the file does not exist, attempt to create it.
'x'	Create and open for writing only. If the file already exists, the fopen call will fail by returning FALSE.
'x+'	Create and open for reading and writing. If the file already exists, the fopen call will fail by returning FALSE.

Note that different operating systems have different line-ending conventions. When you write a text file and want to insert a line break, you need to use the correct line-ending character(s) for your operating system. Unix-based systems use \n as the line-ending character, Windows-based systems use \r\n as the line-ending characters, and Macintosh-based systems use \r as the line-ending character. (PHP has a constant named PHP_EOL that holds the line-ending character for the system you are on.)

In Windows, you can use a text-mode translation flag ('t'), which will translate \n to \r\n when working with the file. In contrast, you can also use 'b' to force binary mode, which will not translate your data. To use these flags, specify either 'b' or 't' as the last character of the mode parameter, such as 'wt'.

Currently, the default mode is set to binary for all platforms that distinguish between binary and text mode. If you are having problems with your scripts, try using the 't' flag.

Here's an example, which opens the file /home/file.txt for reading:

```
$handle = fopen("/home/file.txt", "r");
```

When you open a file, you get a file *handle*, which represents an open file. From then on, you use this handle to work with the file. Now that the file has been opened, you can read from it using the various data-reading functions we'll cover in a few pages, such as fread.

This example opens a file for writing to using text mode, the default:

```
$handle = fopen("/home/file.txt", "w");
```

This example opens a file for binary writing:

```
handle = fopen("/home/file.txt", "wb");
```

In Windows, you should be careful to escape any backslashes used in the path to the file (or use forward slashes):

```
$handle = fopen("c:\\data\\file.txt", "r");
```

You're not limited to files in the local file system, either. Here's how you might open a file on a different web site, as specified by URL:

```
$handle = fopen("http://www.superduperbigco.com/file.txt", "r");
```

You can also open files using the FTP protocol:

```
$handle = fopen("ftp://user:password@superduperbigco.com/file.txt", "w");
```

As mentioned, when you open a file, you get a file handle to work with, and you can pass that file handle to other file functions to work with the file. We'll take a look at those other functions in the following chunks.

Reading Lines of Text: *fgets*

You can use the fgets function to get a string of text from a file; here's how you use it in general:

```
fgets (resource handle [, int length])
```

You pass this function the file *handle* corresponding to an open file, and an optional *length*. The function returns a string of up to length - 1 bytes read from the file corresponding to the file handle. Reading ends when length - 1 bytes have been read, on a newline (which is included in the return value), or on encountering the end of file, whichever comes first. If no length is specified, the length default is 1024 bytes.

Let's see an example, phpreadfile.php. Say you have a file, file.txt, in the same directory as phpreadfile.php, and you want to read its contents:

```
Here
is
the
text.
```

After opening the file for reading, we'll read it line by line with fgets. To loop over all the lines in the file, you can use a while loop and the *feof* function, which returns TRUE when you've reached the end of the file:

```php
<?php
    $handle = fopen("file.txt", "r");
    while (!feof($handle)){
         .
         .
         .

    }
?>
```

Now all we've got to do is to read text lines using fgets and echo the text:

```php
<?php
    $handle = fopen("file.txt", "r");
    while (!feof($handle)){
        $text = fgets($handle);
        echo $text, "<BR>";
    }
?>
```

When you're done with the file, you close the file handle with *fclose*:

```php
<?php
    $handle = fopen("file.txt", "r");
```

```
        while (!feof($handle)){
            $text = fgets($handle);
            echo $text, "<BR>";
        }
        fclose($handle);
?>
```

You can see this all at work in phpreadfile.php, Example 7-6.

EXAMPLE 7-6   Accessing base class methods, phpreadfile.php

```
<HTML>
    <HEAD>
        <TITLE>
            Reading a file
        </TITLE>
    </HEAD>
    <BODY>
        <CENTER>
            <H1>
                Reading a file
            </H1>
            <?php
                $handle = fopen("file.txt", "r");
                while (!feof($handle)){
                    $text = fgets($handle);
                    echo $text, "<BR>";
                }
                fclose($handle);
            ?>
        </CENTER>
    </BODY>
</HTML>
```

That's it; you can see the results in Figure 7-6.

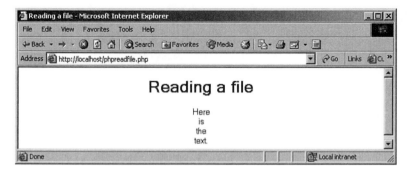

FIGURE 7-6   Reading from a file.

Reading Characters: *fgetc*

Here's another reading function—the `fgetc` function, which lets you read a single character from an open file. You can see how this works in Example 7-7, phpfgetc.php, where we're reading the contents of file.txt character by character and echoing it in a browser window.

EXAMPLE 7-7   Accessing base class methods, phpfgetc.php

```
<HTML>
    <HEAD>
        <TITLE>Reading a file with fgetc</TITLE>
    </HEAD>
    <BODY>
        <CENTER>
            <H1>Reading a file with fgetc</H1>
            <?php
                $handle = fopen("file.txt", "r");
                while ($char = fgetc($handle)) {
                    if($char == "\n"){
                        $char = "<BR>";
                    }
                    echo "$char";
                }
                fclose($handle);
            ?>
        </CENTER>
    </BODY>
</HTML>
```

The results appear in Figure 7-7 (note that the code changes line endings to <BR>).

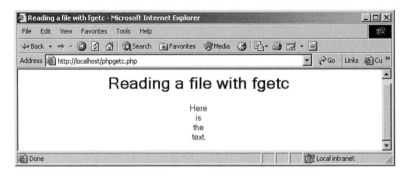

FIGURE 7-7   Reading from a file using `fgetc`.

Binary Reading: *fread*

You don't have to read data from files line by line; you can read as much or as little as you want with the *fread* function. The fgets function treats files as text, but fread treats files as binary files, making no guesses as to where lines end or performing other interpretation—the file is just treated as a simple binary file of bytes. Here's how you use fread in general:

```
fread (resource handle, int length)
```

This function reads up to *length* bytes from the file pointer referenced by *handle*. Reading stops when *length* bytes have been read or when the EOF (end of file) is reached.

On systems like Windows, you should open files for binary reading (mode 'rb') to work with fread. Because adding 'b' to the mode does no harm on other systems, we'll include it here for portability:

```php
<?php
    $handle = fopen("file.txt", "rb");
        .
        .
        .
?>
```

Using fread, you can read a whole file into a string by asking fread to read the number of bytes corresponding to the file's length, which you can find with the filesize function:

```php
<?php
    $handle = fopen("file.txt", "rb");
    $text = fread($handle, filesize("file.txt"));
        .
        .
        .
?>
```

This reads the entire file into $text if there wasn't an error, which you can check by making sure $text doesn't hold an empty string. To convert line endings in the text into <BR> elements, we'll use the str_replace function:

```php
<?php
    $handle = fopen("file.txt", "rb");
    $text = fread($handle, filesize("file.txt"));

    $br_text = str_replace("\n", "<BR>", $text);
        .
        .
        .
?>
```

All that's left is to echo the HTML-prepared text to the browser window and close the file, as you see in phpread.php, Example 7-8.

EXAMPLE 7-8   Using fread, phpread.php

```
<HTML>
    <HEAD>
        <TITLE>
            Reading a file with fread
        </TITLE>
    </HEAD>

    <BODY>
        <CENTER>
            <H1>
                Reading a file with fread
            </H1>

            <?php
                $handle = fopen("file.txt", "rb");
                $text = fread($handle, filesize("file.txt"));

                $br_text = str_replace("\n", "<BR>", $text);

                echo $br_text;
                fclose($handle);
            ?>

        </CENTER>
    </BODY>
</HTML>
```

The results appear in Figure 7-8, where we've read and displayed the file. Not bad.

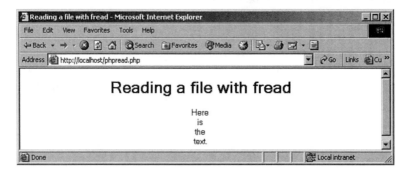

FIGURE 7-8   Reading from a file using fread.

Reading a Whole File: *file_get_contents*

Do you simply want to read the entire contents of a file into a string, as we've been doing? Here's an easy way: use the `file_get_contents` function. It's easy; just pass the name and path of the function to work with (no file handle needed), as you see in phpfilegetcontents.php, Example 7-9.

EXAMPLE 7-9   Using `file_get_contents`, phpfilegetcontents.php

```
<HTML>
    <HEAD>
        <TITLE>
            Reading a file with file_get_contents
        </TITLE>
    </HEAD>

    <BODY>
        <CENTER>
            <H1>
                Reading a file with file_get_contents
            </H1>

            <?php
                $text = file_get_contents("file.txt");
                $br_text = str_replace("\n", "<BR>", $text);
                echo $br_text;
            ?>
        </CENTER>
    </BODY>
</HTML>
```

You can see this at work in Figure 7-9. Very simple.

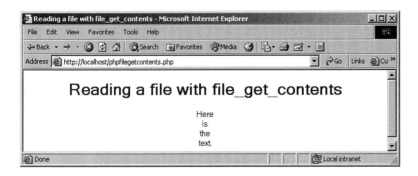

FIGURE 7-9   Reading from a file using `file_get_contents`.

Parsing a File: *fscanf*

To make it easier to extract data from a file, you can format that file (using, for example, tabs) and use fscanf to read your data from the file. Here's how you use fscanf in general:

```
fscanf (resource handle, string format)
```

This function takes a file handle, *handle*, and *format*, which describes the format of the file you're working with. You set up the format in the same way as with sprintf, which was discussed in Chapter 3, "Handling Strings and Arrays." For example, say the following data was contained in a file named tabs.txt, where the first and last names are separated by a tab:

```
George      Washington
Benjamin    Franklin
Thomas      Jefferson
Samuel      Adams
```

Reading this kind of file with fscanf is easy. Start by opening the file:

```
<?php
    $handle = fopen("tabs.txt", "rb");
        .
        .
        .

?>
```

The format in this case is "%s\t%s\n" (string, tab, string, newline character), so here's how we read and parse a line of data from a file into an array named $names:

```
<?php
    $handle = fopen("tabs.txt", "rb");
    while ($names = fscanf($handle, "%s\t%s\n")) {
        .


        .
        .
    }
?>
```

That array can be dissected using the list function:

```
<?php
    $handle = fopen("tabs.txt", "rb");
    while ($names = fscanf($handle, "%s\t%s\n")) {
        list ($firstname, $lastname) = $names;
            .
            .
            .

    }
?>
```

And we can echo the results as shown in phpfscanf.php, Example 7-10.

EXAMPLE 7-10   Using `fscanf`, phpfscanf.php

```
<HTML>
    <HEAD>
        <TITLE>
            Reading a file with fscanf
        </TITLE>
    </HEAD>

    <BODY>
        <CENTER>
            <H1>
                Reading a file with fscanf
            </H1>

            <?php
                $handle = fopen("tabs.txt", "rb");
                while ($names = fscanf($handle, "%s\t%s\n")) {
                    list ($firstname, $lastname) = $names;
                    echo $firstname, " ", $lastname, "<BR>";
                }
                fclose($handle);
            ?>
        </CENTER>
    </BODY>
</HTML>
```

That's all it takes; you can see the results in Figure 7-10.

FIGURE 7-10   Reading from a file using `fscanf`.

Writing to a File: *fwrite*

Want to write to a file? You can use `fwrite`, which works like this:

```
fwrite (resource handle, string string [, int length])
```

The `fwrite` function writes the contents of *string* to the file stream represented by *handle*. If the *length* argument is given, writing will stop after *length* bytes have been written or the end of the string is reached, whichever comes first.

Note also that `fwrite` returns the number of bytes written or FALSE if there was an error. In addition, if you're working on a system that differentiates between binary and text files (that is, Windows), the file must be opened with `'b'` included in the `fopen` mode parameter.

Here's an example, phpfwrite.php, Example 7-11. In this case, we're just going to write some multi-line text to a file, text.txt. We start by opening this new file for binary writing; if the file doesn't exist, it'll be created automatically:

```
$handle = fopen("text.txt", "wb");
      .
      .
      .
```

Now we use some multi-line text, with embedded newline (\n) characters, and we write that text to the file. If there was a problem, we report it; otherwise, we report success:

```
$handle = fopen("text.txt", "wb");

$text = "Here\nis\nthe\ntext.";

if (fwrite($handle, $text) == FALSE) {
    echo "Cannot write to text.txt.";
}
else {
    echo "Created the file text.txt.";
}
      .
      .
      .
```

All that's left is to close the file, as you see in Example 7-11.

EXAMPLE 7-11   Using `fwrite`, phpfwrite.php

```
<HTML>
    <HEAD>
        <TITLE>
            Writing a file with fwrite
        </TITLE>
```

```
    </HEAD>
    <BODY>
        <CENTER>
            <H1>
                Writing a file with fwrite
            </H1>

            <?php
                $handle = fopen("text.txt", "wb");

                $text = "Here\nis\nthe\ntext.";

                if (fwrite($handle, $text) == FALSE) {
                    echo "Cannot write to text.txt.";
                }
                else {
                    echo "Created the file text.txt.";
                }
                fclose($handle);
            ?>
        </CENTER>
    </BODY>
</HTML>
```

You can see the report we get from this application in Figure 7-11, where it's telling us that it wrote the file text.txt successfully.

FIGURE 7-11 Writing to a file using `fwrite`.

Typing out the file confirms that it was indeed written correctly:

```
Here
is
the
text.
```

Appending to a File: *fwrite*

In the previous chunk, we created and wrote to a new file, text.txt. But you may not want to do that—you may want to *append* new text to the file instead of overwriting what's already there, as when someone has added a new comment to a guest book.

In this case, you open the file for appending, using the file mode 'a':

```
$handle = fopen("text.txt", "ab");
    .
    .
    .
```

We'll append this text to text.txt:

```
And
here
is
more
text.
```

You can do that with fwrite much as we wrote the original text, as you see here:

```
$handle = fopen("text.txt", "ab");

$text = "\nAnd\nhere\nis\nmore\ntext.";

if (fwrite($handle, $text) == FALSE) {
    echo "Cannot write to text.txt.";
}
else {
    echo "Appended to the file text.txt.";
}
```

All that's left is to close the file, as you see in phpappend.php, Example 7-12.

EXAMPLE 7-12   Using fwrite to append text to a file, phpappend.php

```
<HTML>
    <HEAD>
        <TITLE>
            Appending to a file with fwrite
        </TITLE>
    </HEAD>

    <BODY>
        <CENTER>
            <H1>
                Appending to a file with fwrite
```

```
        </H1>

        <?php

        $handle = fopen("text.txt", "ab");

        $text = "\nAnd\nhere\nis\nmore\ntext.";

        if (fwrite($handle, $text) == FALSE) {
            echo "Cannot write to text.txt.";
        }
        else {
            echo "Appended to the file text.txt.";
        }

        fclose($handle);
        ?>
    </CENTER>
  </BODY>
</HTML>
```

This example reports success, as you see in Figure 7-12.

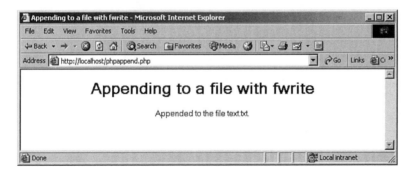

FIGURE 7-12   Appending to a file using `fwrite`.

You can confirm what's happened by typing out text.txt, which shows this result:

```
Here
is
the
text.
And
here
is
more
text.
```

Writing the File at Once: *file_put_contents*

Here's a shortcut if you want to write some text to a file—use the `file_put_contents` function. This function writes a string to a file, and here's how you use it in general:

```
file_put_contents (string filename, string data [, int flags [, resource context]])
```

Here, *filename* is the name of the file you want to write, *data* is the string text to write, *flags* can be `FILE_USE_INCLUDE_PATH`, `FILE_APPEND`, or both, and *context* is a file context (which is beyond the scope of this book). The function returns the number of bytes that were written to the file.

This function is very much the same as calling `fopen`, `fwrite`, and `fclose` automatically—you don't have to open or close the file yourself, and you don't need a file handle. Here's an example, phpfileputcontents.php, Example 7-13. All you have to do is decide on the text you want to store:

```
$text = "Here\nis\nthe\ntext.";
        .
        .
        .
```

Then you can use `file_put_contents` to store the text in a file you give by name, not by handle:

```
$text = "Here\nis\nthe\ntext.";

if (file_put_contents("text.txt", $text) == FALSE) {
    echo "Cannot write to text.txt.";
}
        .
        .
        .
```

If a problem occurs, you can report it, as shown in phpfileputcontents.php, Example 7-13.

EXAMPLE 7-13   Using `file_put_contents` to write text to a file, phpfileputcontents.php

```
<HTML>
    <HEAD>
        <TITLE>
            Appending to a file with file_put_contents
        </TITLE>
    </HEAD>

    <BODY>
        <CENTER>
```

```
    <H1>
        Appending to a file with file_put_contents
    </H1>

    <?php

        $text = "Here\nis\nthe\ntext.";

        if (file_put_contents("text.txt", $text) == FALSE) {
            echo "Cannot write to text.txt.";
        }
        else {
            echo "Wrote to the file text.txt.";
        }

    ?>
    </CENTER>
  </BODY>
</HTML>
```

You can see the results in Figure 7-13, where the application is telling us that it was successful.

FIGURE 7-13   Writing a file using `file_put_contents`.

Here's what was written to the file:

```
Here
is
the
text.
```

Not bad. That completes our discussion in this chapter of OOP and file handling. In the next chapter, we're going to dig deeper into storing and working with data on the server by handling databases for a big lift in programming power.

Summary

This chapter took a look at object-oriented programming and file handling. Functions let you break up your programs into smaller sections, which is good because that makes them easier to write, maintain, and debug. OOP takes the next step, letting you wrap both functions and data into objects. In addition, being able to work with files on the server is very powerful, letting you create and store everything from guest books to inventory management. Here are some of the salient points in this chapter:

- You create classes with the `class` statement.

- You create objects with the `new` statement.

- You can access methods and data members of an object with the arrow operator.

- Public access means "Accessible to all".

- Private access means "Accessible in the same class".

- Protected access means "Accessible in the same class and classes derived from that class".

- Constructors are special methods that let you initialize objects.

- Inheritance lets you base one class on another.

- You can override a method in a base class with a new version of the method simply by redefining the method in the inherited class.

- You can open a file with the `fopen` function.

- The `fgets` function gets a string of text from a file.

- The `fread` function reads data from binary files.

- If you want to read the entire contents of a file into a string, use the `file_get_contents` function.

- If you want to write to a file, you can use the `fwrite` function.

- There's also a shortcut if you want to write text to a file: you can use the `file_put_contents` function.

CHAPTER 8

Working with Databases

PHP comes packed with support for databases, which is good because developers often want to manage and store their data on a server. All kinds of database servers are supported in PHP; you can see the list in Table 8-1.

TABLE 8-1 Supported Database Applications

Database		
Adabas	Ingres	Oracle
dBase	InterBase	Ovrimos
Empress	FrontBase	PostgreSQL
FilePro	mSQL	Solid
Hyperwave Direct	MS-SQL	Sybase
IBM DB2	MySQL	Velocis
Informix	ODBC	SQLite
Unix dbm		

As you can see, there are many different database servers out there. We can't cover them all here, so we'll focus on the database that's the most popular to work with PHP: MySQL, which you can get for free from http://www.mysql.com. The current production release of MySQL is 4.0, which is what we're going to use in this chapter.

We'll also take a look at the PHP DB *module* later in this chapter, which provides a layer of abstraction over database operations, letting you work with many different database servers, such as the ones you see in Table 8-1, in addition to MySQL, using the same function calls.

If you want to use the built-in PHP support for the various database servers in Table 8-1, you can find the manuals for them at http://www.php.net/*dbname*, where *dbname* is the database name, such as mysql, sybase, mssql, and so on. For ODBC, use the name uodbc; for Oracle, use oci8. The DB module lets you access all these database servers in the same way, but using the native built-in support is much faster.

What Are Databases?

So what are databases? The fundamental concept is a simple one—databases organize data for access and manipulation under programmatic or application control.

The most popular database construct is the *table*, which provides our conceptual starting point. To see how a database table works, say that you are in charge of teaching a class and must store a grade for each student. You might make up a table like Table 8-2 to record the grade for each student.

TABLE 8-2 Student grades

Name	Grade
Ann	C
Mark	B
Ed	A
Frank	A
Ted	A
Mabel	B
Ralph	B
Tom	B

This table exactly mimics a table in a database. The database, however, offers far more advantages than paper: with a computer, you can sort, index, update, and organize large tables of data easily (and without a great waste of paper). You can even connect tables together in various ways, creating what are called *relational* databases.

Each individual data entry in a table, such as a student's name, goes into a field in the table. A collection of fields, such as the Name and Grade fields in our table, make up a record.

Each record gets its own row in a table, and each column in that row represents a different field. A collection of records—that is, rows of records where each column is a field—forms a table.

What, then, is a database? In its most conventional form, a database is just a collection of one or more tables. To access the data in those tables, you use SQL in PHP, which is coming up in the next chunk.

Some Basic SQL

To interact with databases in PHP, you use SQL (Structured Query Language). This chapter is designed to give you the experience you need to work with SQL in PHP. Say that you have a database table named "fruit" you want to work with. To get a copy of that table to work with in your code, you can execute this SQL statement, called a *query*:

```
SELECT * FROM fruit
```

To interact with MySQL, you'd use the mysql_query function to execute that SQL query like this:

```
$query = "SELECT * FROM fruit";
$result = mysql_query($query)
    or die("Query failed: ".mysql_error());
```

We'll go through a few SQL statements here to get up to speed. You may already have a good handle on SQL, in which case you can skip this chunk; otherwise, take a look because we'll be using SQL throughout the chapter. We'll assume we have a database table named fruit, which has two fields, *name* (such as "apples" or "oranges") and *number* (representing the number of a particular kind of fruit you have in stock).

You use the *SELECT* statement to retrieve fields from a table; here's an example where we're retrieving all the records in the fruit table, using the wildcard character *:

```
SELECT * FROM fruit
```

This returns a recordset that holds all the records in the fruit table. You can also select specific fields from a table like this, where we're selecting the name and number fields from the fruit table:

```
SELECT name, number FROM fruit
```

Using the WHERE clause, you can set up selection criteria that the records in the recordset generated by the query must meet. For example, to select all the records in the fruit table where the name field equals apples, you can execute this statement:

```
SELECT * FROM fruit WHERE name= "apples"
```

You don't have to use an equals sign here; you can test fields using these operators:

- < (less than)
- <= (less than or equal to)
- \> (greater than)
- >= (greater than or equal to)

You can use an IN clause to specify a set of values that fields can match. For example, here's how you can retrieve records that have values in the name field that match apples or oranges:

```
SELECT * FROM fruit WHERE name IN ("apples", "oranges")
```

You can also use logical operations on the clauses in your SQL statements. Here's an example where we're specifying two criteria: the name field must hold either "apples" or "oranges", and there must be some value in the number field—you use the NULL keyword to test if there's anything in a field:

```
SELECT * FROM fruit WHERE name NOT IN ("apples", "oranges") AND number IS NOT NULL
```

You can use these logical operators to connect clauses: AND, OR, and NOT. Using AND means that both clauses must be true, using OR means either one can be true, and using NOT flips the value of a clause from TRUE to FALSE or FALSE to TRUE.

As you might expect, you can also order the records in the recordset produced by a SQL statement. Here's an example where we're ordering the records in the fruit table using the name field:

```
SELECT * FROM fruit ORDER BY name
```

You can also sort records in descending order with the DESC keyword:

```
SELECT * FROM fruit ORDER BY name DESC
```

You can use the DELETE statement to delete records like this, where we're removing all records from the fruit table that have name values that are not apples or oranges:

```
DELETE  FROM fruit WHERE name NOT IN ("apples", "oranges")
```

You use the UPDATE statement to update a database when you want to make changes. For example, here's how to change the value of the number field in the record that contains the number of apples:

```
UPDATE fruit SET number = "2006" WHERE name = "apples"
```

You can also insert new data into a table—here's an example that inserts a new row into the fruit table:

```
INSERT INTO fruit (name, number) VALUES('apricots', '203')
```

OK, we've gotten as much SQL under our belts as we'll need. Now how about connecting database servers to PHP?

Setting Up Database Support in PHP

Adding database support to PHP can be a little involved, and how you do it depends on your operating system. We'll take a look at the most common choices here.

In Unix, Linux, and the Mac, you specify support for your database server during installation with configuration options, as detailed in the PHP installation directions. You'll find the directions for your specific database server in the server's PHP manual at www.php.net/*dbname*. For example, by using the `--with-mysql[=DIR]` configuration option, you enable PHP to access MySQL 4.0 databases, where *DIR* is the directory in which MySQL is installed, and it's set to /usr/local/mysql by default. For MySQL 4.1 databases (version 4.1 is being tested as of this writing and is not recommended for general use), use `--with-mysql[=DIR]`. In this case, *DIR* has no default value and should be set to the path to the file mysql_config, which is part of the MySQL 4.1 installation. For Oracle, you use the configuration option `--with-oci8[=DIR]`, where *DIR* defaults to your environment variable `ORACLE_HOME`. PHP installations on ISPs are usually already configured for MySQL and other database servers as well; ask your ISP's tech support for the details.

In Windows, you'll find a dynamic link library (DLL) for every supported database server in PHP's ext directory (depending on your PHP installation, that could be, for example, c:\php\ext). Find the correct DLL for the database server you want in that directory and copy it to the main directory (such as c:\php). For example, for MySQL version 4.0 or earlier, this file is php_mysql.dll; for MySQL version 4.1 or later, it's php_mysqli.dll; for Oracle, it's php_oci8.dll; for Microsoft's SQL Server, it's mssql.dll; and so on. After copying the DLL file, you activate the support for the database server by uncommenting its "extension=" line in php.ini by removing the semi-colon at the start of the line. For example, here's how you'd activate support for MySQL version 4.0 in php.ini:

```
;extension=php_mime_magic.dll
;extension=php_mssql.dll
;extension=php_msql.dll
extension=php_mysql.dll
;extension=php_oci8.dll
;extension=php_openssl.dll
;extension=php_oracle.dll
;extension=php_pdf.dll
;extension=php_pgsql.dll
            .
            .
            .
```

After making these configuration changes in Windows, restart PHP.

Creating a Database Using MySQL

We're going to create a sample database by using MySQL from the command line. You can run the MySQL server from the command line (a DOS window in Windows) by changing to the directory mysql/bin and entering this command:

```
%mysqld --console
```

This starts the server. Now we'll start a MySQL session that will connect to the server. Open a new command line window and change to the directory mysql/bin. If you set a username and password, start MySQL using -u and -p options:

```
%mysql -u user -p
Enter password: ********
```

If you don't have a username and password, enter mysql -u root, or just mysql, to start:

```
%mysql -u root
Welcome to the MySQL monitor.  Commands end with ; or \g.
mysql>
```

At the mysql> prompt that appears, enter SELECT VERSION(), CURRENT_DATE; to confirm that MySQL is working:

```
mysql> SELECT VERSION(), CURRENT_DATE;
+---------------+--------------+
| VERSION()     | CURRENT_DATE |
+---------------+--------------+
| 4.0.20a       | 2004-09-06   |
+---------------+--------------+
1 row in set (0.05 sec)
```

Want to see what databases MySQL already comes with? Enter the SHOW DATABASES command, and you'll get something like this:

```
mysql> SHOW DATABASES;
+----------+
| Database |
+----------+
| mysql    |
| test     |
+----------+
2 rows in set (0.01 sec)
```

MySQL comes with two databases built-in—mysql, which holds administrative data for MySQL, and test, which is a sample database. To store data about a variety of fruits and vegetables, you might create a new database named, say, "produce," with the CREATE DATABASE command:

```
mysql> CREATE DATABASE produce;
Query OK, 1 row affected (0.01 sec)
```

To make this database the default one to work with, enter the USE produce command:

```
mysql> USE produce
Database changed
```

Are there any tables in the produce database yet? Try the SHOW TABLES command:

```
mysql> SHOW TABLES;
Empty set (0.01 sec)
```

The response is "Empty set," which means there are no tables yet. To create a table named fruit, you need to create its data fields. There are various data types for fields; here are a few (we'll use strings in this example):

- VARCHAR(length). Creates a variable length string

- INT. Creates an integer

- DECIMAL(totaldigits, decimalplaces). Creates a decimal value

- DATETIME. Creates a date and time object, such as 2006-11-15 20:00:00

Here's how to create the fruit table with name and number fields, both stored in strings:

```
mysql> CREATE TABLE fruit (name VARCHAR(20), number VARCHAR(20))
Query OK, 0 rows affected (0.13 sec)
mysql> SHOW TABLES;
+-------------------+
| Tables_in_produce |
+-------------------+
| fruit             |
+-------------------+
1 row in set (0.00 sec)
```

To get a description of this new table, use the DESCRIBE command:

```
mysql> DESCRIBE fruit;
+--------+-------------+------+-----+---------+-------+
| Field  | Type        | Null | Key | Default | Extra |
+--------+-------------+------+-----+---------+-------+
| name   | varchar(20) | YES  |     | NULL    |       |
| number | varchar(20) | YES  |     | NULL    |       |
+--------+-------------+------+-----+---------+-------+
2 rows in set (0.01 sec)
```

Adding Data to the Database

In the previous chunk, we created a database named produce in MySQL and added a table named fruit to hold data about various fruits. In this chunk, we'll add the data you see in Table 8-3 to the fruit database table.

TABLE 8-3 Fruit data

Name	Number
apples	1020
oranges	3329
bananas	8582
pears	235

To enter this data in the fruit table, continue the MySQL session started in the previous chunk, or start a new one in a command window:

```
%mysql -u root
Welcome to the MySQL monitor.  Commands end with ; or \g.
```

Switch to the produce database and use INSERT to load the data into the fruit table:

```
mysql> USE produce
Database changed
mysql> INSERT INTO fruit VALUES ('apples', '1020');
Query OK, 1 row affected (0.00 sec)
mysql> INSERT INTO fruit VALUES ('oranges', '3329');
Query OK, 1 row affected (0.00 sec)
mysql> INSERT INTO fruit VALUES ('bananas', '8582');
Query OK, 1 row affected (0.00 sec)
mysql> INSERT INTO fruit VALUES ('pears', '235');
Query OK, 1 row affected (0.00 sec)
```

That's it; you can list the data in this table with SELECT to confirm that everything's as it should be, and then end the session with quit, completing our new database table:

```
mysql> SELECT * FROM fruit;
+---------+--------+
| name    | number |
+---------+--------+
| apples  | 1020   |
| oranges | 3329   |
| bananas | 8582   |
| pears   | 235    |
+---------+--------+
4 rows in set (0.00 sec)
mysql>quit
```

Accessing a MySQL Database

Now it's time to access our MySQL database from PHP. To do so, you need to run the MySQL server (unless you're working on an ISP or machine where it's always running). As we've already seen, that involves running `mysqld` in the mysql/bin directory:

```
%mysqld --console
```

To stop the server, you enter this command in the mysql/bin directory in another command line window:

```
%mysqladmin -u root shutdown
```

To actually connect to the MySQL database, you use the `mysql_connect` function, providing hostname, username, and password, if any:

```
$connection = mysql_connect("localhost","root","")
    or die ("Couldn't connect to server");
```

After you've connected, you use the `$connection` object with the `mysql_select_db` function to select a database to work with, which is "produce" for us:

```
$connection = mysql_connect("localhost","root","")
    or die ("Couldn't connect to server");
$db = mysql_select_db("produce", $connection)
    or die ("Couldn't select database");
```

Now you're connected to the produce database. To get all the data from the fruit table, you can execute a SQL query that looks like this using the `mysql_query` function—note also that the `mysql_error` function returns any MySQL error:

```
$query = "SELECT * FROM fruit";
$result = mysql_query($query)
    or die("Query failed: " . mysql_error());
```

Besides `mysql_connect`, `mysql_select_db`, and `mysql_query`, other functions are available for use with MySQL; here's a sampling (if you're using another database server, you can find the list of available functions for that server at www.php.net/*dbname*, where *dbname* is the name of the server):

- `mysql_affected_rows`. Get the number of rows affected by the previous MySQL operation
- `mysql_change_user`. Change the logged-in user
- `mysql_client_encoding`. Return the name of the current character set
- `mysql_close`. Close a MySQL connection

- `mysql_connect.` Open a connection to a MySQL Server

- `mysql_create_db.` Create a MySQL database

- `mysql_data_seek.` Seek data in the database

- `mysql_db_name.` Get the name of the database

- `mysql_db_query.` Send a MySQL query

- `mysql_drop_db.` Drop (that is, delete) a MySQL database

- `mysql_error.` Return the text of the error message from the previous MySQL operation

- `mysql_fetch_array.` Fetch a result row as an associative array, a numeric array, or both

- `mysql_fetch_assoc.` Fetch a result row as an associative array

- `mysql_fetch_row.` Get a result row as an enumerated array

- `mysql_field_len.` Return the length of a given field

- `mysql_field_name.` Get the name of the given field in a result

- `mysql_field_seek.` Seek to a given field offset

- `mysql_field_table.` Get name of the table the given field is in

- `mysql_field_type.` Get the type of the given field in a result

- `mysql_get_server_info.` Get MySQL server info

- `mysql_info.` Get information about the most recent query

- `mysql_list_dbs.` List databases available on a MySQL server

- `mysql_list_fields.` List MySQL table fields

- `mysql_list_tables.` List the tables in a MySQL database

- `mysql_num_fields.` Get the number of fields in result

- `mysql_num_rows.` Get the number of rows in result

- `mysql_pconnect.` Open a persistent connection to a MySQL server

- `mysql_query.` Send a MySQL query

- `mysql_result.` Get result data

- `mysql_select_db.` Select a MySQL database

- `mysql_tablename.` Get the table name of a field

Displaying a Data Table

We're ready to see some SQL and PHP action in a browser. Here, we're going to extr.
the fruit table from the produce database and display its data in an HTML table. We'll
start by connecting, selecting the database, and getting an object named $result that
corresponds to the fruit table:

```
$connection = mysql_connect("localhost","root","")
    or die ("Couldn't connect to server");
$db = mysql_select_db("produce", $connection)
    or die ("Couldn't select database");

$query = "SELECT * FROM fruit";
$result = mysql_query($query)
    or die("Query failed: " . mysql_error());
```

Now you can use the mysql_fetch_array function to get successive rows from the table in
a while loop and get the name and number fields from each row by name like this:

```
while ($row = mysql_fetch_array($result))
{
    echo "<TR>";
    echo "<TD>", $row['name'], "</TD><TD>", $row['number'], "</TD>";
    echo "</TR>";
}
```

Not bad. All we need is the code to wrap the results in an HTML table, as you see in php-
datatable.php, Example 8-1. Note that we also close the connection at the end with
mysql_close, which you should do when you're finished with a database.

EXAMPLE 8-1 Displaying a database table, phpdatatable.php

```
<HTML>
    <HEAD>
        <TITLE>
            Displaying tables with MySQL
        </TITLE>
    </HEAD>

    <BODY>
        <CENTER>
            <H1>Displaying tables with MySQL</H1>

            <?php
                $connection = mysql_connect("localhost","root","")
                    or die ("Couldn't connect to server");
```

continues

EXAMPLE 8-1   continued

```
                    $db = mysql_select_db("produce", $connection)
                        or die ("Couldn't select database");

                    $query = "SELECT * FROM fruit";
                    $result = mysql_query($query)
                        or die("Query failed: ".mysql_error());

                    echo "<TABLE BORDER='1'>";
                    echo "<TR>";
                    echo "<TH>Name</TH><TH>Number</TH>";
                    echo "</TR>";

                    while ($row = mysql_fetch_array($result))
                    {
                        echo "<TR>";
                        echo "<TD>", $row['name'], "</TD><TD>", $row['number'],
                            "</TD>";
                        echo "</TR>";
                    }

                    echo "</TABLE>";

                    mysql_close($connection);

            ?>
        </CENTER>
    </BODY>
</HTML>
```

The results appear in Figure 8-1, where you can see the whole fruit table. Very cool.

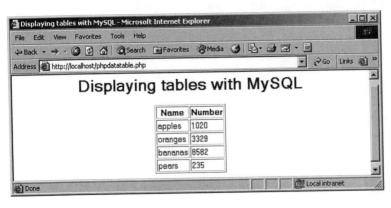

FIGURE 8-1 Displaying a database table.

That's it—we've been able to create a MySQL database and extract data from it in a web page.

Updating Your Data

When your data changes, it's easy to update your database with the appropriate SQL statement. Here's an example—say that someone buys a pear, which would change the number of pears in our database from 235 to 234. You can make that change by connecting to MySQL and selecting the produce database:

```
$connection = mysql_connect("localhost","root","")
    or die ("Couldn't connect to server");

$db = mysql_select_db("produce",$connection)
    or die ("Couldn't select database");
```

Now you can update the value in the pears row of the fruit table like this, where we're setting the value of the number field to 234:

```
$query = "UPDATE fruit SET number = 234 WHERE name = 'pears'";
                    .
                    .
                    .
```

Then you just execute that query like this:

```
$query = "UPDATE fruit SET number = 234 WHERE name = 'pears'";
$result = mysql_query($query)
    or die("Query failed: ".mysql_error());
```

That's all it takes; you can see all this code in phpdataupdate.php, Example 8-2.

EXAMPLE 8-2   Updating database data, phpdataupdate.php

```
<HTML>
    <HEAD>
        <TITLE>
            Updating database data
        </TITLE>
    </HEAD>

    <BODY>
        <CENTER>
            <H1>Updating database data</H1>

            <?php
                $connection = mysql_connect("localhost","root","")
                    or die ("Couldn't connect to server");
                $db = mysql_select_db("produce",$connection)
                    or die ("Couldn't select database");
```

continues

EXAMPLE 8-2   continued

```
                    $query = "UPDATE fruit SET number = 234 WHERE name =
                        'pears'";
                    $result = mysql_query($query)
                        or die("Query failed: ".mysql_error());

                    $query = "SELECT * FROM fruit";
                    $result = mysql_query($query)
                        or die("Query failed: " . mysql_error());

                    echo "<TABLE BORDER='1'>";
                    echo "<TR>";
                    echo "<TH>Name</TH><TH>Number</TH>";
                    echo "</TR>";

                    while ($row = mysql_fetch_array($result))
                    {
                        echo "<TR>";
                        echo "<TD>", $row['name'], "</TD><TD>",
                                    $row['number'], "</TD>";
                        echo "</TR>";
                    }

                    echo "</TABLE>";

                    mysql_close($connection);

                ?>
            </CENTER>
        </BODY>
</HTML>
```

That's all you need; you can see the results in the fruit table in Figure 8-2, where the number of pears has been updated from 235 to 234.

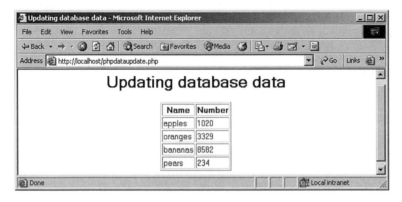

FIGURE 8-2   Updating data.

Inserting New Data

What if you start to carry new stock, such as a new kind of fruit? How can you add a new item to a database table? We'll take a look at this in a new example where we're adding a new type of fruit—say, apricots—to the fruit table. First, we connect to the produce database:

```
$connection = mysql_connect("localhost","root","")
    or die ("Couldn't connect to server");

$db = mysql_select_db("produce",$connection)
    or die ("Couldn't select database");
```

To create a new row for apricots, you can use the SQL INSERT statement like this:

```
$query = "INSERT INTO fruit (name, number) VALUES('apricots',
    '203')";
        .
        .
        .
```

Then you execute this new SQL query to insert the new row:

```
$query = "INSERT INTO fruit (name, number) VALUES('apricots',
    '203')";
$result = mysql_query($query)
    or die("Query failed: " . mysql_error());
```

After the insertion, you can view the new table, as you see in phpdatainsert.php, Example 8-3.

EXAMPLE 8-3 Inserting new data, phpdatainsert.php

```
<HTML>
    <HEAD>
        <TITLE>
            Inserting new data
        </TITLE>
    </HEAD>
    <BODY>
        <CENTER>
            <H1>Inserting new data</H1>

            <?php
                $connection = mysql_connect("localhost","root","")
                    or die ("Couldn't connect to server");
                $db = mysql_select_db("produce",$connection)
                    or die ("Couldn't select database");
```

continues

EXAMPLE 8-3 continued

```
                $query = "INSERT INTO fruit (name, number) VALUES('apricots',
                    '203')";
                $result = mysql_query($query)
                        or die("Query failed: " . mysql_error());


                $query = "SELECT * FROM fruit";
                $result = mysql_query($query)
                        or die("Query failed: " . mysql_error());

                echo "<TABLE BORDER='1'>";
                echo "<TR>";
                echo "<TH>Name</TH><TH>Number</TH>";
                echo "</TR>";

                while ($row = mysql_fetch_array($result))
                {
                    echo "<TR>";
                    echo "<TD>", $row['name'], "</TD><TD>",
                                $row['number'], "</TD>";
                    echo "</TR>";
                }

                echo "</TABLE>";

                mysql_close($connection);

            ?>
        </CENTER>
    </BODY>
</HTML>
```

The results appear in Figure 8-3—complete with apricots. Not bad.

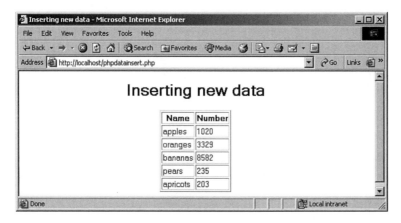

FIGURE 8-3 Inserting data.

Deleting Data

What about deleting data? Say that the apricot supplier isn't coming through, so you need to remove the entry just added in the previous chunk. As usual, you start by connecting to the database:

```
$connection = mysql_connect("localhost","root","")
    or die ("Couldn't connect to server");

$db = mysql_select_db("produce",$connection)
    or die ("Couldn't select database");
```

Then you can use the `SQL DELETE` statement to delete the apricots row, which you can identify by name. Here's what it looks like in SQL:

```
$query = "DELETE FROM fruit WHERE name = 'apricots'";
    .
    .
    .
```

Then you simply execute that new SQL query to delete the apricots row:

```
$query = "DELETE FROM fruit WHERE name = 'apricots'";
$result = mysql_query($query)
    or die("Query failed: " . mysql_error());
```

After deleting the apricots row, we can display the new version of the fruit table as you see in phpdatadelete.php, Example 8-4.

EXAMPLE 8-4   Deleting data, phpdatadelete.php

```
<HTML>
    <HEAD>
        <TITLE>
            Displaying tables with MySQL
        </TITLE>
    </HEAD>

    <BODY>
        <CENTER>
            <H1>Displaying tables with MySQL</H1>

            <?php
                $connection = mysql_connect("localhost","root","")
                    or die ("Couldn't connect to server");
                $db = mysql_select_db("produce",$connection)
                    or die ("Couldn't select database");
```

continues

EXAMPLE 8-4 continued

```
                    $query = "DELETE FROM fruit WHERE name = 'apricots'";
                    $result = mysql_query($query)
                        or die("Query failed: " . mysql_error());

                    $query = "SELECT * FROM fruit";
                    $result = mysql_query($query)
                        or die("Query failed: " . mysql_error());

                    echo "<TABLE BORDER='1'>";
                    echo "<TR>";
                    echo "<TH>Name</TH><TH>Number</TH>";
                    echo "</TR>";

                    while ($row = mysql_fetch_array($result))
                    {
                        echo "<TR>";
                        echo "<TD>", $row['name'], "</TD><TD>",
                                    $row['number'], "</TD>";
                        echo "</TR>";
                    }

                    echo "</TABLE>";

                    mysql_close($connection);

                ?>
            </CENTER>
        </BODY>
    </HTML>
```

You can see the results in Figure 8-4, where the apricots row has indeed been deleted. Now we're able to insert and delete data rows from database tables.

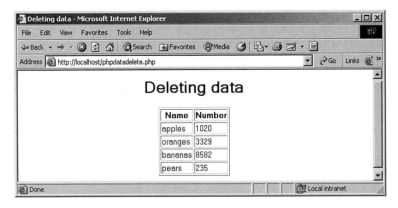

FIGURE 8-4 Deleting data.

Creating a New Table

What if you want to create a whole new table in a database? For example, say that business is so good that you want to start selling vegetables, too. How about creating a vegetables table on-the-fly? No problem. To create a new table, use the CREATE TABLE SQL statement, as here, where we're configuring the name and number fields in the new vegetables table:

```
$query = "CREATE TABLE vegetables (name VARCHAR(20), number
    VARCHAR(20))";
$result = mysql_query($query)
    or die("Query failed: " . mysql_error());
```

Now you can insert data into the new vegetables table with INSERT:

```
$query = "INSERT INTO vegetables (name, number) VALUES('corn',
    '2083')";
$result = mysql_query($query)
    or die("Query failed: " . mysql_error());
```

The full code appears in phpcreate.php, Example 8-5.

EXAMPLE 8-5 Creating a new table, phpdatacreate.php

```
<HTML>
    <HEAD>
        <TITLE>Creating a new table</TITLE>
    </HEAD>
    <BODY>
        <CENTER>
            <H1>Creating a new table</H1>
            <?php
                $connection = mysql_connect("localhost","root","")
                    or die ("Couldn't connect to server");
                $db = mysql_select_db("produce",$connection)
                    or die ("Couldn't select database");

                $query = "CREATE TABLE vegetables (name VARCHAR(20),
                    number VARCHAR(20))";
                $result = mysql_query($query)
                    or die("Query failed: " . mysql_error());

                $query = "INSERT INTO vegetables (name, number) VALUES(
                    'corn', '2083')";
                $result = mysql_query($query)
                    or die("Query failed: " . mysql_error());

                $query = "INSERT INTO vegetables (name, number)
                    VALUES('spinach', '1993')";
```

continues

EXAMPLE 8-5   continued

```
$result = mysql_query($query)
       or die("Query failed: " . mysql_error());

$query = "INSERT INTO vegetables (name, number)
       VALUES('beets', '437')";
$result = mysql_query($query)
       or die("Query failed: " . mysql_error());

$query = "SELECT * FROM vegetables";
$result = mysql_query($query)
       or die("Query failed: " . mysql_error());

echo "<TABLE BORDER='1'>";
echo "<TR>";
echo "<TH>Name</TH><TH>Number</TH>";
echo "</TR>";

while ($row = mysql_fetch_array($result))
{
    echo "<TR>";
    echo "<TD>", $row['name'], "</TD><TD>",
                 $row['number'], "</TD>";
    echo "</TR>";
}
echo "</TABLE>";

mysql_close($connection);
?>
    </CENTER>
  </BODY>
</HTML>
```

You can see the new table in Figure 8-5. Very cool.

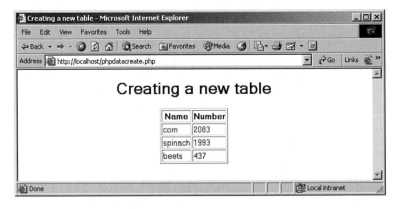

FIGURE 8-5   Creating a new table.

Creating a Database

You can even create a whole new database from PHP. Here's an example, where we're creating a database named foods using the CREATE DATABASE command:

```
$query = "CREATE DATABASE IF NOT EXISTS foods";
$result = mysql_query($query)
    or die("Query failed: " . mysql_error());
```

And we'll add a new table to this database, snacks:

```
$db = mysql_select_db("foods", $connection)
    or die ("Couldn't select database");

$query = "CREATE TABLE snacks (name VARCHAR(20), number
    VARCHAR(20))";
$result = mysql_query($query)
    or die("Query failed: " . mysql_error());
```

All it takes now is some INSERT statements in phpdatacreatedb.php, Example 8-6.

EXAMPLE 8-6   Creating a new database, phpdatacreatedb.php

```
<HTML>
    <HEAD>
        <TITLE>Creating a new database</TITLE>
    </HEAD>
    <BODY>
        <CENTER><H1>Creating a new database</H1>
            <?php
                $connection = mysql_connect("localhost","root","")
                    or die ("Couldn't connect to server");

                $query = "CREATE DATABASE IF NOT EXISTS foods";
                $result = mysql_query($query)
                    or die("Query failed: " . mysql_error());

                $db = mysql_select_db("foods", $connection)
                    or die ("Couldn't select database");

                $query = "CREATE TABLE snacks (name VARCHAR(20), number
                    VARCHAR(20))";
                $result = mysql_query($query)
                    or die("Query failed: " . mysql_error());

                $query = "INSERT INTO snacks (name, number) VALUES('tacos',
                    '2843')";
                $result = mysql_query($query)
                    or die("Query failed: " . mysql_error());
```

continues

EXAMPLE 8-6 continued

```
$query = "INSERT INTO snacks (name, number) VALUES('pizza',
    '1955')";
$result = mysql_query($query)
    or die("Query failed: " . mysql_error());
$query = "INSERT INTO snacks (name, number)
    VALUES('cheeseburgers', '849')";
$result = mysql_query($query)
    or die("Query failed: " . mysql_error());

$query = "SELECT * FROM snacks";
$result = mysql_query($query)
    or die("Query failed: " . mysql_error());

echo "<TABLE BORDER='1'>";
echo "<TR>";
echo "<TH>Name</TH><TH>Number</TH>";
echo "</TR>";

while ($row = mysql_fetch_array($result))
{
    echo "<TR>";
    echo "<TD>", $row['name'], "</TD><TD>",
                $row['number'], "</TD>";
    echo "</TR>";
}
echo "</TABLE>";

mysql_close($connection);

?>
    </CENTER>
  </BODY>
</HTML>
```

The results, including the new database, appear in Figure 8-6. Outstanding.

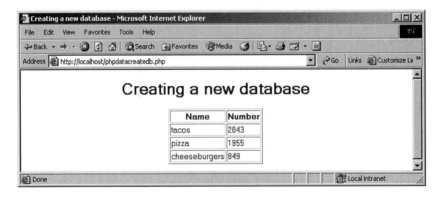

FIGURE 8-6 Creating a new database.

Sorting Data

How about sorting your data? Couldn't be easier. Just connect to the database as usual:

```
$connection = mysql_connect("localhost","root","")
    or die ("Couldn't connect to server");

$db = mysql_select_db("produce",$connection)
    or die ("Couldn't select database");
```

Then when you read your data, use the ORDER BY clause to indicate what field you want to sort on. For example, if you want to sort by name of the various fruits, use this statement:

```
$query = "SELECT * FROM fruit ORDER BY name";
        .
        .
        .
```

And then execute this new SQL statement:

```
$query = "SELECT * FROM fruit ORDER BY name";

$result = mysql_query($query)
    or die("Query failed: ".mysql_error());
```

You can see how this works in phpdatasort.php, Example 8-7.

EXAMPLE 8-7 Sorting data, phpdatasort.php

```
<HTML>
    <HEAD>
        <TITLE>
            Sorting data
        </TITLE>
    </HEAD>

    <BODY>
        <CENTER>

            <H1>
                Sorting data
            </H1>

            <?php

                $connection = mysql_connect("localhost","root","")
                    or die ("Couldn't connect to server");
```

continues

EXAMPLE 8-7 continued

```
                    $db = mysql_select_db("produce",$connection)
                        or die ("Couldn't select database");

                    $query = "SELECT * FROM fruit ORDER BY name";

                    $result = mysql_query($query)
                        or die("Query failed: ".mysql_error());

                    echo "<TABLE BORDER='1'>";
                    echo "<TR>";
                    echo "<TH>Name</TH><TH>Number</TH>";
                    echo "</TR>";

                    while ($row = mysql_fetch_array($result))
                    {
                        echo "<TR>";
                        echo "<TD>", $row['name'], "</TD><TD>",
                                    $row['number'], "</TD>";
                        echo "</TR>";
                    }

                    echo "</TABLE>";

                    mysql_close($connection);

                ?>
            </CENTER>
        </BODY>
</HTML>
```

The results appear in Figure 8-7, where the fruit table's data has been sorted by name. Sorting rows is useful when you're preparing your data to display to users.

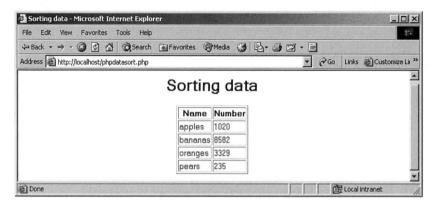

FIGURE 8-7 Sorting data.

Getting the PEAR DB Module

Besides the individual support for various database servers, PHP also supports the DB module, which gives you a level of abstraction that smoothes over the details of working with different database servers. When you use DB, you can use the same functions to access your data; if you switch database server types, you just have to change the name of the database sever you're using.

DB is a PHP extension managed by *PEAR*, the PHP Extension and Application Repository. If you compiled PHP yourself, PEAR was already installed as pear.php in your PHP directory, and if not, there's a script that will install PEAR for you at go-pear.org. To run PEAR, change to the PHP directory and type pear at the command line.

In Windows, PEAR comes with the manual installation version (not the Windows installer version). There should be a .bat file named go-pear.bat in your PHP directory (e.g., C:\PHP); run it by entering go-pear at the command line or by double-clicking go-pear.bat. This .bat file will ask you a few questions and then create pear.bat, which you use to run PEAR.

There are a number of PEAR modules, including the DB module, that are loaded by default when PEAR is loaded, so if you have PEAR, you should have them already (in Windows, go-pear.bat offers to install them for you). To check what modules you have installed, run PEAR and give it the list command like this:

```
%php>pear list
INSTALLED PACKAGES:
===================
PACKAGE         VERSION STATE
Archive_Tar     1.2      stable
Console_Getopt  1.2      stable
DB              1.6.5    stable
Mail            1.1.3    stable
Net_SMTP        1.2.6    stable
Net_Socket      1.0.2    stable
PEAR            1.3.1    stable
PHPUnit         1.0.1    stable
XML_Parser      1.2.0    stable
XML_RPC         1.1.0    stable
```

This lists the PEAR modules that are already installed, and you can see the DB module among them. If you don't see DB among the installed modules, you can install it with the install DB command, which looks like this:

```
%pear install DB
```

If you want to find out what other modules are available in the PEAR repository, use the list-all command:

```
%pear list-all
ALL PACKAGES:
=============
PACKAGE                    LATEST    LOCAL
APC                        2.0.4
Cache                      1.5.4
Cache_Lite                 1.3.1
apd                        1.0
memcache                   1.3
perl                       0.6
PHPUnit                    1.0.1     1.0.1
PHPUnit2                   2.0.2
PHP_Compat                 1.1.0
Var_Dump                   1.0.0
Xdebug                     1.3.2
Archive_Tar                1.2       1.2
bz2                        1.0
Contact_Vcard_Build        1.1
Contact_Vcard_Parse        1.30
File_Fstab                 2.0.0
File_HtAccess              1.1.0
File_Passwd                1.1.0
File_SMBPasswd             1.0.0
MP3_ID                     1.1.3
zip                        1.0
Auth                       1.2.3
Auth_HTTP                  2.0
Auth_PrefManager           1.1.3
Auth_RADIUS                1.0.4
Auth_SASL                  1.0.1
radius                     1.2.4
Benchmark                  1.2.1
Config                     1.10.2
        .
        .
        .
```

If you want to read the PEAR help file, enter "pear help".

To actually use a PEAR module in PHP, you can use the require statement in your code; for example, this statement loads the DB support:

```
require 'DB.php';
```

You can also use "include 'DB.php';", but that's slightly different—if a file you want to use doesn't exist, require considers that a fatal error and ends the script, while include just issues a warning. We'll put the DB module to work in the next chunk.

Displaying a Table with DB

Here's an example of using the DB module's functions to read our MySQL database. First, you add the support for the DB module using the require statement:

```
require 'DB.php';
        .
        .
        .
```

Next, you connect using the DB::connect method (recall that you can use :: to indicate what class a method belongs to). Here's how you use this method in general:

```
DB:connect('dbname://username:password@server/databasename);
```

If you're working locally, use localhost as the server. For example, to connect to the produce database locally with the username root with no password, you'd do this:

```
require 'DB.php';
$db = DB::connect('mysql://root:@localhost/produce');
        .
        .
        .
```

Now you can use the query method of the $db object to execute a SQL query like this one, which reads the entire fruit table:

```
require 'DB.php';
$db = DB::connect('mysql://root:@localhost/produce');

$query = "SELECT * FROM fruit";

$result = $db->query($query);
```

You can recover a row of data using the fetchRow method, as you see in phpdb.php, Example 8-8—the DB_FETCHMODE_ASSOC constant makes this method return data as an associative array, so the rest of the code is just as it was with the MySQL functions we used earlier.

EXAMPLE 8-8   Displaying a table with DB, phpdb.php

```
<HTML>
    <HEAD>
        <TITLE>
            Using DB to display a table
        </TITLE>
    </HEAD>
```

continues

EXAMPLE 8-8   continued

```
    <BODY>
        <CENTER>
            <H1>Using DB to display a table</H1>
            <?php

                require 'DB.php';

                $db = DB::connect('mysql://root:@localhost/produce');

                $query = "SELECT * FROM fruit";

                $result = $db->query($query);

                echo "<TABLE BORDER='1'>";
                echo "<TR>";
                echo "<TH>Name</TH><TH>Number</TH>";
                echo "</TR>";

                while ($row = $result->fetchRow(DB_FETCHMODE_ASSOC))
                {
                    echo "<TR>";
                    echo "<TD>", $row['name'], "</TD><TD>", $row['number'],
                        "</TD>";
                    echo "</TR>";
                }
                echo "</TABLE>";

            ?>
        </CENTER>
    </BODY>
</HTML>
```

The results appear in Figure 8-8. Not bad.

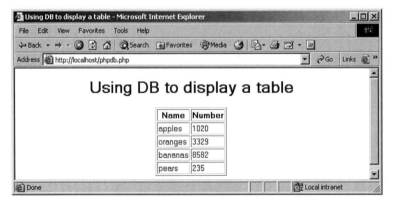

FIGURE 8-8   Using the DB module to display a table.

Inserting New Data with DB

What about inserting new data into a table using the DB module, such as the apricots data we added earlier? No problem, just start by connecting to the database using the DB::connect method:

```
$db = DB::connect('mysql://root:@localhost/produce');
    .
    .
    .
```

We'll use SQL to insert a data row for apricots into the fruit table like this:

```
$db = DB::connect('mysql://root:@localhost/produce');

$query = "INSERT INTO fruit (name, number)
    VALUES('apricots', '203')";
    .
    .
    .
```

And now you can execute this query with the $db->query method:

```
$db = DB::connect('mysql://root:@localhost/produce');

$query = "INSERT INTO fruit (name, number)
    VALUES('apricots', '203')";

$result = $db->query($query);
```

After inserting the new row, we'll display the entire table, as you see in phpdbinsert.php, Example 8-9.

EXAMPLE 8-9 Inserting database data, phpdbinsert.php

```
<HTML>
    <HEAD>
        <TITLE>
            Using DB to insert data
        </TITLE>
    </HEAD>

    <BODY>
        <CENTER>
            <H1>Using DB to insert data</H1>

            <?php
```

continues

EXAMPLE 8-9 continued

```
        require 'DB.php';

        $db = DB::connect('mysql://root:@localhost/produce');

        $query = "INSERT INTO fruit (name, number)
            VALUES('apricots', '203')";

        $result = $db->query($query);

        $query = "SELECT * FROM fruit";

        $result = $db->query($query);

        echo "<TABLE BORDER='1'>";
        echo "<TR>";
        echo "<TH>Name</TH><TH>Number</TH>";
        echo "</TR>";

        while ($row = $result->fetchRow(DB_FETCHMODE_ASSOC))
        {
            echo "<TR>";
            echo "<TD>", $row['name'], "</TD><TD>",
                        $row['number'], "</TD>";
            echo "</TR>";
        }

        echo "</TABLE>";

    ?>
        </CENTER>
    </BODY>
</HTML>
```

The results appear in Figure 8-9, where the apricots row has been added, as we wanted.

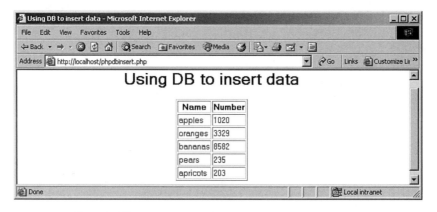

FIGURE 8-9 Using the DB module to insert data.

Updating Data with DB

Here's another one—updating data with the DB module. As before, we'll reduce the number of pears in the fruit table from 235 to 234. Because we've got a handle on using SQL with the DB module, there's no problem here either; just set up the correct SQL query and then execute that query:

```
$query = "UPDATE fruit SET number = 234 WHERE name = 'pears'";

$result = $db->query($query);
```

You can see an example of this in Example 8-10, phpdbupdate.php.

EXAMPLE 8-10   Updating database data, phpdbupdate.php

```
<HTML>
    <HEAD>
        <TITLE>
            Using DB to update data
        </TITLE>
    </HEAD>

    <BODY>
        <CENTER>
            <H1>Using DB to update data</H1>

            <?php

                require 'DB.php';

                $db = DB::connect('mysql://root:@localhost/produce');

                $query = "UPDATE fruit SET number = 234 WHERE name = 'pears'";

                $result = $db->query($query);

                $query = "SELECT * FROM fruit";

                $result = $db->query($query);

                echo "<TABLE BORDER='1'>";
                echo "<TR>";
                echo "<TH>Name</TH><TH>Number</TH>";
                echo "</TR>";

                while ($row = $result->fetchRow(DB_FETCHMODE_ASSOC))
                {
                    echo "<TR>";
```

continues

EXAMPLE 8-10   continued

```
                    echo "<TD>", $row['name'], "</TD><TD>",
                              $row['number'], "</TD>";
                echo "</TR>";
            }

            echo "</TABLE>";

        ?>
      </CENTER>
    </BODY>
</HTML>
```

The results appear in Figure 8-10, where we've been able to change the number of pears stored in the database.

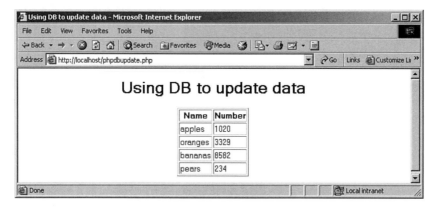

FIGURE 8-10   Using the DB module to update data.

The DB module also includes a DB::isError method to handle errors. Whenever you get a result from a DB module method, you can pass it to the DB::isError method. If that method returns TRUE, there was an error, and you can display the appropriate error message with the result object's getMessage method:

```
$db = DB::connect('mysql://root:@localhost/produce');

if(DB::isError($db)){
    die($db->getMessage());
}
```

Now that you can execute SQL statements using the DB module, you have access to most database applications—all you have to do to select a different type of database server is to change the name of the server type in the connection string.

Summary

This chapter took a look at working with databases and the various options that PHP gives you here. Being able to handle databases in your PHP code is very powerful because you can manage and store data on the server. Here are some of this chapter's salient points:

- You can connect to database servers with PHP functions such as `mysql_connect`, and you can select a database with functions such as `mysql_select_db`.

- You can create a database with the `CREATE` statement.

- You can also create tables and specify the type of data they'll hold with the `CREATE` statement.

- You can store data in a database with the `INSERT` statement.

- You can recover data from a database table with the `SELECT` statement.

- You can update data in a database table with the `UPDATE` statement.

- You can also delete data from database tables with the `DELETE` statement.

CHAPTER 9

Cookies, Sessions, FTP, Email, and More

This chapter covers some very powerful PHP web programming techniques: working with cookies, FTP (File Transfer Protocol), email, sessions, and more. We'll start by seeing how to set and read cookies, those data strings of text that you can store on the user's computer. Using cookies from PHP, you can store text on someone's computer and access it later, keeping track of his or her purchases, custom web page settings, and much more.

FTP is another powerful tool we're going to see in this chapter. FTP is great for sending files back and forth on the Internet, and you can use FTP from PHP scripts. A good many FTP functions are built into PHP, and we're going to use them to connect to remote servers, upload files, download files, and more in this chapter.

Another handy tool you have access to in PHP is email. You can send email from your scripts, which is great if you want to be notified when something happened in a web page. You can have a script send you email notification of new customer orders, signups for a newsletter, and more. We'll also take a look at handling *sessions* in this chapter. Normally, when you navigate to a PHP script, all the data in the variables in that script are initialized to their original values. That's usually OK, but what if you have an online shop and want to keep track of customer purchases as the user browses around your site? You could do that with cookies, but sessions give you an easier alternative.

Setting Cookies

Cookies hold text that you can store on the user's computer and retrieve later. You can set cookies using the `setcookie` function:

```
setcookie(string name [, string value [, int expire [, string path [, string domain [,
int secure]]]]])
```

This function defines a cookie to be sent to the user's machine. Here is what the various parameters mean:

- *name.* The name of the cookie.
- *value.* The value of the cookie. (This value is stored on the client's computer, so you should not store sensitive information.)
- *expire.* The time the cookie expires. This is the number of seconds since January 1, 1970. You'll most likely set this with the PHP `time` function plus the number of seconds before you want it to expire.
- *path.* The path on the server on which the cookie will be available.
- *domain.* The domain for which the cookie is available.
- *secure.* Indicates that the cookie should only be transmitted over a secure HTTPS connection. When set to 1, the cookie will only be set if a secure connection exists. The default is 0.

Note that cookies are part of the HTTP headers sent to the browsers, and so they must be sent before any other output from your script. This means that you should place calls to this function before any other output, including <HTML> and <HEAD> tags. If some output exists before calling this function, `setcookie` may fail and return FALSE. If `setcookie` runs successfully, it will return TRUE—but that does not indicate whether the user accepted the cookie.

Here's an example. In this case, we're going to create a cookie named *message* that will hold the text "No worries.", and we do that with `setcookie`:

```
<?php
    setcookie("message", "No worries.");
?>
```

This PHP goes at the beginning of the script phpsetcookie.php, as you can see in Example 9-1.

EXAMPLE 9-1   Setting a cookie, phpsetcookie.php

```
<?php
    setcookie("message", "No worries.");
?>

<HTML>
    <HEAD>
        <TITLE>
            Setting a cookie
        </TITLE>
    </HEAD>

    <BODY>
        <CENTER>
            <H1>
                Setting a cookie
            </H1>
            Cookie has been set! Look at
                <A HREF="phpgetcookie.php">phpgetcookie.php</A> next.
        </CENTER>
    <BODY>
</HTML>
```

This page appears in Figure 9-1, where PHP has sent the cookie to the browser, and it's already been set.

FIGURE 9-1   Setting a cookie.

Now the cookie's been set, but how do we read it? When the user clicks the hyperlink in this page, he or she will be redirected to phpgetcookie.php, which is coming up in the next chunk.

Getting Cookies

After you set a cookie, it won't be visible to your scripts until the next time you load a page. That's because the cookie is sent to the server from the user's machine, so immediately after you set a cookie, you won't be able to read it; you need to get a page back from the browser first. Note also that cookies are sent in the HTTP headers in pages sent to you by the browser, and if your cookie-handling page is in domain A (such as www.ultra-giantbigco.com), only the cookies that came from domain A are sent to you.

After the cookies have been set, they can be accessed on the next page load with the $_COOKIE array. We set a cookie named message in the previous chunk—so now we'll read it here. The values of cookies are automatically loaded into the global array $_COOKIES, much like how the values of web page data are stored in $_REQUEST.

To read the text from the message cookie, we'll check $_COOKIE['message']. If that variable is set, some cookie data is waiting for us:

```php
<?php
    if (isset($_COOKIE['message'])) {
        .
        .
        .
    }
?>
```

In this case, we'll just echo the recovered data from the cookie to the browser's window:

```php
<?php
    if (isset($_COOKIE['message'])) {
        echo $_COOKIE['message'];
    }
?>
```

You can see how this works in Example 9-2, phpgetcookie.php.

EXAMPLE 9-2   Reading a cookie, phpgetcookie.php

```
<HTML>
    <HEAD><TITLE>
            Getting a cookie
        </TITLE></HEAD>
    <BODY><CENTER>
            <H1>Getting a cookie</H1>
            The cookie says:
            <?php
                if (isset($_COOKIE['message'])) {
                    echo $_COOKIE['message'];
```

```
            }
        ?>
    </CENTER><BODY>
</HTML>
```

After setting the cookie with phpsetcookie.php, you can navigate to phpgetcookie.php, as you see in Figure 9-2, to read the data from the cookie. Very cool.

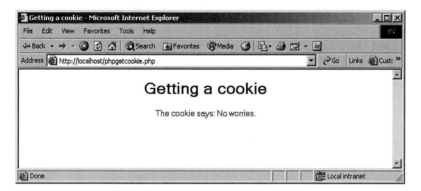

FIGURE 9-2 Reading a cookie.

Cookies names can also be set as array names and will be available to your PHP scripts as arrays. For example, if you did this:

```
setcookie("cookie[one]", "No");
setcookie("cookie[two]", "worries");
setcookie("cookie[three]", "today.");
```

Then after these cookies have been set, you could read them next time the browser sends you a page like this:

```
if (isset($_COOKIE['cookie'])) {
    foreach ($_COOKIE['cookie'] as $data) {
        echo "$value <BR>";
    }
}
```

Now you've got the ability to set and retrieve cookies. Not bad.

Setting a Cookie's Expiration Time

There's more to setcookie than simply setting a cookie's text value. You can also specify how long the cookie should exist on the user's machine. If you don't, the cookie will be deleted when the user ends the current browser session (which usually means closing all browser windows). But you can specify how long a cookie should last by giving a value for the *expire* parameter in setcookie:

```
setcookie(string name [, string value [, int expire [, string path [, string domain [, int secure]]]]])
```

The time stored in this parameter is a Unix timestamp, holding the number of seconds since January 1st, 1970, and specifying the time when the cookie should be deleted. To get the current number of seconds since January 1st, 1970, you can use the PHP time function. For example, to specify that a cookie should be deleted in an hour, you can do something like this, where you specify an expiration time of time() + 3600 seconds:

```
<?php
    setcookie("mycookie", $value, time() + 3600);
?>
```

We'll create a cookie in phpsetconfiguredcookie.php, which will last 30 days and hold the text "No worries for 30 days." as you can see in Example 9-3.

EXAMPLE 9-3   Setting a timed cookie, phpsetconfiguredcookie.php

```
<?php
    setcookie("message", "No worries for 30 days.", time()+60*60*24*30);
?>

<HTML>
    <HEAD>
        <TITLE>
            Setting a configured cookie
        </TITLE>
    </HEAD>

    <BODY>
        <CENTER>
            <H1>Setting a configured cookie</H1>
            Cookie has been set to expire in 30 days! Look at
                <A HREF="phpgetcookie.php">phpgetcookie.php</A> next.
        </CENTER>
    <BODY>
</HTML>
```

You can see what this page looks like in Figure 9-3, where we're setting the cookie that will last 30 days (unless intentionally deleted).

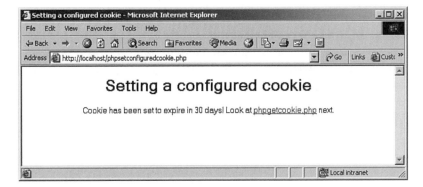

FIGURE 9-3 Setting a timed cookie.

When you click the hyperlink in Figure 9-3, phpgetcookie.php appears, correctly showing the text of the 30-day cookie, as you see in Figure 9-4.

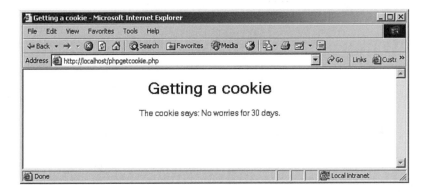

FIGURE 9-4 Getting a timed cookie.

Specifying the expiration time of a cookie is a good idea if you need a long-term cookie that should last beyond the current browser session. If you don't extend your cookie's life, it'll be deleted when the browser session ends.

Deleting Cookies

Want to delete a cookie? Just set the cookie's value to "" and call setcookie with the same parameters as the cookie was set with. When you set the *value* argument to an empty string (""), and all other arguments match a previous call to setcookie, then the cookie with the specified name will be deleted from the user's machine:

```php
<?php
    setcookie ("message", "");
?>
```

When deleting a cookie, it's also best to make sure you set the expiration date in the past in order to trigger the cookie removal mechanism in the browser:

```php
<?php
    setcookie ("message", "", time() - 3600);
?>
```

Here's an example. In this case, we'll delete the message cookie like this:

```php
<?php
    setcookie("message", "", time() - 3600);
?>
```

And we'll also direct the user to phpgetcookie.php to confirm that the cookie is gone:

```php
<?php
    setcookie("message", "", time() - 3600);
?>
<HTML>
    <HEAD>
        <TITLE>
            Deleting a cookie
        </TITLE>
    </HEAD>

    <BODY>
        <CENTER>
            <H1>Deleting a cookie</H1>
            Cookie was deleted. Look at
                <A HREF="phpgetcookie.php">phpgetcookie.php</A>.
        </CENTER>
    <BODY>
</HTML>
```

When you reload this page, the phpgetcookie.php script won't be able to find the cookie any longer.

Using FTP

FTP is great for transferring files back and forth on the Internet, and you can use FTP from PHP. In order to use FTP functions, you should add the `--enable-ftp` option when installing PHP 4. The Windows version of PHP has built-in support for this extension.

Using FTP is not hard. To connect to an FTP server, you use `ftp_connect`:

```
ftp_connect(string host [, int port [, int timeout]])
```

This function opens an FTP connection to the specified *host* (note that host shouldn't have any trailing slashes and shouldn't be prefixed with ftp://). The *port* parameter specifies an alternate port to connect to; if it is omitted or set to zero, then the default FTP port, 21, will be used. The timeout parameter specifies the timeout for all subsequent network operations. If omitted, the default value is 90 seconds. This function returns an FTP stream on success or FALSE on error.

After you connect with `ftp_connect`, you must log in with `ftp_login`, which you use this way:

```
ftp_login(resource ftp_stream, string username, string password)
```

This function passes your *username* and *password* to the FTP server, and it returns TRUE on success or FALSE on failure.

For example, here's how you can connect to and log into an FTP server:

```php
<?php
    $connect = ftp_connect("ftp.ispname.com");
    $result = ftp_login($connect, $username, $password);
    .
    .
    .
```

We'll use this kind of code to connect to FTP servers in the following chunks. Besides `ftp_connect` and `ftp_login`, there are plenty of other FTP functions in PHP; here's a starter list:

- `ftp_alloc`. Allocates space for a file to be uploaded
- `ftp_cdup`. Changes to the parent directory
- `ftp_chdir`. Changes directories on an FTP server
- `ftp_chmod`. Sets permissions on a file via FTP
- `ftp_close`. Closes an FTP connection

- `ftp_connect.` Opens an FTP connection
- `ftp_delete.` Deletes a file on the FTP server
- `ftp_exec.` Requests execution of a program on the FTP server
- `ftp_fget.` Downloads a file from the FTP server and saves to an open file
- `ftp_fput.` Uploads from an open file to the FTP server
- `ftp_get_option.` Retrieves run-time behaviors of the current FTP stream
- `ftp_get.` Downloads a file from the FTP server
- `ftp_login.` Logs in to an FTP connection
- `ftp_mdtm.` Returns the last modified time of the given file
- `ftp_mkdir.` Creates a directory
- `ftp_nb_continue.` Continues retrieving/sending a file
- `ftp_nb_fget.` Retrieves a file from the FTP server and writes it to an open file
- `ftp_nb_fput.` Stores a file from an open file to the FTP server
- `ftp_nb_get.` Retrieves a file from the FTP server and writes it to a local file
- `ftp_nb_put.` Stores a file on the FTP server
- `ftp_nlist.` Returns a list of files in the given directory
- `ftp_put.` Uploads a file to the FTP server
- `ftp_pwd.` Returns the current directory name
- `ftp_quit.` An alias of `ftp_close`
- `ftp_raw.` Sends an arbitrary command to an FTP server
- `ftp_rawlist.` Returns a detailed list of files in the given directory
- `ftp_rename.` Renames a file on the FTP server
- `ftp_rmdir.` Removes a directory
- `ftp_set_option.` Sets miscellaneous run-time FTP options
- `ftp_site.` Sends a SITE command to the server
- `ftp_size.` Returns the size of the given file
- `ftp_ssl_connect.` Opens a secure SSL-FTP connection
- `ftp_systype.` Returns the system type identifier of the remote FTP server

We'll put a number of these functions to work in the following chunks.

FTP: Getting a Directory Listing

We'll start our FTP work by using the `ftp_nlist` function to get a listing of a remote directory; here's how you use this function:

```
array ftp_nlist(resource ftp_stream, string directory)
```

This function returns an array of filenames from the specified *directory* on success or FALSE on error. In this case, we'll connect to an FTP server and get a listing of the directory code22 on that server. Here's how we connect to the FTP server:

```php
<?php
    $connect = ftp_connect("ftp.ispname.com");
    $result = ftp_login($connect, "username", "password");
        .
        .
        .
?>
```

We get the listing of the files in the code22 directory this way:

```php
<?php
    $connect = ftp_connect("ftp.ispname.com");
    $result = ftp_login($connect, "username", "password");

    $a = ftp_nlist($connect, "code22");
        .
        .
        .
?>
```

And we'll display the files in that directory this way:

```php
<?php
    $connect = ftp_connect("ftp.ispname.com");
    $result = ftp_login($connect, "username", "password");

    $a = ftp_nlist($connect, "code22");

    foreach($a as $value){
        echo $value, "<BR>";
    }
?>
```

All this is put to work in phpftp.php, Example 9-4.

EXAMPLE 9-4   Getting a remote directory listing, phpftp.php

```
<HTML>
    <HEAD>
        <TITLE>
            Getting a directory listing with FTP
        </TITLE>
    </HEAD>

    <BODY>
        <CENTER>
            <H1>
                Getting a directory listing with FTP
            </H1>
            Here's what's in the remote directory:
            <BR>
            <BR>
            <?php
                $connect = ftp_connect("ftp.ispname.com");
                $result = ftp_login($connect, "username", "password");

                $a = ftp_nlist($connect, "code22");

                foreach($a as $value){
                    echo $value, "<BR>";
                }

            ?>
        </CENTER>
    <BODY>
</HTML>
```

You can see the results in Figure 9-5, where we've successfully retrieved a directory listing of the remote directory.

FIGURE 9-5   Getting a remote directory listing.

FTP: Downloading a File

What if you want to move around an FTP site and download files? To change to a directory on an FTP site after you're logged in, use ftp_chdir:

```
ftp_chdir(resource ftp_stream, string directory)
```

This function changes your current directory on the FTP site to the specified directory. It returns TRUE on success or FALSE on failure.

How about getting a file from the new directory? For that, use ftp_get:

```
ftp_get(resource ftp_stream, string local_file, string remote_file, int mode [,
int resumepos])
```

This function retrieves *remote_file* from the FTP server and saves it to *local_file* locally (which can include a pathname). The transfer *mode* specified must be either FTP_ASCII or FTP_BINARY. It returns TRUE on success or FALSE on failure. Here's an example, where we're connecting to an FTP site and downloading a file, a.php, storing it locally as script.php. We connect to the FTP site and use ftp_get to retrieve the file, testing the results like this:

```php
$connect = ftp_connect("ftp.ispname.com");
$result = ftp_login($connect, "username", "password");

if(!$result){
    echo "Could not connect.";
    exit;
}

$result = ftp_get($connect, "script.php", "a.php", FTP_ASCII);

if($result){
    echo "Got the file.";
}
else {
    echo "Did not get the file.";
}
```

You can see the whole thing in phpftpget.php, Example 9-5.

EXAMPLE 9-5   Downloading a file, phpftpget.php

```html
<HTML>
    <HEAD>
        <TITLE>
            Getting a file with FTP
```

continues

EXAMPLE 9-5 continued

```
            </TITLE>
        </HEAD>

        <BODY>
            <CENTER>
                <H1>Getting a file with FTP</H1>
                Downloading the file....
                <BR>
                <?php
                    $connect = ftp_connect("ftp.ispname.com");
                    $result = ftp_login($connect, "username", "password");

                    if(!$result){
                        echo "Could not connect.";
                        exit;
                    }

                    $result = ftp_get($connect, "script.php", "a.php", FTP_ASCII);

                    if($result){
                        echo "Got the file.";
                    }
                    else {
                        echo "Did not get the file.";
                    }

                    ftp_close($connect);
                ?>
            </CENTER>
        <BODY>
</HTML>
```

The results appear in Figure 9-6, where we've successfully downloaded the file.

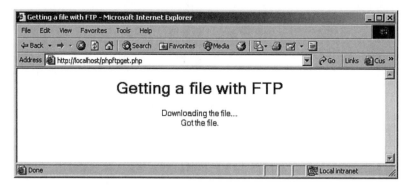

FIGURE 9-6   Downloading a file.

Note that this stores the file in the same directory as phpftpget.php; if you want to store it elsewhere, include a path when you give the name of the local file.

FTP: Uploading a File

In the previous chunk, we downloaded a file by using FTP. In this chunk, we're going to upload a file by using ftp_put:

```
ftp_put(resource ftp_stream, string remote_file, string local_file, int mode [, int startpos])
```

This function stores *local_file* (which can be specified with a pathname) on the FTP server as *remote_file*. The transfer *mode* specified must be either FTP_ASCII or FTP_BINARY. It returns TRUE on success or FALSE on failure. As an example, we'll upload a file named newscript.php to an FTP site as script.php. We start by connecting:

```
$connect = ftp_connect("ftp.ispname.com");
$result = ftp_login($connect, "username", "password");

if(!$result){
    echo "Could not connect.";
    exit;
}
```

Then we use ftp_put to upload the file, and we check the result:

```
$connect = ftp_connect("ftp.ispname.com");
$result = ftp_login($connect, "username", "password");

if(!$result){
    echo "Could not connect.";
    exit;
}

$result = ftp_put($connect, "newscript.php", "script.php", FTP_ASCII);

if($result){
    echo "Sent the file.";
}
else {
    echo "Did not send the file.";
}
```

You can see this all at work in Example 9-6, phpftpput.php.

EXAMPLE 9-6 Uploading a file, phpftpput.php

```
<HTML>
    <HEAD>
        <TITLE>
```

continues

EXAMPLE 9-6 continued

```
                Putting a file with FTP
            </TITLE>
    </HEAD>

    <BODY>
        <CENTER>
            <H1>Putting a file with FTP</H1>
            Uploading the file....
            <BR>
            <?php
                $connect = ftp_connect("ftp.ispname.com");
                $result = ftp_login($connect, "username", "password");

                if(!$result){
                    echo "Could not connect.";
                    exit;
                }

                $result = ftp_put($connect, "newscript.php", "script.php",
                            FTP_ASCII);

                if($result){
                    echo "Sent the file.";
                }
                else {
                    echo "Did not send the file.";
                }

                ftp_close($connect);
            ?>
        </CENTER>
    <BODY>
</HTML>
```

The results appear in Figure 9-7, where, as you can see, we've successfully uploaded the file.

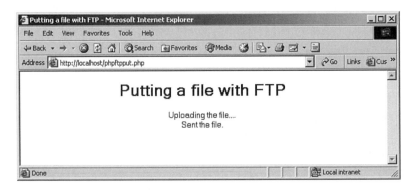

FIGURE 9-7   Uploading a file.

Sending Email

Your PHP scripts can send email as well. To enable email, edit this section in php.ini:

```
[mail function]
; For Win32 only.
SMTP = localhost
; For Win32 only.
sendmail_from = me@localhost.com
; For Unix only.  You may supply arguments as well (default: "sendmail -t -i").
;sendmail_path =
```

Windows users should list the SMTP host they want to use (such as mail.ispname.com or smtp.ispname.com) and set their return address. Linux and Unix users may not have to make any changes, but if things don't work as they are, uncomment the sendmail_path and set it to the appropriate value (such as /usr/bin/sendmail).

To actually send mail, you use the mail function:

```
mail(string to, string subject, string message [, string additional_headers [,
string additional_parameters]])
```

This sends mail to the email address in *to*, with subject *subject* and message *message*. You can also set additional mail headers and parameters to mail. You can see an example in phpemail.html, Example 9-7 and in phpemail.php, Example 9-8.

EXAMPLE 9-7   Sending email, phpemail.html

```
<HTML>
    <HEAD>
        <TITLE>
            Send me some email
        </TITLE>
    </HEAD>

    <BODY>
        <CENTER>
            <H1>Send me some email</H1>
            <BR>
            <FORM METHOD=POST ACTION="phpemail.php">
                Please enter your message and click Submit:
                <BR>
                <TEXTAREA NAME="message" COLS="50" ROWS="5"></TEXTAREA>
                <BR>
                <BR>
                <INPUT TYPE="SUBMIT" VALUE="Submit">
            </FORM>
        </CENTER>
    <BODY>
</HTML>
```

The phpemail.html page displays a text area for the text to send in the email, as you see in Figure 9-8.

FIGURE 9-8 Accepting email.

The message is sent using the mail function, as shown in phpemail.php, Example 9-8.

EXAMPLE 9-8 Sending email, phpemail.php

```
<HTML>
    <HEAD>
        <TITLE>Sending email</TITLE>
    </HEAD>

    <BODY>
        <CENTER>
            <H1>Sending email</H1>
            Your email was sent.
            <BR>
            <?php
                $result = mail("steve@ispname.com", "Web mail",
                    $_REQUEST["message"]);
            ?>
        </CENTER>
    <BODY>
</HTML>
```

And that's it—we've sent some email from a PHP script. Very cool.

Sending Email with Headers

You can do more with the `mail` function—for example, you can set additional email headers to cc ("carbon copy") or bcc ("blind carbon copy," where the recipient doesn't know a copy was also sent to someone else) people. To set such headers, you use the *additional_headers* parameter in the call to the `mail` function:

```
mail(string to, string subject, string message [, string additional_headers [,
string additional_parameters]])
```

Note that you use \r\n to separate headers (although some Unix mail transfer agents may work with just a single newline, \n). Example 9-9, phpemailheaders.html, lets the user set "cc" and "bcc" addresses.

EXAMPLE 9-9   Using headers, phpemailheaders.html

```
<HTML>
    <HEAD><TITLE>Send me some email with headers</TITLE></HEAD>
    <BODY><CENTER>
            <H1>Send me some email with headers</H1>
            <BR>
            <FORM METHOD=POST ACTION="phpemailheaders.php">
                Please enter your message and click Submit:
                <BR>
                cc: <INPUT TYPE="TEXT" NAME="cc">
                bcc: <INPUT TYPE="TEXT" NAME="bcc">
                <BR>
                <TEXTAREA NAME="message" COLS="50" ROWS="5"></TEXTAREA>
                <BR>
                <INPUT TYPE="SUBMIT" VALUE="Submit">
            </FORM>
        </CENTER></BODY>
</HTML>
```

You can see what this page looks like in Figure 9-9.

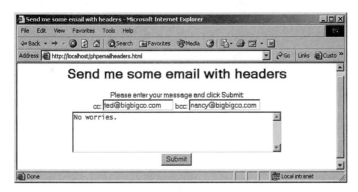

FIGURE 9-9   Sending email with headers.

In phpemailheaders.php, Example 9-10, we check the cc and bcc data, and if either exists, we add them to the variable $headers:

```
if(isset($_REQUEST["cc"])){
    $headers .= "cc:" . $_REQUEST["cc"] . "\r\n";
}

if(isset($_REQUEST["bcc"])){
    $headers .= "bcc:" . $_REQUEST["bcc"] . "\r\n";
}
```

After we've set the headers as needed, we use the mail function to send the email, as you see in phpemailheaders.php, Example 9-10.

EXAMPLE 9-10 Sending email with headers, phpemailheaders.php

```
<HTML>
    <HEAD><TITLE>Sending email</TITLE></HEAD>
    <BODY>
        <CENTER>
            <H1>Sending email</H1>
            Your email was sent.
            <BR>
            <?php
                $headers = "";

                if(isset($_REQUEST["cc"])){
                    $headers .= "cc:" . $_REQUEST["cc"] . "\r\n";
                }

                if(isset($_REQUEST["bcc"])){
                    $headers .= "bcc:" . $_REQUEST["bcc"] . "\r\n";
                }

                $result = mail("steve@chooseanisp.com", "Web mail",
                    $_REQUEST["message"], $headers);
            ?>
        </CENTER>
    <BODY>
</HTML>
```

This script sends the email to steve@chooseanisp.com, along with the cc and bcc addresses.

Sending Email with Attachments

You can also send email with attachments, but that takes some effort. To show how this works, we'll send an email with our image file from the previous chapter, image.jpg, attached. In this script, phpemailattachment.php, you specify whom the email is to, the subject, the message, the file you want to attach, and its MIME type (change the MIME type from image/jpeg to the correct type if you're not sending a JPEG):

```
//Set these variables yourself:
$to = "steve@ispname.com";
$subject = "Web mail";
$message = "This email has an attachment.";
$attachment = "image.jpg";
$attachment_MIME_type = "image/jpeg";
```

Then the script reads in the file, storing its data in $data:

```
$handle = fopen ($attachment, "rb");
$data = fread ($handle, filesize($attachment));
fclose ($handle);
```

To send an attachment, you need to create a multipart form and encode the data using the PHP functions chunk_split and base64_encode:

```
$boundary = "---Multipart_Boundary---";

$headers = "\nMIME-Version: 1.0\n" .
"Content-Type: multipart/mixed;\n" .
" boundary=\"" . $boundary . "\"";

$data = chunk_split(base64_encode($data));
```

Then you add the encoded attachment, as in phpemailattachment.php, Example 9-11.

EXAMPLE 9-11   Sending email with an attachment, phpemailattachment.php

```
<HTML>
    <HEAD>
        <TITLE>Sending email with attachments</TITLE>
    </HEAD>
    <BODY>
        <CENTER>
            <H1>Sending email with attachments</H1>
            <?php
            //Set these variables yourself:
            $to = "steve@ispname.com";
            $subject = "Web mail";
```

continues

EXAMPLE 9-11   continued

```
                $message = "This email has an attachment.";
                $attachment = "image.jpg";
                $attachment_MIME_type = "image/jpeg";

                $handle = fopen ($attachment, "rb");
                $data = fread ($handle, filesize($attachment));
                fclose ($handle);

                $boundary = "---Multipart_Boundary---";

                $headers = "\nMIME-Version: 1.0\n" .
                "Content-Type: multipart/mixed;\n" .
                " boundary=\"" . $boundary . "\"";

                $data = chunk_split(base64_encode($data));

                $text = "--" . $boundary . "\n" .
                "Content-Type:text/plain\nContent-Transfer-Encoding: 7bit\n\n" .
                $message . "\n\n--" . $boundary . "\n" .
                "Content-Type: " . $attachment_MIME_type . ";\n name=\"" .
                $attachment . "\"\nContent-Transfer-Encoding: base64\n\n" .
                $data . "\n\n--" . $boundary . "--\n";

                $result = @mail($to, $subject, $text, $headers);
                if($result) {
                    echo "The email was sent.";
                } else {
                    echo "The email was not sent.";
                }
            ?>
            </CENTER>
        <BODY>
    </HTML>
```

The results appear in Figure 9-10, where we've sent an email with a JPEG attachment from PHP. Very impressive.

FIGURE 9-10   Sending email with an attachment.

Working with Sessions

When the user is working with the various pages in your web application, all the data in the various pages is reset to its original values when those pages are loaded. That means all the data in those pages is wiped out between page accesses, which is not ideal if your web application is a large one, holding many pages. To preserve that data between page accesses, you can use cookies, as we've already seen, or you can use *sessions*.

Sessions are designed to hold data on the server. Each user is given a cookie with his or her session ID, which means that PHP will be able to reinstate all the data in each user's session automatically, even over multiple page accesses. If the user has cookies turned off, PHP can encode the session ID in URLs instead.

Using sessions, you can store and retrieve data by name. To work with a session, you start by calling session_start. To store data in the session, you use the $_SESSION array. For example, here we're storing "blue" under the key "color":

```
session_start();
$_SESSION['color'] = "blue";
```

Now in another page access (either of the same or a different page), you can access the data under the key "color" using $_SESSION again:

```
session_start();
$color = $_SESSION['color'];
```

In this way, you're able to preserve data between page accesses. Session support is enabled in PHP by default. If you would not like to build your PHP with session support, you should specify the --disable-session option. The Windows version of PHP has built-in support for this extension.

Session behavior is affected by these settings in php.ini—note for example that you can set how long a session lasts by setting a value for session.cache_expire in minutes:

- session.save_path "/tmp"

- session.name "PHPSESSID"

- session.save_handler "files"

- session.auto_start "0"

- session.gc_probability "1"

- session.gc_divisor "100"

- session.gc_maxlifetime "1440"

- `session.serialize_handler "php"`
- `session.cookie_lifetime "0"`
- `session.cookie_path "/"`
- `session.cookie_domain ""`
- `session.cookie_secure ""`
- `session.use_cookies "1"`
- `session.use_only_cookies "0"`
- `session.referer_check ""`
- `session.entropy_file ""`
- `session.entropy_length "0"`
- `session.cache_limiter "nocache"`
- `session.cache_expire "180"`
- `session.use_trans_sid "0" PHP_INI_SYSTEM | PHP_INI_PERDIR`

In particular, it's important to note that all data for a particular session will be stored in a file in the directory specified by the `session.save_path` item. A file for each session (whether or not any data is associated with that session) will be created.

In Windows, you must set this item yourself. By default, it's set this way (change this value in Linux and Unix as well if no /tmp is available):

`session.save_path "/tmp"`

Set this item to the location you want to use for session files, which are automatically handled by PHP. For example, in Windows, if you have a PHP directory, that might look something like this:

`session.save_path "\PHP"`

That's it; we're set to use sessions. We'll put them to work starting in the next chunk.

Storing Session Data

You use the $_SESSION array to store data in a session. This array is a global variable just like $_POST, $_GET, and $_REQUEST. Note that you must start your session using session_start before you can use $_SESSION.

Here's an example, where we'll use session_start and then store some data in the session under the name temperature, setting it to 72:

```php
<?php
    session_start();
    $_SESSION['temperature'] = "72";
?>
```

After storing that data in a session, we'll let the user move to another page, phpsession2.php, before recovering that data, so we'll also include a hyperlink to phpsession2.php in phpsession.php, as you can see in Example 9-12.

EXAMPLE 9-12   Storing data in a session, phpsession.php

```html
<HTML>
    <HEAD><TITLE>Storing data in sessions</TITLE></HEAD>

    <BODY><CENTER>
        <H1>
            Storing data in sessions
        </H1>

        <?php
            session_start();
            $_SESSION['temperature'] = "72";
        ?>

        Stored the temperature as 72 degrees.
        <BR>
        To read the temperature in a new page, <a href="phpsession2.php">
            click here</a>.
    </CENTER><BODY>
</HTML>
```

You can see this page at work in Figure 9-11, where we've stored the data in the session.

FIGURE 9-11 Storing data.

If the user navigates to phpsession2.php, Example 9-13, before the session expires, we'll be able to recover the stored data and display it. You can see the retrieved data displayed in phpsession2.php, Figure 9-12. Cool.

EXAMPLE 9-13 Retrieving data in a session, phpsession2.php

```
<HTML>
    <HEAD>
        <TITLE>
            Retrieving data in sessions
        </TITLE>
    </HEAD>
    <BODY>
        <CENTER>
            <H1>
                Retrieving data in sessions
            </H1>

            <?php
                session_start();

                if(isset($_SESSION["temperature"])){
                    echo "Welcome. The temperature is " .
                    $_SESSION['temperature'];
                }
            ?>
        </CENTER>
    <BODY>
</HTML>
```

FIGURE 9-12 Retrieving data.

Creating a Hit Counter

Here's an example that points out the advantages of using sessions. Say you want to create a hit counter that keeps track of the number of times a user has visited a specific page. If you try to simply increment a variable, $count, as shown in phpcounter.php, Example 9-14, there will be a problem because the data in that variable is not preserved between page accesses.

EXAMPLE 9-14   Hit counter first try, phpcounter.php

```
<HTML>
    <HEAD>
        <TITLE>
            A hit counter
        </TITLE>
    </HEAD>
    <BODY>
        <CENTER>
            <H1>
                A hit counter
            </H1>
            Welcome. You've been here
            <?php
                $count++;

                echo $count ;
            ?>
            times before.
        </CENTER>
    <BODY>
</HTML>
```

As shown in Figure 9-13, no matter how many times you load the page, the counter will always be reset (and you'll get a notice about incrementing an undefined variable).

FIGURE 9-13   First attempt at a hit counter.

The solution is to store the count in a session, as you see in Example 9-15.

EXAMPLE 9-15 Corrected hit counter, phpcounter.php

```
<HTML>
    <HEAD>
        <TITLE>
            A hit counter
        </TITLE>
    </HEAD>
    <BODY>
        <CENTER>
            <H1>
                A hit counter
            </H1>
            Welcome. You've been here
            <?php
                session_start();
                if (!isset($_SESSION['count'])) {
                    $_SESSION['count'] = 0;
                } else {
                    $_SESSION['count']++;
                }
                echo $_SESSION['count'];
            ?>
            times before.
        </CENTER>
    <BODY>
</HTML>
```

You can see the final working version in Figure 9-14. Nice.

FIGURE 9-14 The working hit counter.

Using Sessions Without Cookies

PHP stores a user's session ID in a cookie, so it can determine which set of session data it should load as needed. But what if the user has cookies turned off? In that case, PHP can try to encode the session ID in all URLs accessed by the user. To enable that capability, set the session.use_trans_sid item in php.ini to 1 (you can also specify that PHP use only cookies for session IDs by enabling session.use_only_cookies):

```
; trans sid support is disabled by default.
; Use of trans sid may risk your users security.
; Use this option with caution.
; - User may send URL contains active session ID
;   to other person via. email/irc/etc.
; - URL that contains active session ID may be stored
;   in publically accessible computer.
; - User may access your site with the same session ID
;   always using URL stored in browser's history or bookmarks.
session.use_trans_sid = 0
```

This way, the user's URLs will look something like this:

```
script.php?PHPSESSID=322fe03120041e6c5285480a4fbf1037
```

This item, session.use_trans_sid, is turned off by default because explicitly listing the session ID like this is a security problem. So what if the user has cookies turned off and session.use_trans_sid is turned off too? In that case, you can explicitly pass the session ID to other pages yourself. You do that by storing the session ID, which you can get with the function session_id, in a hidden variable named PHPSESSID, as shown in phpsession-nocookies.php, Example 9-16.

EXAMPLE 9-16 Passing session ID without cookies, phpsessionnocookies.php

```
<HTML>
    <HEAD>
        <TITLE>Storing data in sessions without cookies</TITLE>
    </HEAD>
    <BODY>
        <CENTER>
            <H1>Storing data in sessions without cookies</H1>
            <?php
                session_start();
                $_SESSION['temperature'] = "72";
            ?>
            Stored the temperature as 72 degrees.
            <BR>
            To read the temperature in a new page, click Submit.
            <BR>
```

continues

EXAMPLE 9-16 continued

```
                <FORM ACTION="phpsession2.php" METHOD="POST">
                    <INPUT TYPE="HIDDEN" NAME="PHPSESSID" VALUE="
                    <?php
                        echo session_id();
                    ?>
                    ">
                    <INPUT TYPE='SUBMIT' VALUE='Submit'>
                </FORM>
            </CENTER>
        <BODY>
</HTML>
```

You can see this page at work in Figure 9-15.

FIGURE 9-15 Handling sessions without cookies.

No further programming is needed to pick up the session ID in the target page, phpsession2.php, which is unchanged from Example 9-13. You can see the successful results in Figure 9-16. Nice.

FIGURE 9-16 Using session data without cookies.

Removing Data in Sessions

Want to remove some data that you've stored in a session? In that case, you can use the unset function. Here's an example; say that you've stored the temperature as 72 in a session using a data item named temperature, as you see in phpsessionunset.php:

```
<H1>Removing data from sessions</H1>
<?php
    session_start();
    $_SESSION['temperature'] = "72";
?>
Stored the temperature as 72 degrees.
<BR>
To read the temperature in a new page, <a href="phpsession2.php">
    click here</a>.
```

You can see what this page looks like in Figure 9-17.

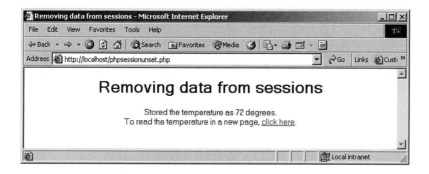

FIGURE 9-17   Removing data from sessions.

This page links to phpsessionunset2.php, where we'll unset the temperature item:

```
Removing the "temperature" item....<BR>
<?php
    session_start();
    unset($_SESSION["temperature"]);
?>
To continue, <a href="phpsessionunset3.php">click here</a>.
```

You can see what this page looks like in Figure 9-18.

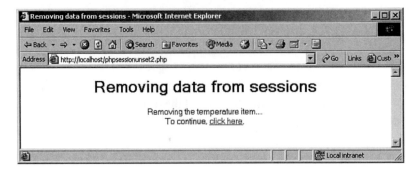

FIGURE 9-18 Removing an item.

Finally, in the linked-to page, phpsessionunset3.php, we'll search for the `temperature` item:

```
<H1>Removing data from sessions</H1>
Looking for the temperature item...<BR>
<?php
    session_start();
    if(isset($_SESSION["temperature"])){
        echo "The temperature is " . $_SESSION["temperature"];
    }
    else {
        echo "Can't find the temperature item.";}
?>
```

You can see the results in Figure 9-19—as expected, the `temperature` item has indeed been removed. Perfect.

FIGURE 9-19 The item was removed.

That completes our work with sessions—and that completes our book. We've come far in this book, from the very beginning up to some advanced techniques. PHP gives you outstanding power, and I hope you enjoy working and playing with it as much as I do—all that's left is to put it all to use for yourself!

Summary

This chapter covered a number of very powerful PHP techniques: cookies, sessions, FTP, email, and more. These are all advanced PHP techniques that can really beef up your PHP arsenal. Here are some of this chapter's salient points:

- You can set a cookie with the setcookie function.

- To check if a cookie has been set, use the isset function.

- To recover the data in a cookie, use the $_COOKIE array with the cookie name, like this: $_COOKIE['message'].

- To connect to an FTP server, you use ftp_connect.

- After you connect with ftp_connect, you log in with ftp_login.

- There are many FTP functions in PHP, such as ftp_nlist to get a directory listing, ftp_chdir to change directories, ftp_get to get a file, ftp_put to upload a file, and so on.

- To enable email, you need to edit php.ini.

- To actually send email, use the mail function.

- You can start a session with the session_start function to preserve user data.

- To store data in the session, you use the $_SESSION array.

PHP Language Elements

Creating Scripts

```
<?php
    .
    .
    .
?>
```

You usually surround a PHP script with the markup <?php...?>, which tells a PHP-enabled server that you're going to be using PHP. A number of keywords, which appear in Table A-1, are reserved for PHP's own use.

TABLE A-1   PHP Keywords

__CLASS__	__FILE__	__FUNCTION__	__LINE__	__METHOD__
and	default	endif	global	print
array	die	endswitch	if	require
as	do	endwhile	include	require_once
break	echo	eval	include_once	return
case	else	exception	isset	static
cfunction	elseif	exit	list	switch
class	empty	extends	new	unset
const	enddeclare	for	old_function	use
continue	endfor	foreach	or	while
declare	endforeach	function	php_user_filter	xor

Scripts are composed of PHP statements, which end with a semicolon in PHP, unless they're compound statements surrounded with curly braces, { and }. Here's an example of both:

```
<?php
    if ($test) {
        echo "No worries.";
    }
?>
```

You can also interleave PHP with HTML; here's an example:

```
<?php
    if ($test) {
?>
    <b>No worries.</b>
<?php
    } else {
?>
    <b>Could be a problem.</b>
<?php
    }
?>
```

Data Types

Data items are apparently untyped in PHP because you don't have to declare types of variables, but behind the scenes, data types are important because mixing them or going beyond their allowed bounds can cause problems.

Booleans are the simplest built-in PHP data type; booleans express a truth value, which can be either TRUE or FALSE.

Integers hold a number from in the range {...-3, -2, -1, 0, 1, 2, 3 ...}. Integers can be given in decimal (base 10), hexadecimal (base 16), or octal (base 8) notation and can include a sign (- or +). If you use the octal notation, you must precede the number with a 0 (zero); to use hexadecimal notation, you must precede the number with 0x.

Here are a few examples:

```
234
-234
0123 An octal integer
0x1A A hexadecimal integer
```

Floating point numbers hold floating point values. The size of a float is platform-dependent, although a maximum of about 1.8e308 with a precision of roughly 14 decimal digits is common.

Here are some examples:

```
<?php
    $value1 = 1.234;
    $value2 = 1.23e4;
    $value3 = 1E-23;
?>
```

Strings are series of characters (in PHP, a character is the same as a byte). PHP imposes no practical bound to the size of strings. Strings can be specified in three different ways:

- single quoted
- double quoted
- Using "heredoc" syntax

The easiest way to specify a string is to enclose it in single quotes, which just stores text in a string:

```php
<?php
    echo 'No worries.';
    echo 'Some multi-line
        text looks
        like this.';
?>
```

If you enclose a string in double quotes, PHP can interpret more escape sequences for special characters:

\n	Linefeed (LF or 0x0A (10) in ASCII)
\r	Carriage return (CR or 0x0D (13) in ASCII)
\t	Horizontal tab (HT or 0x09 (9) in ASCII)
\\	Backslash
\$	Dollar sign
\"	Double-quote

The values in variables can be *interpolated* if you put them into double-quoted (not single-quoted) strings, which means that their values are inserted directly into the string. You can do that like this:

```php
$value = 1;
echo "The number is $value.";
```

This example prints out "The number is 1."

Another way to delimit strings is by using heredoc syntax ("<<<"). You need to provide an identifier after <<<, then the string, and then the same identifier to end (note that the closing identifier must begin in the first column). Here's an example:

```php
echo <<<END
This example uses
"here document" syntax to display all
the text until the ending token is reached.
END;
```

Creating Variables

Variables in PHP are represented by a dollar sign followed by the name of the variable, which is case-sensitive. Variable names follow the same rules as other labels in PHP: a valid variable name starts with a letter or underscore, followed by any number of letters, numbers, or underscores.

Here's an example where we're creating two variables by assigning values to them:

```php
<?php
    $variable = 5;
    $another_variable = $variable;
?>
```

By default, PHP variables are assigned by value—when you assign an expression to a variable, the entire value of the original expression is copied into the destination variable. This means, for example, that after assigning one variable's value to another, changing one of those variables will have no effect on the other. You can also assign values to variables by reference. This means that the new variable references the original variable, so changes to the new variable affect the original (note that this also means that no copying is performed).

To assign by reference, simply prepend an ampersand (&) to the variable being assigned. Here's an example:

```php
<?php
    $variable = 5;
    $new_variable = &$variable;
    $variable = 6;     // Alters both $variable and $new_variable
?>
```

Predefined Variables

PHP provides a large number of predefined variables to any script that it runs. These variables are superglobals, which are available anywhere in a script. Here's a list of the primary ones:

- $_GLOBALS. Contains every variable that is currently available within the global scope of the script. The keys of this array are the names of the global variables.

- $_SERVER. Variables set by the web server or otherwise directly related to the execution environment of the current script.

- $_GET. Variables provided to the script via HTTP GET.

- $_POST. Variables provided to the script via HTTP POST.

- $_COOKIE. Variables provided to the script via HTTP cookies.

- $_FILES. Variables provided to the script via HTTP POST file uploads.

- $_ENV. Variables provided to the script via the environment.

- **$_REQUEST.** Variables provided to the script via the GET, POST, and COOKIE input mechanisms.

- **$_SESSION.** Variables that are currently registered to a script's session.

Arrays

```
$array[index] = value;
$array = array(value1, value2);
$array = array(key1 => value1, key2 => value2);
```

Arrays are indexed collections of data items, starting by default with an index of 0. You can create arrays by assigning data to them, and you can give arrays the same names as you give to standard variables. Like variable names, array names begin with a $. PHP knows you're working with an array if you include [] after the name, like this:

```
$array[1] = "No worries.";
```

This creates an array named $array and sets the element at index 1 to "No worries.". From now on, you can refer to this element as you would any simple variable—you just include the index value to make sure you reference the data you want, like this:

```
echo $array[1];
```

This statement would echo "No worries.". This example stored a string using a numeric index, but you can also use string indexes. Here's an example of using string indexes:

```
$data["Ralph"] = 123;
$data["Tom"] = 567;
$data["Ted"] = 980;
```

You can now refer to the values in this array by string, as $data["Ralph"], and so on.

You can also use a shortcut for creating arrays—you can simply use [] after the array's name, and PHP increments the array's index as you add new elements; the created index values will be numeric. Here's an example:

```
$data[] = 123;
$data[] = "Hello";
$data[] = "Good day";
```

In this case, $data[0] will hold 123, $data[1] will hold "Hello", and $data[2] will hold "Good day".

Here's an even shorter shortcut for creating an array, using the PHP array function:

```
$data = array(123, "Hello", "Good day");
```

This creates the same array, starting from an index value of 0. If you wanted to start with an index value of 1, you could use the => operator like this:

```
$data = array(1 => 123, "Hello", "Good day");
```

Now the array would look like this:

```
$data[1] = 123;
$data[2] = "Hello";
$data[3] = "Good day";
```

Operators

PHP comes with a number of operators for working on your data, and they appear in Table A-1.

TABLE A-2   Operators in Descending Order of Precedence

Operators
new
[
! ~ ++ -- (int) (float) (string) (array) (object)
@
* / %
+ - .
<< >>
< <= > >=
== != === !==
&
^
|
&&
||
? :
= += -= *= /= .= %= &= |= ^= <<= >>=
print
and
xor
or
,

For example, here are the PHP math operators:

- +   Adds two numbers

- -   Subtracts one number from another

* Multiplies two numbers together

/ Divides one number by another

% Returns the remainder when one number is divided by another (modulus)

You can see them all at work in this example:

```
<HTML>
    <BODY>
        <H1>Using the PHP math operators</H1>
        <?php
            echo "9 + 4 = ", 9 + 4;
            echo "9 - 4 = ", 9 - 4;
            echo "9 * 4 = ", 9 * 4;
            echo "9 / 4 = ", 9 / 4;
            echo "9 % 4 = ", 9 % 4;
        ?>
    </BODY>
</HTML>
```

Operator precedence is also an issue—if you evaluate this statement, what would be the result?

```
<?php
    echo 4 + 2 * 9;
?>
```

Will this be 4 + 2 * 9 = 6 * 9 = 54, or will the * be evaluated first, giving 4 + 2 * 9 = 4 + 18 = 22? In this case, you get 22 because the * operator has precedence over the + operator when you mix them up. Operator precedence, from highest to lowest, is shown in Table A-2.

You can always use parentheses to tell PHP what to do if you're unsure about precedence. If you change this expression to (4 + 2) * 9, then you'll get 6 * 9 = 54:

```
<?php
    echo "4 + 2 * 9 = ", 4 + 2 * 9;
    echo "(4 + 2) * 9", (4 + 2) * 9;
    echo "4 + (2 * 9)", 4 + (2 * 9);
?>
```

Here, you'd get 22, 54, and 22.

The *if* statement

```
if (expr)
    statement
```

The if statement is one of the most important statements in PHP because it allows for conditional execution of code fragments. Here, *expr* is evaluated, and if it evaluates to TRUE, PHP will execute *statement*, whereas if *expr* evaluates to FALSE, PHP will ignore *statement*.

Sometimes you will want to execute more than a single statement conditionally. In that case, you can group several statements into a compound statement. For example, this code displays a message if $value1 is bigger than $value2 and, if so, swaps the values:

```php
<?php

if ($value1 > $value2) {
    echo "$value1 is bigger than $value2\n";
    echo "Swapping the values.";
    $temp = $value1;
    $value1 = $value2;
    $value2 = $value1;
}
?>
```

The *else* Statement

```
if (expr)
    statement
else
    other_statement
```

Sometimes you will want to execute a statement if a certain condition is true, but a different statement otherwise. That's what else does; it extends an if statement to execute a different statement in case the condition in the if expression evaluates to FALSE.

For example, this code indicates which is bigger, $value1 or $value2:

```php
<?php
    if ($value1 > $value2) {
        echo "$value1 is larger than $value2";
    } else {
        echo "$value1 is not larger than $value2";
    }
?>
```

The else statement is only executed if the if condition evaluates to FALSE.

The *elseif* Statement

```
if (expr)
    statement0
elseif
    statement1

        .

        .

        .

elseif
    statementN-1
else
    statementN
```

The elseif statement works much like if and else together. Like else, it extends an if statement to execute a different statement in case the original if expression evaluates to FALSE. But unlike else, elseif will execute that alternative expression only if the elseif conditional expression evaluates to TRUE.

For example, this displays various messages depending on whether $value1 is larger than $value2, equal to $value2, or less than $value2:

```php
<?php
    if ($value1 > $value2) {
        echo "$value1 is larger than $value2";
    } elseif ($$value1 == $value2) {
        echo "$value1 is equal to $value2";
    } else {
        echo "$value1 is less than $value2";
    }
?>
```

You can use several elseifs in the same if statement. Note that in PHP, you can also write "else if" (two words).

The *switch* Statement

```php
switch ($expr) {
    case test1:
        statement1
        break;
    case test2:
        statement2
        break;
    case test3:
        statement3
        break;
    default:
        statement4
    }
```

The switch statement is much like a series of successive if statements using the same expression. The idea is to compare the same expression with many different test values, executing different code depending on which test value it matches.

For example, here's how you might test the value in $expr using a ladder of if and elseif statements:

```php
<?php
    if ($expr == 1) {
        echo "Expr is 1";
    } elseif ($expr == 1) {
        echo "Expr is 2";
    } elseif ($expr == 3) {
        echo "Expr is 3";
    }
?>
```

And here's how this would look as a `switch` statement:

```
switch ($expr) {
case 1:
    echo "Expr is 1";
    break;
case 2:
    echo "Expr is 2";
    break;
case 3:
    echo "Expr is 3";
    break;
}
```

When a case statement is found with a value that matches the value of the `switch` expression, PHP continues to execute the statements until the end of the `switch` block, or until it encounters a `break` statement. If you don't write a `break` statement at the end of a `case` statement, PHP will go on executing the statements of the following case(s). For example, take a look at this `switch` statement:

```
switch ($expr) {
case 1:
    echo "Expr is 1";
case 2:
    echo "Expr is 2";
case 3:
    echo "Expr is 3";
}
```

If $expr is 1, PHP will execute all of the echo statements.

You can also use the `default` keyword, which will match anything that wasn't matched by the other cases. If you use it, the `default` statement should be the last `case` statement because no case statement after it will be executed. Here's an example:

```
switch ($expr) {
case 1:
    echo "Expr is 1";
case 2:
    echo "Expr is 2";
case 3:
    echo "Expr is 3";
default:
    echo "Sorry, expr didn't match 1, 2, or 3.";
}
```

This `switch` statement works just as this `if` statement does:

```
<?php
    if ($expr == 1) {
        echo "Expr is 1";
    } elseif ($expr == 1) {
```

```
        echo "Expr is 2";
    } elseif ($expr == 3) {
        echo "Expr is 3";
    } else {
        echo "Sorry, expr didn't match 1, 2, or 3.";
    }
?>
```

The *while* Statement

```
while (expr) statement
```

The while loop is the simplest type of loop in PHP. It tells PHP to execute *statement* (which could be a compound statement) repeatedly, as long as *expr* evaluates to TRUE. The value of the expression is checked each time at the beginning of the loop, so even if this value changes during the execution of the nested statement, execution will not stop until the end of the iteration. If the while expression evaluates to FALSE from the very beginning, the nested statement won't even be run once.

As with the if statement, you can group multiple statements within the same while loop by surrounding a group of statements with curly braces:

```
<?php
    $loop_index = 1;
    while ($loop_index <= 10) {
        echo $loop_index++;
    }
?>
```

This example uses a loop index, $loop_index, but you don't have to use a loop index at all in a while loop. For example, some PHP functions, such as feof (which returns TRUE when you're at the end of a file), are designed to be used in while loops. Here's an example:

```
<?php
    $handle = fopen("file.txt", "r");
    while (!feof($handle)){
        $text = fgets($handle);
        echo $text, "<BR>";
    }
?>
```

The *do...while* Statement

```
do {
    statement
} while (expr);
```

The PHP do...while loop is very similar to the while loop, except that *expr* is checked at the end of each iteration instead of at the beginning. Thus, compared to standard while loops, the first iteration of a do...while loop will always run, which is not necessarily true for a while loop (because it depends on the while loop's expression).

Here's an example of using a while loop where the loop condition is false from the very beginning, so this script doesn't echo anything:

```php
<?php
    $value =10;
    while ($value < 5){
        $value += 2;
        echo $value, "<BR>";
    }
?>
```

However, in a do...while loop, the condition is tested at the end, so this script does echo 12 in a browser:

```php
<?php
    $value = 10;
    do{
        echo $value, "<BR>";
        $value += 2;
    } while ($value < 5);
?>
```

The *for* Statement

```
for (expr1; expr2; expr3) statement
```

The for loop is the most involved loop in PHP. In this statement, the first expression, *expr1*, is evaluated once at the beginning of the loop. The continuation expression, *expr2*, is evaluated at the beginning of each iteration. If it evaluates to TRUE, the loop iterates again, and the nested statement(s) are executed. If it evaluates to FALSE, the loop ends. At the end of each iteration, *expr3* is executed, which usually increments a loop counter variable that will be tested in *expr2*.

Here's an example, where the for loop will display text twenty times:

```php
<?php
    for ($loop_counter = 0; $loop_counter < 20; $loop_counter++){
        echo "This will print twenty times.<BR>";
    }
?>
```

In fact, you can reduce this loop to the following script, where the for loop has no body at all:

```php
<?php
    for ($loop_counter = 0; $loop_counter < 20; echo "This will print twenty
        times.<BR>", $loop_counter++);
?>
```

The *foreach* Statement

```
foreach (array_expression as $value) statement
foreach (array_expression as $key => $value) statement
```

The PHP foreach statement gives you an easy way to iterate over arrays. This statement works only on arrays (you'll get an error when you try to use it on anything else).

The first form of this loop as shown here loops over the array given by *array_expression*. In each iteration, the value of the current element in the array is automatically assigned to *$value,* and the loop moves on to the next element.

The second form of this loop does the same thing, except that the current element's key will also be assigned to the variable *$key* in each iteration.

Here's an example:

```php
<?php
    $array = array("grapes", "grapefruit", "bananas");

    foreach ($array as $value) {
        echo "The current value is $value\n";
    }
?>
```

If you prefer, you can also display the key during each iteration:

```php
<?php
    $array = array("grapes", "grapefruit", "bananas");

    foreach ($array as $key => $value) {
        echo "The current key is $key and the current value is $value\n";
    }
?>
```

Creating Functions

```
function function_name([$arg1 [, $arg2, ..., [$argN]]])
{
    [statement]
    [return $return_value;]
}
```

Functions are groups of statements that act together; you can call functions and pass data to them, and they can return results to you. Any valid PHP code can be placed inside a function, including other functions and PHP class definitions.

Here's an example:

```
function echoer()
{
    echo "No worries.";
}
```

When called, this function echoes "No worries.". Here's how you call it from other code:

```
echoer();
```

You can also pass data to functions as arguments by enclosing them inside parentheses. Here's an example that passes an array to a function, which just echoes the contents of the array:

```php
<?php
    $vegetables[0] = "corn";
    $vegetables[1] = "squash";
    $vegetables[2] = "cauliflower";
    $vegetables[3] = "beans";

    echoer($vegetables);

    function echoer($array)
    {
        for ($index = 0; $index < count($array); $index++){
            echo "Element $index: ", $array[$index], "\n";
        }
    }
?>
```

Here's what you'd see:

```
Element 0: corn
Element 1: squash
Element 2: cauliflower
Element 3: beans
```

To return a value from a function, you use the return statement:

```
return (value);
```

The parentheses are optional. For instance, this function increments the value you pass to it and returns the result:

```php
<?php
    function incrementer($value)
    {
        return ++$value;
    }
?>
```

Here's how you could call this function and handle its return value:

```php
<?php
    echo incrementer(9);

    function incrementer($value)
    {
        return ++$value;
    }
?>
```

Classes and Objects

```
[access_modifier] class
{
    [access_modifier] var variable;
        .
        .
        .

    [access_modifier] function function_name (arg1, arg2, ... argN)
    {
        statement
    }
        .
        .
        .

}
```

A class is a collection of variables and functions—in OOP terms, properties and methods. A class is a type, and you create objects of that type and store them in PHP variables.

Here's an example, the Person class, which stores the name of a person with the set_name method and returns that name with the get_name method.

```
class Person
{
    var $name;

    function set_name($text)
    {
        $this->name = $text;
    }

    function get_name()
    {
        return $this->name;
    }
}
```

You can use the new statement to create an object of a class. You don't have to use the new statement when creating simple variables of the built-in types, such as integer or float, but you do when you want to create a variable that holds an object of a class.

For example, to create an object of the Person class in a variable named $doug, you'd do this:

```
<?php
    class Person
    {
        var $name;

        function set_name($text)
        {
```

```
            $this->name = $text;
        }

        function get_name()
        {
            return $this->name;
        }
    }

    $doug = new Person;
?>
```

At this point, you've got an object of the Person class. You can access the methods of the Person class using the arrow operator, like this, where we're setting the name of the person to Douglas:

```
$doug = new Person;
$doug->set_name("Douglas");
            .
            .
            .
```

To access that name, you can use the get_name method:

```
$doug = new Person;
$doug->set_name("Douglas");
echo "The person's name is ", $doug->get_name(), ".";
```

When you run this code, you get:

```
The person's name is Douglas.
```

By default, you can also access properties using the -> operator. Here's an example:

```
<?php
    class Person
    {
        var $name;

        function set_name($text)
        {
            $this->name = $text;
        }

        function get_name()
        {
            return $this->name;
        }
    }

    $doug = new Person;
    echo "The person's name is ", $doug->name, ".";
?>
```

You can access the methods and properties of an object by default, but sometimes that's not a good idea. You might want to have an accessor method that restricts access, like this example, which restricts the values you can assign to the name property:

```
function set_name($text)
{
    if (strlen($text) <= 128){
        $this->name = $text;
    }
}
```

You can also make the properties and methods *private* to the Animal class with the PHP access modifiers:

- public. Means "Accessible to all"

- private. Means "Accessible in the same class"

- protected. Means "Accessible in the same class and classes derived from that class"

By default, all methods and properties are public, so there's no restriction on accessing them from outside an object. If you declare the name property as private, that property can't be accessed from code outside the class itself. Here's how you use it:

```
<?php
    class Person
    {
        private $name;

        function set_name($text)
        {
            $this->name = $text;
        }

        function get_name()
        {
            return $this->name;
        }
    }

    $doug = new Person;
    echo "The person's name is ", $doug->name, ".";     // Will not work.
?>
```

Here's what you'd see:

```
The person's name is PHP Fatal error:  Cannot access private property Person::$name
in lion.php
```

You can also make methods private as well:

```
class Person
{
    var $name;

    private function set_name($text)
    {
        $this->name = $text;
    }

    function get_name()
    {
        return $this->name;
    }
}
```

In this case, you can't access set_name outside an object of this class.

PHP Function Reference

This appendix details the most commonly used PHP functions—the array, file, and string functions.

TABLE B-1 The PHP Array Functions

Function	Does This
array array_change_key_case (array input [, int case])	Changes case of an array's string keys
array array_chunk(array input, int size [, bool preserve_keys])	Divides an array into chunks
array array_combine(array keys, array values)	Makes an array
array array_count_values (array input)	Counts the values of an array
array array_diff_assoc(array array1, array array2 [, array ...])	Returns the difference of two associative arrays
array array_diff_assoc(array array1, array array2 [, array ..., callback key_compare_func])	Returns the difference of arrays with additional index check, performed by a call back function
array array_diff(array array1, array array2 [, array ...])	Returns the difference of two arrays
array array_fill(int start_index, int num, mixed value)	Fills an array with values
array array_filter(array input [, callback callback])	Filters elements of an array using a callback function
array array_flip(array trans)	Exchanges keys with their values in an array
array array_intersect_assoc(array array1, array array2 [, array ...])	Returns the intersection of arrays with additional index check
array array_intersect(array array1, array array2 [, array ...])	Returns the simple intersection of arrays
bool array_key_exists(mixed key, array search)	Checks if the specified key or index exists in the array

TABLE B-1 continued

Function	Does This
array array_keys(array input [, mixed search_value])	Return the keys of an array
array array_map(mixed callback, array arr1 [, array ...])	Applies the callback function to the elements of the arrays
array array_merge_recursive(array array1, array array2 [, array ...])	Merges two or more arrays recursively
array array_merge(array array1, array array2 [, array ...])	Merges two or more arrays simply
bool array_multisort(array ar1 [, mixed arg [, mixed ... [, array ...]]])	Sorts multi-dimensional arrays
array array_pad(array input, int pad_size, mixed pad_value)	Pads array to the given length with a value
mixed array_pop(array array)	Pops an element from the end of an array
int array_push(array array, mixed var [, mixed ...])	Pushes elements onto the end of array
mixed array_rand(array input [, int num_req])	Picks random entries out of an array
mixed array_reduce(array input, callback function [, int initial])	Iteratively reduces the array to a single value using a callback function
array array_reverse(array array [, bool preserve_keys])	Returns array with elements in reverse order
mixed array_search(mixed needle, array haystack [, bool strict])	Searches the array for a specified value; returns the key if successful
mixed array_shift(array array)	Shifts an element off the beginning of array
array array_slice(array array, int offset [, int length])	Extracts a slice of an array
array array_splice(array input, int offset [, int length [, array replacement]])	Removes a part of the array and replaces it
mixed array_sum(array array)	Returns the sum of values in an array
array array_udiff_assoc(array array1, array array2 [, array ..., callback data_compare_func])	Returns the difference of arrays with additional index check; uses a callback function
array array_udiff_uassoc(array array1, array array2 [, array ..., callback data_compare_func, callback key_compare_func])	Returns the difference of arrays with additional index check
array array_udiff(array array1, array array2 [, array ..., callback data_compare_func])	Returns the difference of arrays, using a call back function for comparison

Function	Does This
array array_unique(array array)	Removes duplicate values from an array
int array_unshift(array array, mixed var [, mixed ...])	Prepends elements to the beginning of an array
array array_values(array input)	Returns the values of an array
bool array_walk(array array, callback function [, mixed userdata])	Calls a function on every member of an array
array array([mixed ...])	Makes an array
bool arsort(array array [, int sort_flags])	Sorts an array in reverse order while maintaining index association
bool asort(array array [, int sort_flags])	Sorts an array while maintaining index association
array compact(mixed varname [, mixed ...])	Compacts an array
int count(mixed var [, int mode])	Counts elements in a variable
mixed current(array array)	Returns the current element in an array
array each(array array)	Returns the current key and value pair from an array
mixed end(array array)	Move the internal pointer of an array to the last element
int extract(array var_array [, int extract_type [, string prefix]])	Imports variables into the symbol table from an array
bool in_array(mixed needle, array haystack [, bool strict])	Checks if a value exists in an array
mixed key(array array)	Gets a key from an associative array
bool krsort(array array [, int sort_flags])	Sorts an array by key in reverse order
bool ksort(array array [, int sort_flags])	Sorts an array by key
void list(mixed ...)	Assigns variables as if they were an array
void natcasesort(array array)	Sorts an array using a case-insensitive "natural sort"
void natsort(array array)	Sorts an array using a "natural sort" algorithm
mixed next(array array)	Advances the internal array pointer of an array
mixed pos(array array)	Same as current()
mixed prev(array array)	Moves the internal array pointer back one element
array range(int low, int high [, int step])	Makes an array containing a range of elements
mixed reset(array array)	Sets the internal pointer of an array to the first element

TABLE B-1 continued

Function	Does This
`bool rsort(array array [, int sort_flags])`	Sorts an array in reverse order
`void shuffle(array array)`	Shuffles an array
`int sizeof(mixed var [, int mode])`	Same as count()
`bool sort(array array [, int sort_flags])`	Sorts an array
`bool uasort(array array, callback cmp_function)`	Sorts an array with a user-defined comparison function while maintaining index association
`bool uksort(array array, callback cmp_function)`	Sorts an array by keys using a comparison function
`bool usort(array array, callback cmp_function)`	Sorts an array by values using a comparison function

TABLE B-2 The PHP File Functions

Function	Does This
`string basename(string path [, string suffix])`	Returns the filename part of a path
`bool chgrp(string filename, mixed group)`	Changes a file's group
`bool chown(string filename, mixed user)`	Changes a file's owner
`void clearstatcache(void)`	Clears a file's file status cache
`bool copy(string source, string dest)`	Copies a file
`void delete(string file)`	Deletes a file
`string dirname(string path)`	Returns the directory name part of a path
`float disk_free_space(string directory)`	Returns available space in directory
`float disk_total_space(string directory)`	Returns the total size of a directory
`float diskfreespace(string directory)`	Same as disk_free_space()
`bool fclose(resource handle)`	Closes an open file
`bool feof(resource handle)`	Tests for end-of-file on a file
`bool fflush(resource handle)`	Flushes the output to a file
`string fgetc(resource handle)`	Gets a character from file
`array fgetcsv(resource handle, int length [, string delimiter [, string enclosure]])`	Gets a line from file and parses for CSV fields
`string fgets(resource handle [, int length])`	Gets a line from a file
`string fgetss(resource handle, int length [, string allowable_tags])`	Gets a line from file and strips HTML tags
`bool file_exists(string filename)`	Checks whether a file or directory exists
`string file_get_contents(string filename [, bool use_include_path [, resource context]])`	Reads entire file into a string

Function	Does This
int file_put_contents(string filename, string data [, int flags [, resource context]])	Writes a string to a file
array file(string filename [, int use_include_path [, resource context]])	Reads an entire file into an array
int fileatime(string filename)	Gets the last access time of a file
int filectime(string filename)	Gets the change time of a file
int filegroup(string filename)	Gets a file group
int fileinode(string filename)	Gets a file inode
int filemtime(string filename)	Gets a file's modification time
int fileowner(string filename)	Gets a file's owner
int fileperms(string filename)	Gets a file's permissions
int filesize(string filename)	Gets a file size
string filetype(string filename)	Gets a file type
bool flock(resource handle, int operation [, int &wouldblock])	Sets advisory file locking
array fnmatch(string pattern, string string [, int flags])	Matches a filename against a pattern
resource fopen(string filename, string mode [, int use_include_path [, resource zcontext]])	Opens a file or URL
int fpassthru(resource handle)	Outputs all remaining data on a file
int fputs(resource handle, string string [, int length])	Same as fwrite()
string fread(resource handle, int length)	Binary-safe file read
mixed fscanf(resource handle, string format [, string var1])	Parses input from a file according to a format
int fseek(resource handle, int offset [, int whence])	Seeks in a file
array fstat(resource handle)	Gets information about a file
int ftell(resource handle)	Returns the file read/write position
bool ftruncate(resource handle, int size)	Truncates a file to a specified length
int fwrite(resource handle, string string [, int length])	Binary-safe file write
array glob(string pattern [, int flags])	Return pathnames matching a pattern
bool is_dir(string filename)	Returns whether the filename is a directory
bool is_executable(string filename)	Returns whether the filename is executable
bool is_file(string filename)	Returns whether the filename is a regular file
bool is_link(string filename)	Returns whether the filename is a symbolic link

Function	Does This
`bool is_readable(string filename)`	Returns whether the filename is readable
`bool is_uploaded_file(string filename)`	Returns whether the file was uploaded using HTTP POST
`bool is_writable(string filename)`	Returns whether the filename is writable
`bool is_writeable(string filename)`	Same as is_writable()
`bool link(string target, string link)`	Makes a hard link
`int linkinfo(string path)`	Returns information about a link
`array lstat(string filename)`	Returns information about a file or symbolic link
`bool mkdir(string pathname [, int mode [, bool recursive [, resource context]]])`	Makes a directory
`bool move_uploaded_file(string filename, string destination)`	Moves an uploaded file to a new location
`array parse_ini_file(string filename [, bool process_sections])`	Parses a configuration file
`array pathinfo(string path)`	Returns information about a file path
`int pclose(resource handle)`	Closes a process file
`resource popen(string command, string mode)`	Opens a process file
`int readfile(string filename [, bool use_include_path [, resource context]])`	Outputs a file
`string readlink(string path)`	Returns the target of a symbolic link
`string realpath(string path)`	Returns an absolute pathname
`bool rename(string oldname, string newname [, resource context])`	Renames a file or directory
`bool rewind(resource handle)`	Rewinds the position of a file
`bool rmdir(string dirname [, resource context])`	Deletes a directory
`int set_file_buffer(resource stream, int buffer)`	Same as stream_set_write_buffer()
`array stat(string filename)`	Returns information about a file
`bool symlink(string target, string link)`	Makes a symbolic link
`string tempnam(string dir, string prefix)`	Makes a file with a unique file name
`resource tmpfile(void)`	Makes a temporary file
`bool touch(string filename [, int time [, int atime]])`	Sets access and modification time of file
`int umask([int mask])`	Changes the current umask
`bool unlink(string filename [, resource context])`	Deletes a file

TABLE B-3   The PHP String Functions

Function	Does This
`string addcslashes(string str, string charlist)`	Quotes a string with slashes using the C style
`string addslashes(string str)`	Quotes a string using slashes
`string bin2hex(string str)`	Converts binary data into hexadecimal
`string chop(string str [, string charlist])`	Same as `rtrim()`
`string chr(int ascii)`	Returns a specific character
`string chunk_split(string body [, int chunklen [, string end]])`	Divides a string into smaller chunks
`string convert_cyr_string(string str, string from, string to)`	Converts from one Cyrillic character set to another
`mixed count_chars(string string [, int mode])`	Returns information about characters used in a string
`int crc32(string str)`	Returns the crc32 polynomial of a string
`string crypt(string str [, string salt])`	Creates one-way string encryption
`void echo(string arg1 [, string argn...])`	Outputs one or more strings
`array explode(string separator, string string [, int limit])`	Divides a string using a string
`int fprintf(resource handle, string format [, mixed args])`	Writes a formatted string to a stream
`array get_html_translation_table(int table [, int quote_style])`	Returns the translation table that is used by `htmlspecialchars()` and `htmlentities()`
`string hebrev(string hebrew_text [, int max_chars_per_line])`	Converts logical Hebrew text to visual text
`string hebrevc(string hebrew_text [, int max_chars_per_line])`	Converts logical Hebrew text to visual text including newline conversion
`string html_entity_decode(string string [, int quote_style [, string charset]])`	Converts all HTML entities to their applicable characters
`string htmlentities(string string [, int quote_style [, string charset]])`	Converts all applicable characters to HTML entities
`string htmlspecialchars(string string [, int quote_style [, string charset]])`	Converts special characters to HTML entities
`string implode(string glue, array pieces)`	Joins array elements using a string
`string join(string glue, array pieces)`	Same as `implode()`
`int levenshtein(string str1, string str2)`	Returns the Levenshtein distance between two strings
`array localeconv(void)`	Gets numeric formatting data
`string ltrim(string str [, string charlist])`	Strips whitespace from the beginning of a string

TABLE B-3 continued

Function	Does This
`string md5_file(string filename [, bool raw_output])`	Returns the md5 hash of a specified filename
`string md5(string str [, bool raw_output])`	Returns the md5 hash of a string
`string metaphone(string str)`	Returns the metaphone key of a string
`string money_format(string format, float number)`	Formats a number as a currency string
`string nl_langinfo(int item)`	Queries language and locale information
`string nl2br(string string)`	Inserts HTML line breaks before all newlines in a string
`string number_format(float number [, int decimals])`	Formats a number with grouped thousands
`int ord(string string)`	Returns ASCII value of character
`void parse_str(string str [, array arr])`	Parses the string into variables
`int print(string arg)`	Outputs a string
`void printf(string format [, mixed args])`	Outputs a formatted string
`string quoted_printable_decode(string str)`	Converts a quoted-printable string to an 8-bit string
`string quotemeta(string str)`	Quotes meta characters
`string rtrim(string str [, string charlist])`	Strips whitespace from the end of a string
`string setlocale(mixed category, string locale [, string ...])`	Sets locale information
`string sha1_file(string filename [, bool raw_output])`	Returns the sha1 hash of a file
`string sha1(string str [, bool raw_output])`	Returns the sha1 hash of a string
`int similar_text(string first, string second [, float percent])`	Returns the similarity between two strings
`string soundex(string str)`	Returns the soundex key of a string
`string sprintf(string format [, mixed args])`	Returns a formatted string
`mixed sscanf(string str, string format [, string var1])`	Parses input from a string according to a format
`mixed str_ireplace(mixed search, mixed replace, mixed subject [, int &count])`	Case-insensitive version of `str_replace()`
`string str_pad(string input, int pad_length [, string pad_string [, int pad_type]])`	Pads a string to a certain length with another string
`string str_repeat(string input, int multiplier)`	Repeats a string
`mixed str_replace(mixed search, mixed replace, mixed subject [, int &count])`	Replaces all occurrences of the search string with the replacement string

Function	Does This
string str_rot13(string str)	Performs the rot13 transform on a string
string str_shuffle(string str)	Randomly shuffles a string
array str_split(string string [, int split_length])	Converts a string to an array
mixed str_word_count(string string [, int format])	Returns information about words used in a string
int strcasecmp(string str1, string str2)	Binary safe case-insensitive string comparison
string strchr(string haystack, string needle)	Same as strstr()
int strcmp(string str1, string str2)	Compares strings in a binary-safe way
int strcoll(string str1, string str2)	Compares strings in a locale-based way
int strcspn(string str1, string str2)	Returns length of initial segment not matching mask
string strip_tags(string str [, string allowable_tags])	Strips HTML and PHP tags
string stripcslashes(string str)	Un-quotes string quoted with addcslashes()
int stripos(string haystack, string needle [, int offset])	Returns position of first occurrence of a case-insensitive string
string stripslashes(string str)	Un-quotes string quoted with addslashes()
string stristr(string haystack, string needle)	Case-insensitive strstr()
int strlen(string str)	Gets string length
int strnatcasecmp(string str1, string str2)	Case insensitive string comparisons using a "natural sort" algorithm
int strnatcmp(string str1, string str2)	String comparisons using a "natural sort" algorithm
int strncasecmp(string str1, string str2, int len)	Binary-safe case-insensitive string comparison of a given number of characters
int strncmp(string str1, string str2, int len)	Binary-safe string comparison of a given number of characters
int strpos(string haystack, string needle [, int offset])	Returns the position of first occurrence of a string
string strrchr(string haystack, char needle)	Returns the last occurrence of a character in a string
string strrev(string string)	Reverses a string
int strripos(string haystack, string needle [, int offset])	Returns position of last occurrence of a case-insensitive string in a string

Function	Does This
int strrpos(string haystack, string needle [, int offset])	Returns position of last occurrence of a char in a string
int strspn(string str1, string str2)	Returns length of initial segment matching mask
string strstr(string haystack, string needle)	Returns first occurrence of a string
string strtok(string arg1, string arg2)	Tokenizes a string
string strtolower(string str)	Makes a string lowercase
string strtoupper(string string)	Makes a string uppercase
string strtr(string str, string from, string to)	Translates characters
int substr_compare(string main_str, string str, int offset [, int length [, bool case_sensitivity]])	Binary-safe comparison of two strings from an offset, up to length characters
int substr_count(string haystack, string needle)	Counts the number of substring occurrences
string substr_replace(string string, string replacement, int start [, int length])	Replaces text in a part of a string
string substr(string string, int start [, int length])	Returns part of a string
string trim(string str [, string charlist])	Strips whitespace from both the beginning and end of a string
string ucfirst(string str)	Uppercases a string's first character
string ucwords(string str)	Uppercases the first character of each word in a string
void vprintf(string format, array args)	Outputs a formatted string
string vsprintf(string format, array args)	Creates and returns a formatted string
string wordwrap(string str [, int width [, string break [, boolean cut]]])	Wraps a string to a specified number of characters

Index

strip tags, 189
validate data, 167, 181-182
variable functions, creating, 126-127
fwrite, 228-231

G

GATEWAY INTERFACE, 170
GET, 137
get name, 200, 203
getrandmax, 35
global variables, 122-123

H

headers
HTTP headers. *See* HTTP headers
sending email, 287-288
"here" documents, printing, 16-17
hexdec, 35
hidden controls, creating, 150, 152
hit counters, 295-296
HTML
creating
checkboxes, 144-145
PHP pages, 4
text areas, 142-143
FORM, 136-137
hidden controls, 150, 152
image maps, 154-156
listboxes, creating, 148-150
mixing with PHP, 10-12
password controls, creating, 152-154
radio buttons, creating, 146-148
text fields, creating, 138-139
uploading files, 156, 158
HTML controls, 135
HTML tags
displaying text in browsers, 14
encoding, 191-192
removing, 189-190
HTTP, authentication, 197
HTTP ACCEPT, 172
HTTP ACCEPT CHARSET, 172
HTTP ACCEPT ENCODING, 172
HTTP ACCEPT LANGUAGE, 172
HTTP CONNECTION, 172
HTTP headers, 172
determining browser type, 173-174
redirecting users, 175-176
HTTP HOST, 172
HTTP REFERER, 172

HTTP USER AGENT, 172
hyperbolic cosine (cosh), 35
hyperbolic sine (sinh), 36
hyperbolic tangent (tanh), 36
hypot, 35

I

IDE (integrated development
environment), 5
if statements, 33, 45-46, 50, 309-310
image maps, creating, 154-156
implode, 85
imploding arrays, 85
include files, 131-132
incrementing, 38-39
indexes, 65
inheritance, 210-212
protected inheritance, 212-214
initializing objects with constructors,
208-209
INSERT, 242
inserting data
into databases, 249-250
with DB, 263-264
installing PHP, 2-3
integers, 304
integrated development environment
(IDE), 5
interactions, skipping with continue
statements, 62
interpolated, 305
interpolating, 24-25, 27
inverse hyperbolic cosine (acosh), 35
inverse hyperbolic sine (asinh), 35
inverse hyperbolic tangent (atanh), 35
is finite, 35
is infinite, 36
is nan, 36
ISPs (internet service providers),
transporting PHP pages to, 5

J-K

JavaScript, validating data, 195-196
joiner, 111

key/value pairs, 73
keys, 65
keywords, 29, 303
DESC, 238
Komodo, 5

L

lcg value, 36
lista, creating variable-length argument lists, 111-112
listbox.php, 149
listboxes, creating, 148-150
lists
    argument lists, 104
    returning from functions, 117-118
log, 36
log10, 36
log1p, 36
logical operators, 49-50, 238
looping
    arrays, 77-78
    multidimensional arrays, 95-96
loops, 33
    breaking out of, 61
    do, while loops, 59
    for loops, 55-56
    foreach loops, 60
    while loops, 57-58

M

Maguma, 5
mail, 287
manipulating data in arrays, 91-92
math functions, 35-36
math operators, 34
max, 36
merging arrays, 88
METHOD, 136
methods
    base class methods, accessing, 216-217
    overriding, 214-215
    restricting access to, 206-207
Microsoft Word, creating PHP documents, 5
min, 36
mixing
    data types, 31
    HTML and PHP, 10-12
modifying arrays, 74-75
mt getrandmax, 36
mt rand, 36
mt srand, 36
multidimensional arrays, 93-96
MySQL, 235
    accessing databases, 243-244
    creating databases, 240-241

N

name, 200
nav bar, 102-103
navigating through arrays, 83-84
nesting comments, 19
next, 83
NOT, 238
numbers, validating data, 185-186

O

object-oriented programming, 199-200
objects, 200, 317-320
    creating, 200, 204-205
    initializing with constructors, 208-209
ODBC, 235
ooctdec, 36
OOP (object-oriented programming), 199-200
opening files, fopen, 218-219
operator precedence, 40-41
operators, 308-309
    And, 50
    array operators, 97-98
    assignment operators, 37
    bitwise operators, 44
    comparison operators, 47-48
    decrementing, 38-39
    execution operators, 42
    incrementing, 38-39
    logical operators, 49-50, 238
    math operators, 34
    operator precedence, 40-41
    Or, 50
    PHP operators, 33
    string operators, 43
    ternary operators, 52-53
Or operators, 50, 238
ORDER BY clause, 257
overriding methods, 214-215

P

padding specifier, 69
parsing files, fscanf, 226-227
passing
    arguments by reference, 109-110
    arrays to functions, 106
    data to functions, 104-105
password controls, creating, 152-154
PATH TRANSLATED, 170